*Gender and the Politics of Social Reform
in France, 1870–1914*

To Joan –
with great
admiration and
appreciation.

Rachel

Gender and the Politics of Social Reform in France, 1870–1914

Elinor A. Accampo, Rachel G. Fuchs, and Mary Lynn Stewart

with contributions by

Linda L. Clark, Theresa McBride, and Judith F. Stone

The Johns Hopkins University Press

Baltimore and London

© 1995 The Johns Hopkins University Press
All rights reserved. Published 1995
Printed in the United States of America on acid-free paper
04 03 02 01 00 99 98 97 96 95 94   5 4 3 2 1

The Johns Hopkins University Press
2715 North Charles Street
Baltimore, Maryland 21218-4319
The Johns Hopkins Press Ltd., London

Library of Congress Cataloging-in-Publication Data
will be found at the end of this book.
A catalog record for this book is available from the British Library.

ISBN 0-8018-5060-6
ISBN 0-8018-5061-4 (pbk.)

Frontispeice: Honoré Daumier, *La Republique*. Musée d'Orsay. © Photo R.M.N.

Contents

Preface

THIS COLLECTION OF essays was conceived in the café Ma Bourgogne, where the three coauthors gathered after a day of research in the Public Assistance Archives in Paris. We discussed our respective projects, which were in various stages of formulation, and remarked on a similarity: they examined bourgeois men, politicians and administrators, who were defining and proposing solutions to a series of problems involving working-class women and their children. After speaking about the possibility of compiling a collection of essays, each of us went back to the archives with more focused intentions of exploring why these privileged men, and possibly other politicians and administrators, were so interested in the plight of poor women and children; why they began in the 1880s; and how viewing their motives, strategies, and programs through the lenses of class and gender might explicate the politics of social reform in France.

Over the next few years, despite our locations in two countries and research carried out on two continents, we managed to work in a truly collaborative way. In addition to sessions of conceptualizing, writing, and revising in Paris, we presented our ideas about class, gender, and social reform in a panel with early versions of our individual projects at an annual meeting of the Social Science History Association in New Orleans. At subsequent annual meetings of the Society for French Historical Studies and the Western Society for French History, we heard interesting presentations on related topics and approached the presenters about contributing to our collection. Later, at least four or five of the contributors at a time were able to gather at annual meetings to discuss progress on the essays and to exchange suggestions about the joint project. Finally, all six contributors read and critiqued all the essays and communicated suggestions for revision and overall cohesion via electronic and regular mail, fax, and telephone.

The essays and the collection benefited from regular, informed, and constructive criticism by each contributor and from the intellectual cross-fertilization of revising in response to the other essays, and especially in response to the contextualizing introduction and final essay. Several outside readers have made invaluable and helpful suggestions toward the end of the process of writing this volume. We would especially like to thank Steve Hause and Bob Nye for their knowledgeable and constructive suggestions. Henry Tom of the Johns Hopkins University Press has lent his clear vision and encouragement to making this a more unified volume, and we appreciate his support. We owe an intellectual debt to two influential scholars: Karen Offen's work on depopulation, feminism, and the state had a profound bearing on most of the essays in this book; Joan Scott's outstanding theoretical work has infused the word *gender* with new meaning and has redefined the parameters in which we think about history. We have all profited from their work.

To the archivists and librarians who facilitated the primary research, we express our collective gratitude. Although they are too numerous to mention by name here, we want to acknowledge the assistance of archivists and librarians at the Archives de l'Assistance Publique; Archives Nationales; Archives de Paris; Archives Départementales of the Nord, Seine-Maritime, and Eure-et-Loir; Archives Municipales de Tourcoing, of the Musée Sociale; the Bibliothèque Historique de la Ville de Paris; the Bibliothèque Marguerite Durand; the Bibliothèque Nationale; and the Library of Congress.

Finally, we thank Patricia Current, of Arizona State University for help in compiling the bibliography and Grace Buonocore for her most meticulous and considerate copyediting.

Gender and the Politics of Social Reform
in France, 1870–1914

One

Gender, Social Policy, and the Formation of the Third Republic

An Introduction

ELINOR A. ACCAMPO

> Could I forget that precious half of the Republic which creates the happiness of the other and whose gentleness and wisdom maintain peace and good morals? Amiable and virtuous countrywomen [*citoyennes*], the fate of your sex will always be to govern ours. It is fortunate when your chaste power, exercised solely in conjugal union, makes itself felt only for the glory of the State and the public happiness.
>
> ROUSSEAU

JEAN-JACQUES ROUSSEAU may not have forgotten the "precious half," but historians have long ignored or dismissed the centrality gender had for the conceptualization and practice of republicanism. Several recent works focused on the manner in which republicanism at once depended upon "separate spheres" for women and men and reconstructed male and female roles appropriate for a new society during the French Revolution and the early American Republic.[1] No one has yet offered any such systematic analysis for France's third and longest effort at republicanism. Yet failure to do so leaves unresolved many of the paradoxes so often associated with the Third Republic and its origins and leaves unexplored the very nature of the welfare state and its relationship to twentieth-century republicanism.

Textbook histories of the early Third Republic have traditionally concentrated on the bitter struggles surrounding its consolidation against monarchists, the emerging nationalist Right and socialist Left, and the all-consuming conflict between the church and anticlericals. Successive crises, party rivalries, and the apparent absence of coherent policies obscured the very meaning of republicanism in a state that seemed to have a perpetual crisis of identity. Historians have paid far less attention to social reform and the interrelated themes of gender, family, and the state as agents governing republican politics and culture than to the political intrigues that made the consolidation of the Republic so problematic.[2]

Judith Stone and Sanford Elwitt did, however, focus on "the social question" as the vehicle that fundamentally shaped republican culture, politics, and reform efforts. Both identified the social question as class conflict between working-class and bourgeois men which resulted from industrialization. Social reform consisted of national legislation and programs that applied to men or to the nation in general.[3] But these histories, all attempting to untangle the complex strands of the early Third Republic, or to generalize from them, have overlooked women and the issue of gender itself. After all, if the "social question" amounted to enfranchised workers threatening the Republic with socialism and anarcho-syndicalism, women played but a small role. Nor did women factor into the very conceptualization of citizenship, whose ingredients included political equality, property ownership, liberty, individualism, independence, and suffrage. Historians have not included women in any analysis of the Third Republic political dynamics because political theory itself and French republicanism since the eighteenth century had systematically denied them any of these attributes or rights.[4] And yet, it has become increasingly clear that the men of the Third Republic did not simply ignore women as they built the state and implemented legislation; they had women very much in mind. Without understanding how conceptions of gender influenced their thinking, we cannot understand the nature of the twentieth-century state.

Several historians, including the contributors to this collection, have begun to review Third Republic politics through the lens of gender. They offer at least two corrections to the above analysis. First, they demonstrate that women, children, and the family constituted major subjects of discussion among politicians, social hygienists, and physicians throughout the political spectrum from the inception of the Third Republic, and even prior to it. Legislation regulating the treatment of children and female and child labor, as well as regulating motherhood itself, began in the 1870s and 1880s. Although this legislation developed independently of labor reform for men, an examination of its history demonstrates that "the social question" cannot be separated from "the woman question" and that the very conceptualization of these "questions" and responses to them linked directly to the ideology of republicanism itself. Second, this legislation and the abundant discourse behind reform efforts demonstrate that the republican conception of citizenship and the theory and practice of republicanism that shaped politics after 1870 were highly gendered. Indeed, public and private policies operated to redefine womanhood in the service of the state. Legislators and the parapoliticals who lobbied them urgently felt the need to control and reshape women's roles and their relationships to men in the industrializing, republican society. Their manner of thinking about women not only constructed gender roles through legislation and bureaucracy, and thereby laid the foundations for a welfare state, but it also played a major role in defining the Third Republic itself. The position of women presented at once a problem that needed resolution and an opportunity to mold civil society. By turning motherhood and other private family responsibilities into political and social concerns, Third Republic politicians ironically increased women's public function.

What, then, precisely was the thinking behind all this legislation that defined women's relationship to the state and to men? Did lawmakers' attitudes toward women and their definitions of gender vary by the social class to which women belonged? Were different laws meant to apply to different women? Did legislators share a single concept of womanhood, or did competing concepts make legislation difficult to pass?

The essays in this collection focus primarily on bourgeois men who formulated republican ideology, who studied society, medicine, and hygiene, and who engineered social reform. Specifically, they introduce us to the gendered thinking of Jules Michelet, Victor Hugo, Eugène Pelletan, Alfred Naquet, Gustave Dron, Richard Waddington, and Paul Strauss—all men who, directly or indirectly, exercised major influence on state policy. It has been our primary intention to concentrate on how men in power conceived of gender because they set the parameters for women and workers who were the objects of social reform. Only Linda Clark's essay focuses on women; by scrutinizing women whose job it was to implement reform, she indicates how male concepts of gender interacted with those of women and how that interaction played out in the bureaucracy that instituted social reform.

Our shared assumption in these essays is that gender is a social construct whose meaning constantly fluctuates. We are primarily concerned here with how these men, individually or collectively, defined gender and, more important, how they attempted to implement their definitions of gender through the republican state. As these essays readily reveal, we do not assume that men shared a single definition of womanhood. Nor do we mean to suggest that women's experience and conception of gender, their role in social reform, or their responses to legislation had any less importance than those of men. Our focus on bourgeois men arose from an acute awareness that the decisions they made circumscribed the lives of women, and we wished to discover more about those decisions.

These essays collectively suggest that three interrelated developments in the second half of the nineteenth century strongly influenced the way men with political power thought about women: industrialization, decline in the rate of population growth, and the culture of republicanism. Each of these developments in some way rendered women's private and public roles problematic; at the same time, they created the context and the parameters within which men tried to redefine women's roles.

Large-scale industrialization, which had intensified during the 1850s and 1860s, in many areas restructured work for both women and men, often forcing them to leave the home to work in factories or migrate from rural villages to larger towns. The proportion of French women in the labor force increased steadily from about 24 percent in 1850 to about 43 percent by 1920.[5] Apart from domestic service, the primary industry that employed women outside their own homes was that of textiles—cotton, wool, linen, and silk. Contemporary apologists for large-scale industry argued that women in factories simply continued to perform tasks they had once performed in the home, only such work was less tiresome because machines "assume[d] all the difficult part of the labor."[6] However, until the law of 1892 restricted and began to regulate women's work, most female factory workers stood tending machines in twelve-hour night and day shifts, with few or no breaks. Factories harbored deplorable conditions, with extreme temperatures of hot or cold, humidity, air filled with infectious textile particles, and poor lighting. Some workers and observers testified that night shifts also ruined workers' health by inducing severe fatigue and by destroying the appetite, thus causing poor nutrition. Pregnant women would continue to tend machines in these conditions up to the moment of delivery. Working-class men and women throughout the industrial centers of France complained bitterly that industrial work ruined women's health and caused an increase in miscarriages, stillbirths, and maternal mortality.[7]

Removal of work from the home also disrupted family life because it meant that mothers and fathers had less opportunity to tend to children and women had less time to devote to homemaking. Although many women abandoned factory labor once they had children, some did not have that option, and few could abandon wage labor altogether. Only the most highly paid male workers could support a family on a single salary, and even they had difficulty doing so after the births of several children. In areas where mechanization eliminated traditional forms of domestic industry, women had little choice but to resume factory work as soon as they could. In most industrial areas, however, old forms of domestic industry persisted or new forms emerged, and mothers continued to earn wages in the home. But women earned far lower wages with this type of work than those they could earn in the factory. And in order for women laboring in their homes to make any sort of adequate contribution to the family income, they had to work at least twelve hours per day without interruption. In short, the productive labor that remained available in the home rarely permitted women to give any more attention to their child-rearing and household responsibilities than did factory labor.[8]

Although large-scale industrialization occurred only in several regions and coexisted with the traditional forms of production that persisted throughout much of France, its visible impacts jolted middle-class observers into a new awareness of social problems. For example, the conservative and considerably influential Frederick LePlay and his followers became appalled by what they considered to be moral changes associated with industrial labor. By leaving the home to work at unskilled labor, men lost domestic authority vis-à-vis their wives and children. To the absence of women from the home, Abbé Cetty, a follower of LePlay, attributed the "almost irredeemable decadence" of the family; yet at the same time he acknowledged that the industrial economy gave women no choice but to leave the home so that they could contribute to the family wage. In the eyes of conservative economists, the Paris Commune of 1871 demonstrated the political extremes to which such demoralization could take workers; and the economic depression of the 1880s made urban working-class misery that much more visible. So, too, did real threats from the Left become more apparent: worker congresses that began to meet in the mid-1870s resulted in organized, increasingly doctrinaire socialist groups in the 1880s. The ranks of anarchists swelled by the 1890s; they made their presence felt through acts of terrorism such as sabotaging railroad lines and assassinating the president of the Republic. These developments made the "social question" ever more poignant: even though the actual number of those adhering to socialist, anarchist, and anarcho-syndicalist groups remained relatively small, the government feared that social conditions would increase the appeal these groups might have for disgruntled workers.[9] Left-wing politics also corrupted working-class women. *Les petroleuses* of the Paris Commune, similar to the revolutionary women of 1793, became repulsive and threatening when they transgressed their "natural" role. Other women made similar transgressions as they attended worker congresses, joined socialist organizations, and founded feminist groups from the mid-1870s.[10]

Most scholarship on industrialization and the working-class family in the last thirty years has played down the disruptive effects of the process and has stressed instead continuity and the adaptability of worker families. The working-class family did indeed survive industrialization, for had it not, the working class itself would have disappeared, along with its culture and the labor movement it produced. However, demography belies the ease with which workers coped. At a time when infant mortality throughout western Europe began to decrease, the rates in industrial cities increased. For example, Mulhouse (Haut-Rhin) averaged 330 deaths per 1,000 births in the 1860s, and Roubaix (Nord) had 239 deaths per 1,000 births between 1873 and 1876. In the department of the Nord as a whole, infant mortality reached its height between 1893 and 1900.[11] Saint Chamond (Loire) registered an increase not only in infant and child mortality as it industrialized but also in stillbirths and maternal mortality.[12] All these areas were centers of textile production in which married women worked outside the home. High rates of infant mortality reflected not just unhealthy living conditions but the stresses associated with industrial labor as well. The necessity for mothers to continue working outside the home meant that they either had to send their infants to wet nurses—which frequently amounted to a death sentence—give them unhealthy or unsanitary substitutes for breast milk, which caused the often fatal gastroenteritis. Even where women did work in the home, combining wage earning with child care proved difficult, and mothers had to take shortcuts with the latter.[13]

Outside the context of marriage and the family, industrialization contributed to a growing moral problem that in turn helped increase the rates of infant mortality: illegitimate births. Industrial, urban centers attracted young women from the countryside who, unprotected by family and rural networks, found themselves seduced, abandoned, and pregnant. Cities also served as magnets for unmarried pregnant women who flocked there to give birth anonymously. These mothers often abandoned their children, which sharply decreased chances for survival. The infant mortality rate among illegitimate babies in Mulhouse, for example, reached 450 deaths per 1,000 births. But during times of economic depression, such as the 1880s, an increased proportion of married women would also abandon their infants.[14] Although the infant mortality rate for all of France had declined from 195 per 1,000 births in the early nineteenth century to 179 in 1880, this rate remained high in comparison with other industrial countries. Clearly, deaths in urban, industrial centers raised the average rate.

The high rates of infant mortality constituted but one element of an increasingly apparent demographic phenomenon: a declining growth rate. Over the course of the nineteenth century, the crude birthrate fell from 281 per 10,000 inhabitants to 202. Despite this drop in births, the number of marriages that took place in France increased, and couples married earlier, two factors that should have increased the birthrate. French couples thus consciously employed means to limit family size. By the 1880s, the French population, numbering about thirty-eight million, exhibited minimal growth. According to the censuses of 1881 and 1886, France experienced an increase of only 3.2 births per 1,000 inhabitants, whereas the German empire could boast 10, Prussia just under 12, and Russia almost 13. Between 1881 and 1901, Germany's population increased by four million (nearly 20%), while that of France increased by only one million (3%). Combined with a high overall mortality rate (23 deaths per 1,000 inhabitants), to which infant deaths contributed so greatly, the number of deaths actually exceeded that of births in 1890–92 and in 1895.[15]

This phenomenon came to be known in France as the "crisis of depopulation," the second development during this period which intensified physicians', social hygienists', and politicians' concerns about women's biological and social roles in motherhood. As Robert Nye demonstrated, the meaning that depopulation had for the French cannot be fully appreciated outside the broader context of the prevailing sense of national "degeneration."[16] The social theory of degeneration derived from biological, medical, and psychopathological theories advanced in the 1860s. Degeneration was defined as "a pathological state of the organism which, in relation to its most immediate progenitors, is constitutionally weakened in its psychophysical resistance and only realizes in part the biological conditions of the hereditary struggle for life. That weakening, which is revealed in permanent stigmata, is essentially progressive, with only intervening regeneration; when this is lacking, it leads more or less rapidly to the extinction of the species."[17] Nye has shown that the language and model of biomedical theory soon came to permeate other modes of thought, so that "by the 1890s degeneracy was no longer simply a clinical theory of abnormal individual pathologies, but a *social* theory of persuasive force and power." [18]

Even prior to the scientific advances of medicine in the 1860s, social and political theorists had viewed society as an organism, a collectivity with integral and interdependent parts. But the elaboration of degeneration theory within the biomedical model infused the metaphor with new inspiration, power, and legitimacy. [19] Within this metaphor, moreover, the theory of degeneration fostered the belief that depopulation resulted from a pathological state in the French social organism that would ultimately lead to its extinction. The organic metaphor and the theory of degeneration led politicians and social hygienists to scrutinize the female population—the reproductive cell of the social organism—all the more closely.

Even prior to 1870, the medical profession's attention to the high infant mortality produced critiques of wet-nursing and a reconceptualization of women's roles as mothers. Many nationalists and populationists blamed urban women for the high rate of infant deaths because they did not nurse infants themselves but instead gave them to wet nurses. This practice not only increased deaths among infants but rendered those who survived infancy weaker and smaller because, deprived of their mothers' breast milk, they were not sufficiently nourished. In 1874, the French National Assembly passed the Roussel law, intended to reduce infant mortality and protect the charges of wet nurses by regulating the wet-nursing industry. As Joshua Cole recently demonstrated, this law represented the culmination of more than a decade of debate about infant protection, wet-nursing, and breast-feeding. And indeed, these debates uncover a conception of womanhood that formed a basis for further legislation. Cole argues that in their testimony to the National Academy of Medicine, Dr. Louis-Adolphe Bertillon, André-Théodore Brochard, and Dr. Charles Monot all emphasized "the mother's responsibility in high rates of infant death while simultaneously downplaying the socio-economic factors which led women to resort to wet-nurses." The work of Alexandre Mayer, founder of the first Société protectrice de l'enfance, also stressed maternal responsibility to the point that "the body of the mother had no integrity of its own, it existed for the child, and not for itself," and thus Cole suggests that motherhood itself dissolved into the realm of "the social." [20]

The Franco-Prussian War left in its wake a deepened sense of national degeneration that offered a framework within which to understand and explain increasing rates of infant mortality and declining birthrates. France's sickly demographic profile coincided with the prevailing belief that population size formed the basis for military strength or weakness, and it thus attracted keen national interest. With a declining and aging population, France would not be able to defend itself against foreign armies, particularly the German army, in the event of another war. The ever intensifying sense of national degeneration, fueled by the stark results of census reports, led to the further scrutinization of women's lives and particularly the dilemma that industrialization posed for them. In general, republican reformers focused on ways to prevent infant mortality, while conservative, Catholic, and nationalist reformers concentrated on increasing natality. The efforts of both groups frequently overlapped. Concluding in 1890 that there was "perhaps no more serious question" for the future of the French than their "weak natality," Henri Napias, general inspector of public assistance, quoted Dr. Proust: "[A woman's] life itself," this doctor argued, "does not belong to her. . . . When she is a young girl, she must preserve her health from all that can prevent the perfect, harmonious, complete development of her being; [as a] woman, she needs to conserve her health and multiply all her forces for her children."[21]

The notion that women's bodies were not their own became translated into law between 1874 and 1919. Concern over reproductive issues became one of the most important factors that led the French legislature to pass numerous measures restricting women's right to work. Article 3 of the child labor law of 1874 prohibited girls younger than age 21 from working at night, and Article 7 prohibited girls and women from working underground in mines, pits, and quarries. The law of 1892 extended restrictions on night work to all women and limited their workday to eleven hours. The law of 1900 further reduced women's workday to ten hours. Women did not receive compensation for these reduced hours until the law on minimum wages was passed in 1915. Women's work and motherhood became explicitly linked in the maternity laws of 1909 and 1913; the former guaranteed jobs after a voluntary leave, and the latter gave pregnant women the right to take an optional leave four weeks prior to the birth of a baby and obligated them to take a four-week leave after the birth. Finally, the law of 23 April 1919 reduced the workday for industrial workers of both sexes to eight hours but further prohibited women from an increasing number of dangerous trades.[22]

Although passage of this legislation came with only a good deal of struggle and debate, it could not have happened without some consensus about womanhood on the part of legislators. We must also stress, however, that even with this legislation, conceptions of womanhood remained

painfully paradoxical for these men. Women could not simply be relegated to the private sphere because they already had a public presence
and public function in the productive labor they performed outside the
home. Moreover, their reproductive functions assumed a new social importance. Concerns about womanhood coincided with the very formation
of the Republic and efforts to implement anew conceptions of citizenship.
Industrialization, high infant mortality and the low birthrate, and notions
of degeneration brought new attention to women and forced legislators not
only to define women's roles explicitly and legally but to reassess the whole
meaning of laissez faire and civil rights. Thus the third point at which the
essays in this volume intersect, and the third site in which women's roles
became contested and redefined, was within the development of republicanism and republican culture.

Republicanism in the second half of the nineteenth century in France,
as well as throughout western Europe and the United States, differed fundamentally from its eighteenth-century manifestations in that it coincided
with the profound philosophical transition that political theorists have
termed the rise of "the social." T. H. Marshall's theory of citizenship, for
example, points to an evolution from due process to political rights and
then to social rights, or "freedom from want." [23] This most recent conception of citizenship arose with the recognized dangers of industrialization,
urbanization, and proletarianization, as well as with the expansion of state
power. The state becomes the "guarantor of society's progress" and attempts to improve conditions for the health, education, and morality of
all members of society. As Jacques Donzelot puts it, the nature of a citizen's work status places him "in the situation of being society's ward in
proportion to the injuries inflicted on him by the social division of labor." [24]

François Ewald elaborates in detail the rise of "the social" and the development of the French welfare state and refers to the 1898 law on work
accidents as the crucial turning point at which the right to life for the
broader good of the society began to take precedence over the classic, individual right to freedom. Not incidentally, this transformation coincided
with the rise of the biomedical metaphor that viewed society as an organism, a collection of individuals whose private well-being and interdependence determined the health of the collectivity as a whole. Ewald points
out that industrialization changed the nature of risk in society at large by
making workers victims in their labor. Accidents became, and continue to
be, a social phenomenon that increases with technological progress. They
happen with regularity and are predictable; they are a product of collective

life and mass society. The modern accident is not centered in dangers of nature, nor in the conduct of individuals, but is rather an objective social phenomenon. Fault, and thus responsibility, lie not with individual will but with relations between individuals. Since no one can be independent of society, society itself must take responsibility for preserving the right to live. Republicanism lent further meaning to scientific knowledge about biology and society. "The problematic of social rights," Ewald explains, "supposes a universal objectification of the living person as wealth that the society must extract, develop and multiply for the well-being of all: the most important capital is the living person. This problematic is turned towards the maximization of life under all its forms." This "biopower," as Michel Foucault called it, appeared in practical politics, economic observations, and problems of natality, public health, and housing.[25] The "contract of solidarity" replaces Rousseau's "social contract," and the task of the state becomes that of governing the life of each individual even in its most private dimensions.

In analyzing the changing meaning of citizenship, these theorists, ironically, consider only male citizenship, the nature of male labor, and the risks to which men were subjected. But clearly, industrialization, urbanization, the depopulation crisis, and all the social scientific studies of problems associated with these developments focused attention on female labor, and reproduction itself as a labor, which put women at a collective risk. It was through women that "the social" began to emerge. Only scholars such as Denise Riley who have reinterpreted the rise of the welfare state with an analysis of gender have recognized the link between women and the philosophical transformation Marshall, Foucault, Donzelot, Ewald, and others have variously described. As Riley notes, "In so far as the concerns of the social *are* familial standards—health, education, hygiene, fertility, demography, chastity and fecundity—and the heart of the family is inexorably woman, then the woman is also solidly inside of that which has to some degree already been feminized."[26]

As theorists have pointed out, "social right" came into direct conflict with "classical right" of citizenship—the right to work—a paradox that permeates the legislative debates of the Third Republic. But women as sociological subjects, and as objects of protection, elided the paradox because they never had rights of citizenship in the classic sense. Because women's bodies were not considered their own, women became easy targets for incursions into private life. They had little liberty to begin with and few civil rights once they married.[27]

In their analysis of women's relationship to the Third Republic, the essays in this volume in various ways point to three dominating elements of republican culture: the legacy of 1789 and the place of women within it; "solidarism"; and the place of physicians and social hygienists in the republican order. As noted above, an examination of republicanism during the 1789 revolution clearly establishes the importance of gender. It shows, moreover, that women came to have public importance as mothers long before the rise of "the social" as it has been defined. Three decades prior to the Revolution, Rousseau insisted that the very integrity of a republic rested on the virtue of both women and men. Gender played a key role in his definition of virtue: men became virtuous through their use of reason, control over their passions, and acting for the public good. Women's virtue rested on a somewhat anomalous set of attributes: on the one hand, strict control of the body through modesty, chastity, and sexual innocence, and on the other hand, motherhood, whereby one loses sexual innocence and bodily control. Motherhood assumed importance not just for family life but for the success of the Republic. Virtuous women would produce and nurture virtuous citizens.[28]

Paradoxically, although it is the public sphere that gives meaning and purpose to woman's activity, Rousseau confines her to the private, domestic realm "as a public sign of her political virtue."[29] The public itself corrupted women while it served as the arena within which men cultivated their virtue. Rousseau's ideas not only shaped revolutionary ideology and action in France but provided a basis for practicing new gender roles. During France's first experience with republicanism in the Revolution of 1789, the revolutionaries—after five years of dealing with women's demands and their presence in public life—officially removed them from the public. The Committee on General Security decided in 1794 that women's popular societies would no longer be permitted, women could not exercise political rights or take an active part in government affairs, and they could not speak at political or popular gatherings. Women, it was declared, had neither the moral nor the physical strength to engage in political deliberations or to resist oppression. Speaking on behalf of the Committee on General Security, André Amar echoed Rousseau's proclamations about women with great precision. Women's function, he declared, was "to begin the education of men, to prepare the minds and hearts of children for public virtue." These were their functions "after taking care of the home." According to Amar, women were "naturally destined to make virtue loved."[30]

Rousseau and his revolutionary disciples thus created the foundation for what has come to be called "republican motherhood."[31] Joan Landes recently argued that the Revolution of 1789 created a new role for women in republican motherhood and that it was a necessary element in the emergence of a bourgeois political culture. She argues that women during the French Revolution, including feminists, embraced this ideal and that it persisted in varying versions well into the nineteenth century. Although the Revolution did not grant women political emancipation, it "bequeathed them a moral identity and a political constitution."[32] The concept of republican motherhood rested uneasily on the proposition that the private act of mothering took on a public function and thus opened itself to public scrutiny and, in principle, state intervention.

Nineteenth-century history of domesticity certainly testifies to the legacy of Rousseau and of the French Revolution. As several historians have shown, Rousseau's thinking about separate spheres became ever more relevant as industrialization and urbanization further increased the spatial separation of home and work, reinforcing the dichotomy between private and public and, indeed, increasing the need or desire for female domesticity. The emphasis on reproductive, maternal, and homemaking activities provided a new gender role for women that sought to replace the corrupt, aristocratic model of womanhood, redress the lingering upheaval caused by the French Revolution and Napoleonic Wars, and provide a moral haven from new challenges of industrialization, urbanization, and growing class tensions.[33] The cult of domesticity, furthermore, created new moral distinctions between working-class and middle-class women. Although few working women had the time, ability, or inclination to pursue it, the middle class held the domestic ideal as a standard against which to judge workers' material and moral lives. But the ideal of domesticity in many ways empowered middle-class women, as Bonnie Smith demonstrated. And because this domesticity most often included a strong devotion to Catholicism, the power and influence of middle-class women actually became problematic for anticlerical republicans who continually struggled to reduce church power.[34]

Republican men used education to combat the conservatism of middle-class women and the perceived degeneracy of working-class women. Education, with the Ferry laws of the early 1880s, became a crucial element in the process of republicanizing France and creating citizens. The Ferry laws intended to create citizens loyal to the Republic by substituting religion with republican patriotism and morality. Just as important, as Linda Clark demonstrated, were the gender roles this education sought to create. Girls became important targets of moralization because women, especially middle-class women, practiced Catholicism and were particularly vulnerable to clerical and antirepublican influence. Instead of Catholicism, the new instruction focused on a republican-centered morality that included "(1) the premise that women's patriotic duties differed from men's, (2) mothers' obligations to teach children love of France, (3) watchfulness to see that a husband fulfilled civic duties and that children learned to obey laws, and (4) bravery if the country called upon a son or husband to fight."[35] But this education meant to moralize working-class women as well, so that they, in turn, could mold their husbands and sons into citizens loyal to the Republic.

Much of the republican thinking about womanhood became articulated in the political ideology of "solidarism." Sharing some of the same etiology as the social theory of degeneration, and indeed complementing it, solidarism rested on the perception of society as a living organism, made up of a large number of interdependent cells. First articulated as a philosophy by Léon Bourgeois in the 1890s, solidarism posited that individuals and social classes were mutually dependent and had social obligations that rose above indivdual interests. Solidarism provided a rationale for restricting laissez-faire economics in order to establish social reform, ameliorate class relations, and prevent social conflict.[36] No political ideology could better represent the rise of "the social."

Family and gender held a central place in solidarist philosophy and policy. In particular, the working-class woman became a potential stabilizer in the face of the working-class-male threat to the bourgeois, republican order. Civil and "social" engineer Émile Cheysson, for example, believed that women "held the secret of the alleviation of misery, of the well-being of the worker, of the reconciliation of classes, of social peace, and of the moral unity and greatness of the nation."[37] Cheysson characterized women as "soft, nurturing, and above all, modest"—adjectives that echo Rousseau's conception of virtuous womanhood in a republic. For Cheysson these qualities were "to be admired in themselves and for their social utility, especially because they dissolved male passions and male tendencies toward precipitous action such as strikes." Furthermore, "because sex knows no class, the uniformity of female social obligations 'brings together all the women of the world, those of the bourgeoisie and those of the people.'"[38] Cheysson viewed women as a single group with common interests—those of nurturing and maintaining a household. Undivided by class, womanhood would convert workers into good citizens.

Middle-class women would educate their working-class sisters so that they, in turn, could moralize men. Through women of both classes, class divisions and tensions would melt away, and France would obtain a moral, national unity. Women, of course, could only fulfill such obligations if they remained at home and learned the skills of household management. Cheysson's vision thus contradicted the reality of working-class women, since the wives of most workers had to perform productive labor of some sort. But such thinking on his part and of those like him contributed to concerns over women's productive and reproductive roles in the new industrial order.

Because the philosophy of solidarism, like the social theory of degeneration, drew on the recent discoveries of biological science, its advocates became especially influenced by the progress of medical science. Medical progress increased the power of physicians, who provided scientific legitimation for a good deal of the political thinking about womanhood. As Jack Ellis recently demonstrated, physicians almost always constituted 10 to 12 percent of the legislature between 1870 and 1914, a presence that greatly overrepresented their proportion in the population. From the 1880s to 1910, one- to two-thirds of those physician-legislators were Radicals. Ellis explains this disposition by noting that the doctrines of revolutionary *fraternité*, which played such an important role in the conception of republicanism, included a collective responsibility for illness. But this republican or democratic concern for public health had a nationalistic corollary: the French population had to overcome its physical inferiority to the Germans. And in this arena, the physicians both inside and outside the National Assembly joined the front lines in the battle against depopulation. Public health, Ellis concludes, "legitimized by bacteriology, was a collective enterprise necessitating the subordination of private interests to the general good."[39] Central to this subordination to private interests was concern over the survival of children. "Few [physicians] were willing to ground their defense of women on much more than the sanctity of their reproductive function."[40] Whether or not a woman was married, reproduction was her most important function.

The essays in this collection demonstrate the ubiquity of physicians throughout the political and bureaucratic structures and the power they exercised through their positions to help define women's biological and social roles. In the effort to reduce infant mortality, legislators looked to physicians, who uttered proclamations about women's special physiology—a physiology that dictated childbearing and breast-feeding and either the removal of women from the labor force or legislation to protect women by restricting their labor. Parallel to the development of physicians' power and authority was that of public health, or *hygiène sociale*. Social hygiene, bolstered by medicine and social science, became an organized, bourgeois movement in response to infant mortality, industrialization, and "the social question." As Sanford Elwitt pointed out, through science and scientific controls, social hygienists attempted to reach workers by "moralizing and educating the working-class family, that is, extending the surveillance of labor to its most private sphere, which had the not incidental effect of inhibiting its collective solidarity."[41]

Policymakers of the Third Republic thus conceptualized social problems and the solutions to them in the context of a multifaceted and complex political culture. It is with a gendered analysis of this culture that our collection begins. Judith Stone's essay, "The Republican Brotherhood: Gender and Ideology," demonstrates that the experience of "fraternity" which nurtured republicanism throughout the nineteenth century included a need among republican men to shape and channel domesticity and womanhood itself to their political worldview even when there was no republic. Republicans such as Jules Michelet and Victor Hugo developed the ideal of republican motherhood to redeem women from the fate of their respective class-determined situations. Bourgeois women were "corrupted by luxury, idleness, and clericalism," and working-class women were "degraded by abject misery." Republican men would shape and define the republican women, who, in turn, would produce and cultivate republican citizens.[42] Like social engineer Émile Cheysson, Victor Hugo viewed the working-class woman as the potential savior of society, through her ability to eliminate class tensions. Here, the central paradox of the separation of spheres which Rousseau had prescribed became once again apparent; for if women really remained confined to the private sphere, they could not fulfill their republican obligations. Thus Eugène Pelletan argued for a far broader education for women, because what they received could no longer meet the task of republican motherhood. He actually made a case for female influence in politics. Unlike Rousseau, he contended that women had a civic role in the public sphere and that they reasoned just like men.

Stone documents how the creation of a male and female industrial working class and women's demands for civil and political rights challenged republican ideology and forced republicans to reformulate their policies. How were industrial workers and women to be incorporated into the Republic and, in turn, be used to stabilize republicanism rather than threaten it? Stone answers that republicans infused their ideology with solidarism, with which they intended to forge peaceful class relations and ensure that a new generation of republican mothers would be created through extended education.

It is clear, however, that republican culture harbored no single conception of womanhood and that conflicting viewpoints forged the legislation proposed or passed during the Third Republic. Theresa McBride's essay, "Divorce and the Republican Family," presents an entirely different kind of thinking about women on the part of a legislator, Alfred Naquet; and the fact that Naquet managed to obtain passage of the divorce law after many versions and much struggle demonstrates that others shared his view. But the contestation surrounding this law also highlights the acute conflict between, on the one hand, the classical conception of citizenship based on individual rights to freedom and, on the other hand, social rights of those "at risk."

Although Naquet's republicanism was rooted in the tradition of individual civil rights, he focused attention on the plight of working women, who suffered not only from the economic system but also from the legal system which denied them any control of family income and property.[43] Naquet firmly believed that the mother was the economic, social, and moral "pivot" of the family, and the debate over divorce obviated a need to rethink the family and legislation affecting it. Implicitly or explicitly, problems of industrialization and depopulation came to the fore. Parliamentarians acknowledged the instability of the working-class family as well as problems of prostitution, infanticide, and abortion. Some believed that divorce would lead to remarriage and, in turn, more stable and prolific families. Other supporters saw the divorce law as a means to regulate the morals of the working class. They worked up considerable moral fervor over the abandonment of pregnant women by their lovers (and the ensuing problem of impoverished single mothers and abandoned children) or even over the hypocrisy of legislation that required a husband's sexual fidelity to his wife only when he was at home.

Naquet faced daunting opposition from those who believed divorce would only destabilize family life and weaken the position of women. McBride also suggests that the debate about marital discord involved legislators in matters that came very close to home—the failings of marriage in their own social milieu. They were terribly concerned about the unhealthy state of middle-class marriages, and many of them were personally familiar with adultery. Their own marriages were often based on interest rather than affection, and in many cases their experience with the judicial system's attempt to cope with family violence and family breakdown gave divorce a special place in the discussion of family life. But a key paradox they faced was how to protect women and the family without restricting the liberty of men by interfering in their private lives. A conservative version of the bill passed partly as a result of changing attitudes about men's responsibility for the family as well as for the society at large. But of no small importance in the passage of this law was the republican association of divorce with anticlericalism and antimonarchism.

The law of 1884 did not reflect a singular definition of womanhood or women's place in society. What came to issue here, as with so much other legislation, was the confrontation between republican ideals about individual liberty and a paternal authority with regard to women which became transferred to the state. Encumbered by a belief in the state's authority over marriage, the legislators chose liberty with deep ambivalence.

But if the divorce law marks a lingering focus on individual freedom for men, and to a lesser degree women, subsequent legislation regarding women, children, and motherhood unveils a transition to "the right to life" over the right to liberty. It is also clear, furthermore, that women's and children's lack of individual liberty provided the basis for early welfare legislation. In her essay "The Right to Life: Paul Strauss and the Politics of Motherhood," Rachel Fuchs closely analyzes the motives, thinking, and activities of one French politician who became obsessed with the problem of infant mortality. Strauss's concerns began with illegitimate infants, since their rates of death loomed so high. In his early efforts, he established departmental and municipal programs to assist unwed mothers so that they could keep their babies rather than abandon them. He then encouraged those who kept their infants to breast-feed them—a difficult task, since single mothers necessarily had to support themselves and their children and thus had to devote most of their waking hours to earning wages. Strauss later extended his concerns to impoverished married women whose circumstances made it difficult to care properly for their children. Policies on the local level eventually became national programs and resulted in a spate of legislation passed between 1904 and 1913 whose purpose was to protect children and the reproductive potential of women.

Strauss's efforts represented some major shifts in policy: single mothers ceased to be morally condemned and came under the paternal protection of the state. All mothers and pregnant women who became objects of this legislation experienced incursions into their private family lives. Inspectors attempted to control their morality, to supervise their hygiene, to ensure that they breast-fed, and to instruct them in child-rearing practices. Family activities, once private, now became the object of public scrutiny for poor women. And women became the vehicle for such intervention into private life because legislators and bureaucrats did not consider them full citizens or individuals with rights to liberty and to privacy. Poor single women and wives of poor men especially lacked rights and privacy. According to Paul Strauss and policymakers who shared his beliefs, motherhood became a public duty. They viewed women as vessels for perpetuating the French "race"; they were to bear and raise children for the good of the nation and place their own interests second to those of the children they bore.

The legislation that Paul Strauss engineered to enhance women's role as mothers came into effect in the same decades as the legislation that restricted women's right to productive labor. In "Setting the Standards: Labor and Family Reformers," Mary Lynn Stewart demonstrates that the thinking behind protective legislation for working women closely paralleled that of Paul Strauss and others who expressed deep concern about the impact of industrialization on the family and about the role of women in depopulation. Her essay examines the public and private agendas of Richard Waddington and Dr. Gustave Dron, republicans who served in the Chamber of Deputies and who held primary responsibility for the passage of protective legislation restricting the paid work of women.

Struggling against objections to the violations of laissez-faire economics and civil rights for men, Waddington and Dron succeeded in forging a parliamentary coalition favoring protective legislation by focusing their rhetoric on the crisis of depopulation and on the reproductive roles of working-class women. Attitudes about gender, the family, and reproduction shaped their vision of industrial production and provided the fuel for their arguments. Both expressed solidarist views combining humanitarianism and republican patriotism. Concerns about military capabilities also motivated Waddington's efforts to protect workers' health. And Dron, like Émile Cheysson and Victor Hugo, wanted working-class women to "inculcate the habits of order and economy," which were the "strength and security of the French worker."[44] As a physician-legislator, Dron used scientific data to argue that the state should restrict women's productive labor in favor of their reproductive responsibilities. For reasons of compassion as well as of practicality, these two politicians made it their goal to try to reconcile the contradictory roles of working women, while at the same time strengthen the republican state.

But Strauss, Waddington, and Dron at no point wanted to remove women entirely from the labor force in order to make them into non-wage-earning housewives. While they wanted working women to acquire more skills in the tasks of mothering and keeping a household and husband, they knew that the French economy and much of the French population as a whole—workers themselves as well as employers in all sectors—would not support the removal of women from the labor force. Indeed, this legislation marks a true effort to reconcile contradictory roles as well as a major change in male attitudes about working women. Whereas in the first half of the nineteenth century the word *ouvrière* brought connotations of impiety and sordidness to the minds of political economists and the like, by the second half the female wage earner had become a given and her importance as producer and reproducer acknowledged.[45] And interestingly, the pervasiveness of this element in French political thinking distinguished it from other industrializing countries. The findings of both Fuchs and Stewart confirm what Jane Jensen recently argued: that French legislators never viewed women only as mothers and never intended to eliminate them from the productive labor force. Jensen argues that in France, protecting infants and limiting hours of work "reproduc[ed] gender relations in which women's place was in the family though not necessarily in the home" and "reconciled paid work and maternity."[46] The United States, by contrast, did not develop policies for working mothers. Protective legislation for American women came later than in France, with the initiative for it coming from women rather than from the state.

Thus, even in the effort to protect motherhood and childhood, the Third Republic legislation also represents an acceptance of women's public, wage-earning role. Public policy regarding middle-class women represented a similar dualism. Middle-class women, as noted above, were also expected to embrace motherhood. But motherhood in the context of republican culture paradoxically became a public as well as private duty in the obligation to create republican citizens. Such instruction literally became public, as women began to become teachers and bureaucrats. The Republic employed the "feminine qualities" of middle-class women to enforce the legislation regarding working-class women and children.

We see how such utilization of middle-class women operates in Linda Clark's essay, "Bringing Feminine Qualities into the Public Sphere: The Third Republic's Appointment of Women Inspectors." The national government began to employ women in supervisory positions as early as the July Monarchy, in recognition that their inherent nurturing abilities could serve children and other women. The ideology of republican motherhood, or "maternalism," became especially pervasive in the functionary roles of women during the Third Republic. As Clark points out, inspectresses of schools, factories, and prisons became "state-supplied mothers or sisters."[47] One of the school inspectresses' most important functions was to make sure that girls of the lower classes received instruction in morality and homemaking.

Just as solidarist and social engineer Émile Cheysson believed women needed to moralize their husbands and children in the private sphere, here the state used middle-class women to moralize working women in the public sphere. Apart from moralization, the state sought to secularize women of both classes, to remove them from the influence of the church and its antirepublican allies. Women spread and bolstered republican ideology through mothering, teaching, and helping regulate women's labor through inspection. Clark points out that these inspectresses generally shared the predominant male view of womanhood, though some did espouse feminism.

Clark's essay also demonstrates that what other historians have termed *maternalism* took root very early in France and assumed a development that ultimately increased the state's power over women. Seth Koven and Sonya Michel defined maternalism as "ideologies that exalted women's capacity to mother and extended to society as a whole the values of care, nurturance and morality. . . . It extolled the private virtues of domesticity while simultaneously legitimating women's public relationships to politics and the state, to community, workplace and marketplace." As they point out, and as Clark demonstrates in her essay, maternalism "challenged the constructed boundaries between public and private, women and men, state and civil society." In their comparison of France with Germany, Great Britain, and the United States between 1880 and 1920, they observe that because the French "regarded family matters as a public concern,"[48] the power of women to shape policy in France became more circumscribed than elsewhere. In Clark's essay, we see just how limited female power was even in woman's capacity as public functionary; and in all the other essays, we note the extensive concern that politicians had for family matters and issues of gender. What the rise of "the social" actually did by the turn of the century was bring Rousseau's republican motherhood more explicitly into the public sphere and further blur the already fuzzy boundaries between private and public.

Through the political construct of solidarism and through the scientific authority of social hygiene, the Third Republic government entered the private sphere of family life and attempted not only to create a version of republican motherhood to serve the family and the state but also to use women to tame working-class men. Because of their emphasis on bourgeois men, these essays do not focus on the issue of women's and workers' responses to these efforts. Did women and working-class men embrace the bourgeois construction of gender? As these essays suggest, women did often resist efforts to regulate their lives, sometimes by protesting protective labor legislation, other times by manipulating the system to their own ends and in fact permanently bending the system itself, as in the case of single and impoverished mothers. Certainly many feminists opposed the gender system that emerged during the Third Republic. But in her groundbreaking article of several years ago, Karen Offen brilliantly demonstrated how mainstream French feminism responded to and appropriated the language of depopulation and nationalism and used it to its own ends.[49]

Much speculation, but little systematic research, has been done on the question of worker response to gender-based reform efforts. To date, the scholarly consensus appears to be that working-class men did seek to establish the bourgeois ideal of domesticity: their efforts to obtain a family wage, the competition they felt from women in the labor force, and the frequent shunning of women in the labor movement all point to such an ideal. Michelle Perrot has written of the French worker's eulogy of the housewife, emphasizing his desire to remove her from the labor force.[50]

But I do not think we should so readily conclude that such eulogy meant that workers—male or female—sought to implement the bourgeois republican ideals about gender and the family. The options workers conceived for themselves stemmed from the physical reality they faced as well as from the entire spectrum of political discourse at the end of the nineteenth century. For example, beginning with the first worker congress after the Paris Commune which took place in October 1876, workers expressed many of the same concerns as bourgeois republicans. The issue of depopulation entered their discussion as workers began to articulate their problems and goals. They conceived of depopulation in the same terms as the pronatalists—that is, as a matter of female reproduction—and seemed to propose the same solutions. At this congress, more than one worker noted "great preoccupation" with the causes of depopulation in France. "The cause is no place other than in the excessive work our period demands of women, which makes for a poor constitution and renders them incapable of raising and suckling their children."[51] Delegates blamed female industrial labor for maternal mortality and for their children's terrible health. The discussion continued at the socialist workers' congress of 1879, where delegate Dauthier presented a solution similar to that of the bourgeois populationists, stating that women should leave the workshop or factory and return to the household because the woman who labored in the workshop could not maintain her home and had to leave it "in a state of disorder."[52] Like his bourgeois, solidarist counterparts of the 1880s and 1890s, he further emphasized that the woman was the soul of the family, the cornerstone of every social edifice. Dauthier also similarly referred to medical reports that specified the physiological responsibilities and physical weaknesses of women. Depopulation, he argued, resulted from moral and physical debilitation, which in turn resulted from the practice of working women sending their infants to wet nurses. Sounding much like the doctors quoted above, Dauthier concluded, "That which renders woman improper for industrial work is precisely that which renders her proper for maternity."[53]

While one can argue that this posture reflects bourgeois values, it also represents the brute reality workers faced. Like the bourgeois observers, workers at these congresses perceived that industrialization and the factory work to which it gave rise had ravaged the health of women and children and undermined the moral fabric of their family lives. Significantly, however, congress participants did not suggest that women could or should devote themselves exclusively to domestic concerns. Indeed, they even criticized the idleness of bourgeois women. A female delegate argued against the very concept of a male wage that could support a family, saying, "Any woman who, able to work, finds it more convenient to be lodged [and] fed by her husband, is only, according to me, a kept woman."[54] Instead of suggesting that women cease participating in productive labor, male and female members of the congress proposed that productive labor be returned to the home and regulated. They argued, for example, that reducing hours and raising wages would solve the problems unique to women workers. Workers of both sexes at these congresses did not conceive of female productive labor as the least bit incompatible with their family goals; it was women's involvement with industrial labor that had weakened, debilitated, and demoralized the family, because it had prevented women from meeting family needs.

Rhetoric about the depopulation crisis and the discourse of degeneration helped workers articulate their own perceptions about how industrialization had undermined their family lives. The scientific information supplied by doctors and health commissioners focused workers' attention on female labor as a central problem. They felt that industrialization, by debilitating family life, had weakened their ability to resist incursions of the bourgeoisie—patriarchal state regulation being one such incursion. And to resist, workers also advocated their own form of republican motherhood. They demanded better education for women, whose goal would be to make their "sons independent men, and [their] daughters [into] mothers capable of rendering their children citizens worthy of . . . 1789." [55]

As the labor and socialist movements became more organized in the 1880s and 1890s and issues of doctrine assumed center stage, the "woman question," which previously had held first place on the congress agendas, ceased to have any place at all. This change has significance, especially as it coincided with emerging feminism and legislation regulating female labor. And certainly, as socialism became more doctrinaire in the 1880s, its adherents viewed women's issues as a detraction from the more important class struggle. But why women's paid work and its relation to the family ceased to be a prominent topic of discussion is a question that has not been adequately addressed, let alone answered.[56] At the same time another predominantly working-class movement emerged that did explicitly address gender issues: the neo-Malthusian, or birth control, movement.

Historians have downplayed the significance of neo-Malthusianism by suggesting that, as a birth control movement, it had little apparent impact on working-class fertility, primarily because workers had already reduced the size of their families. Moreover, neo-Malthusian rhetoric, which divided workers, socialists, and feminists, issued primarily from a fringe group of anarchists and anarcho-syndicalists. I would like to make a preliminary and speculative suggestion, however, that the anarchist and neo-Malthusian movements, whose rhetoric reached far greater numbers of men and women than the adherents, provided the basis for a cultural resistance to Third Republic incursions into private life. Anarchists not only advocated birth control, but they took up other issues of the body so frequently highlighted in the social theory of degeneration and so popular among legislators: alcoholism, tuberculosis, and housing. One might argue that, apart from variations of socialist doctrine and revolution itself, anarchists concerned themselves with reclaiming jurisdiction over the body. While the bourgeois men featured in this collection sought to improve national health through increased state and bureaucratic power, neo-Malthusians and anarchists sought to educate themselves about the same issues as a means to combat the state and enhance (depending on the variety of anarchism) individual or class power.

Most important, while much of the birth control rhetoric did not usually focus directly on women or gender roles, those who spread birth control devices and the instruction to use them certainly addressed women as their audience. The neo-Malthusian movement, along with its advocates among other political groups such as socialists, anarchists, and feminists, provided an alternative image of motherhood for women. Effective birth control and the rationalizations for it allowed women to see themselves as individuals rather than as mothers alone and also provided a basis for them to resist Third Republic proclamations about women's nature. In addition to providing the technology necessary for avoiding births, neo-Malthusianism released the collective and individual imaginations from their previous restraints about gender.[57]

Moreover, the effort to channel women into actual motherhood, or symbolic motherhood in the form of "maternalism," by bringing women into the social, or public, sphere had the paradoxical result of ascribing them with the more classical rights to personal liberty. Parallel to the legislation that seemed to define women as mothers emerged a series of laws that increased women's civil liberties and that began systematically to dismantle or modify some of the articles in the Napoleonic Code oppressive to women: in 1893, single and separated women gained full legal status; in 1897, adult women gained the right to serve as witnesses for civil acts; married women gained the right to control their own wages in 1907. In the early 1880s, the Ferry laws extended and improved education for girls, and soon after, women began to enter universities and professional schools. These gains speak to an increased acknowledgment of women as adult individuals rather than as minors in the custody of men or of the state. These changes, moreover, coincided with the growth of a feminist movement in France and a rise in the number of educated women and of women in occupations such as teaching. Such trends made gender relations increasingly problematic for society as a whole and for politicians and legislators in particular.

Woman as individual remained, and has remained to this day, a problematic construct. Carole Pateman persuasively argued that in Enlightenment political philosophy the concept of the individual in the republican social contract is, in fact, a male construct dependent upon the "sexual contract"—the sexual subordination of woman to man. Woman, she argues, cannot be a free individual in a liberal society.[58] The history of republicanism in France from 1789 through the Third Republic certainly bears testimony, not simply to the nonindividuality of women and their lack of ownership over their own bodies, but to the need of republicanism to emphasize motherhood and domesticity, especially in a society in which "social right"—the need and ability to preserve life—takes precedence over "civil right." This tendency culminated with the law of 1920 which criminalized the sale of contraceptive devices and the publication or distribution of birth control propaganda and stiffened the penalties for abortion. No law better signifies state entry into private life and control over the body, especially the female body.

Every essay in this collection demonstrates that republicans viewed women primarily in their reproductive capacity or potential. However, the political philosophy and practice of republicanism were inconsistent. While bourgeois republicanism in 1793 depended on the dichotomy of public and private, and the relegation of women to the latter sphere, the "private" sphere of domesticity and motherhood necessarily became a public matter even in the First Republic; it became a social and political concern in the industrial and demographic context of the Third Republic. For the reasons these essays demonstrate, motherhood could not remain a private construct in the late nineteenth century because it necessarily had to serve the state for purposes of repopulation, civic education, national self-esteem, military strength, social control, and defense against the all-pervasive sense of degeneration. If republicanism could not live with women in the public sphere, it could not live without them either. Politicians thus had to refashion gender to fit the new order even though no single conception of gender prevailed.

I would, finally, suggest that those conceptions of gender that found constitutional or legislative expression not only provoked resistance movements but may also have served to reinforce class divisions. The different educational tracks of middle-class and working-class girls, and the different uses to which solidarists hoped to put middle-class and working-class women in their effort to consolidate and harmonize the Republic, may well have perpetuated and reinforced the class system and at the same time undermined worker solidarity, as Sanford Elwitt suggested. The various efforts to fit women into the Republic no doubt also contributed to the numerous divisions within the French feminist movement and help explain its fractured nature.

The social reform legislation of the early Third Republic as well as the debates and discourse that led to its creation lend a good deal of irony to Rousseau's comment that it would be women's fate to govern men. For him, of course, the female capacity and imperative to "govern" men lay strictly in the private sphere, where women could exert influence through virtue (or vice). But the actual practice of French republicanism—a republicanism whose theoretical foundations Rousseau helped construct—broke down many of the barriers between private and public. If women did not have political rights in the Third Republic, concepts of womanhood nonetheless governed the minds of reformers and politicians as they attempted to shape the French nation. It follows that the efforts of traditional historians to make sense of the various political intrigues and paradoxes of the Third Republic have fallen short because of their inattention to issues of gender. The essays in this collection, along with other recent scholarship, set a new agenda for political and social history and open the door to new ways of understanding the Third Republic and the twentieth-century state.

Two

The Republican Brotherhood
Gender and Ideology

JUDITH F. STONE

THE FAMILY HAS long served as a metaphor to explain the structures of the state, and the state has provided a model for the functional family.[1] Central in this modeling process are the relations of power and subordination between men and women and between rulers and ruled. Recourse to such models becomes more frequent in periods of political and social transformation. In 1816, as the Bourbon Restoration was being installed, the aristocratic counterrevolutionary Louis de Bonald insisted that power relations within the family must reflect and sustain those of the state. Patriarchal authority must be protected if royal authority was to be maintained. "Just as political democracy allows the people, the weak part of political society, to rise against the established power, so divorce, veritable domestic democracy, allows the wife, the weak part, to rebel against marital authority. . . . In order to keep the state out of the hands of the people, it is necessary to keep the family out of the hands of wives and children."[2] Almost fifty years later, during the decline of the Bonapartist Second Empire, a similar analogy was made, although one whose political content differed significantly. Eugène Pelletan, a leader of the republican opposition, addressed a large audience on the role of women. While subscribing to the dominant ideology of domesticity, he attempted to redefine the governing of the home and simultaneously to endorse a new political regime. "As for woman, her place is at home, directing, administering the house and above all constantly forming those young souls which Providence has confided to her, making them one day citizens worthy of their country. Thus, if I had to define marriage, you must excuse me, I would call it a constitutional government. The husband minister of foreign affairs, the wife minister of the interior, and all household questions decided by the council of ministers."[3] Unlike the Bonald metaphor, in which patriarchal and hierarchical relations of family and state clearly reinforced each other, Pelletan's metaphor lacked such consistency. In this republican model, subordination and equality uneasily coexisted with each other.[4]

Throughout the nineteenth century a rich array of theoretical and practical projects emerged intending to rewrite the domestic and political dramas. Most gave considerable attention to how these realms affected each other, and most had great expectations of achieving happy endings in both the domestic and political spheres. In the more romantic and ambitious of these projects, that happy ending required the full emancipation of the "people," or workers, or women; others aimed to establish "social peace," increased birthrates, and family tranquility. Especially after 1850 these new formulations of state and family coincided with challenges to classical liberal views. "The will of the people," embodied either in its democratic form of universal male suffrage or in its nationalist version, was becoming an accepted source of political legitimacy. In France these transformations were particularly complex. After 1871 France was the only major European republic. At least until 1905, most committed republicans retained a permanent sense of insecurity, perhaps paranoia, about the Republic's survival, despite their electoral and parliamentary victories. They feared the strength of clerical, authoritarian, and traditionalist forces whose supporters were by no means inconsequential. Second, beginning in the 1860s the French economy and society experienced a profound transformation: the relative decline of the agricultural sector and the nationwide expansion of industrialization and the market. This transformation was accompanied by a relatively high participation of women in the labor force and a continuing decline in the birthrate. Third, while republicanism achieved the position of the official and dominant ideology by 1900, it confronted a well-organized and growing socialist opposition. The socialists presented themselves as the authentic heirs to the revolutionary tradition of 1789, which, they claimed, republican governments and politicians had abandoned. Finally, beginning in the 1880s, feminist organizations, which primarily identified themselves as part of the larger republican movement, demanded increased civil rights and, after 1900, the right to vote. They particularly called on the most committed republicans, the Radicals, to make good their support for universal suffrage.

Republicans attempted to adjust their beliefs in order to address these new conditions. This essay examines republicanism at midcentury, demonstrating the central role that gender had in shaping that ideology. The midcentury formulation of republicanism molded a new generation of men who came to dominate the Third Republic by the 1880s. These new men of the new republic preserved and refashioned republican ideology, including its important assumptions about gender. The second part of the study examines how these republican politicians of the late nineteenth and early twentieth centuries responded to two distinct sets of issues: concrete concerns about women's productive and reproductive experiences, and demands for women's civil rights and suffrage.

All republicans of the nineteenth century identified themselves with the Great Revolution. Since 1789, family and gender had always played a critical role in republican ideology. Republicans had asserted the sovereignty of citizens and deposed the traditional authority of patriarchal monarchy. By 1793 the Jacobins had aggressively imposed an exclusively male identity on the key category of citizen which remained unquestioned by most republicans until the second half of the nineteenth century.[5] By then Radical republicans were claiming as their exclusive inheritance the more militant, more popular, more nationalistic, and more patriarchal Jacobinism of 1793. This identification was an intimate, personal, and familial one; the Radicals constantly insisted that they were the "sons of the Revolution." Among the generation that came to political maturity in the 1880s and 1890s, many actually had influential republican fathers. If few of these Third Republican Radicals acknowledged republican mothers, there was always the symbol of the nurturing maternal republic.[6] Jean-Jacques Rousseau remained a principal source of political and moral inspiration. Eminent republicans traveled to Geneva to celebrate the centenary of his death in 1878. Eugène Pelletan, for one, signaled the importance of Rousseau's moral vision of virtue.[7] Egalitarianism and universality were central to this tradition, but they were extended to citizens who "naturally" could only be men. As Carol Blum persuasively argued, Rousseau's most influential texts on education, *Émile* and *La Nouvelle Héloïse*, subordinated women to men and presented new educational models to reinforce that subordination.[8] In Rousseauean political theory and the Jacobin practice of republicanism, women were assigned the domestic sphere, were given the responsibility to rear republican citizens, and were to defer to male authority.[9] Only in the second half of the nineteenth century did some republicans begin to consider whether *la femme au foyer* could actually fulfill her civic functions of republican mother and what the implications of separate spheres might mean for the republican principle of equality. From its origins, then, modern republicanism associated male political equality with a hierarchical family. The apparently universal principles of the public realm depended on the exclusion and subordination of women. Men were individuals and citizens, active in the state; women were mothers who produced and nurtured future citizens.

"Citizen" was perhaps the most important republican concept inherited from the Revolution. The custom of replacing the respectable and polite greeting of "Monsieur" with the militant salutation "Citoyen" continued among Radical republicans until the First World War. The address and the concept always carried assumptions of equality among men and the exclusion of women. "Citizen" was linked to other central and similarly protean republican concepts: equality, individualism, the people, and personal property. The rhetoric on equality embraced equality before the law, equality of political participation for citizens, and equality of opportunities. Although the Civil Code guaranteed citizens legal equality, it relegated married women to the status of minors, therefore barring them from participation in legal actions. Most important, equality was defined by a negative, the absence of privileges—political, social, and to some degree economic. While great wealth and unrestrained capitalism (*la fédodalité financière*) remained suspect, personal property was highly valued. Without it republicans could not imagine authentic individualism and citizenship. Lacking personal property, independence seemed impossible, and without independence an authentic individual identity could not exist. In the second half of the nineteenth century the growing number of propertyless male workers alarmed republicans, who feared that such proletarians would not be able to exercise the rights and responsibilities of citizens. Yet at the same time, most republicans accepted the legal restrictions making it impossible for married women to control property and in effect preventing them from functioning as fully independent individuals with political rights and economic responsibilities.

The 1850s were a critical and traumatic period for republicans. The failure of the Second Republic, armed conflict among republicans over social and economic questions, and Louis-Napoléon Bonaparte's successful coup establishing an authoritarian empire challenged assumptions of republican ideology and marked the young men who came of age during the Second Empire. Republicans struggled to identify the authentic "people," to transform an authoritarian state into a republican one without civil war, and to define the appropriate role of the family. Recovering in the 1860s, the republican movement expanded, becoming increasingly active and self-confident. This growth was sustained by a prolific cultural and intellectual environment, centered in Paris. This literary, intellectual, and political world of opposition to Bonapartism shaped the men who would acquire political power in the early decades of the Third Republic. While every generation of republicans considered themselves the "sons of the Revolution," those born in the 1840s viewed themselves in addition as the heirs of Second Empire republicanism. In some cases they directly inherited their politics from fathers actively opposed to Bonapartism.[10] In all cases they eagerly imbibed the assumptions and beliefs that constituted the broad opposition of the 1860s. All republicans of this 1840s generation would acknowledge the powerful influence of Jules Michelet and Victor Hugo. During the crucial decades of the Second Empire the historian and the poet significantly refashioned an earlier republican tradition. Both explicitly linked the future creation of a republic to the condition of the family and the role of women.

Immediately before and after the unsuccessful revolution of 1848 and the Second Republic, the romantic historian Jules Michelet played a major role in shaping republican ideology.[11] At his death in 1874 Radicals praised him as a "poet of history . . . [who] had remade France." [12] Michelet's histories, which placed 1789 and "*le peuple*" at the center of French identity, were intended to provide a moral and political direction for his contemporaries, especially for his students. His audience, however, reached well beyond narrow academic and political circles. In Michelet's view recent republican disasters and France's moral malaise stemmed from unnatural divisions among the "people," unnecessary enmity caused by the misunderstandings between classes and genders. Divisiveness among what ought to be a republican brotherhood could be politically disastrous, but an even more fundamental danger for France and the republican cause was the woman question. In his view, the absence of authentic republican mothers was undermining France and progressive political movements. Living as an internal exile during the Second Empire, Michelet increasingly stressed issues of "secular morality," in which the conditions of women, their relations with men, and the reform of those relations figured prominently. This persistent theme of women's roles, especially in what he hoped would be a reinvigorated republican France, was drawn together most completely in two tracts, *L'Amour* (1858) and *La Femme* (1860). These were specifically written to refute the views of utopian socialists who had decried the family, marriage, and women's subordination in those institutions. By the 1850s republicans were coming to regard the revolutionary critique of the traditional home, like the call to armed insurrection, as a cause for the disastrous end of the Second Republic.

L'Amour and *La Femme* were widely read; in 1860 alone Hachette published three editions of *La Femme*. Both were marriage manuals addressed to the young men of France and especially to the circle of Left Bank students who followed Michelet's courses and frequented his soirees. They were intended for the next generation of republicans just becoming adults in the 1860s. Michelet argued that these bachelors had a patriotic and moral responsibility to establish families and republican households. There were two obstacles: bourgeois women corrupted by luxury, idleness, and clericalism, and working-class women degraded by abject misery.[13] Supersensitive to conditions of alienation, Michelet opened *La Femme* with a description of these two alienated states. In the first men and women were increasingly unable to communicate with each other; they had such fundamentally different life experiences that they appeared as two distinct peoples.[14] The second was that of the single, working-class woman, *l'ouvrière*, whose isolated, impoverished existence resulted in endless rounds of economic and sexual exploitation. These observations brought Michelet to the categorical conclusion that "woman cannot live without a man."[15]

Unquestionably, the issue of France's declining birthrate, which by mid-century was already becoming a national preoccupation, as well as a personal obsession of Michelet's, provided a strong motive for this insistence that all women were destined to be wives and mothers.[16] According to Michelet, physiology linked women more closely with nature, endowing them with unique nurturing abilities. He was convinced, for example, that all little girls naturally adored gardens and could instinctively raise masses of flowers.[17] But *La Femme* was not simply a plea to increase the birthrate. It called for a specific type of wife and mother, a republican one, drawn from the "popular classes" or from those remaining bourgeois families which had not yet succumbed to moral corruption. Such girls through proper training would become the wives who could create a much needed haven for their republican husbands and could supervise the indispensable moral training of their children. In Michelet's ideal, women were to sustain and nurture not only their own children but future generations and the future republic. Woman would provide an ever present generative support for man's heroic activities. She is destined to live "for others. . . . She is the cradle of the future, she is its school, yet another cradle. In one word: She is the altar." [18]

Michelet's glorification of nursing mothers, like that found in Rousseau's earlier educational tracts, served as a practical call for maternal breast-feeding and as a powerful symbol of the fecund, harmonious family and state. [19] Such mothers provided a forceful example of the expected, heroically silent sustenance that women must provide for the nation. Women must be trained from childhood to fulfill their nature, which was "to live for others" and to experience suffering. [20] This maternal image, with its undercurrent of eroticism and pain, so powerfully affected Michelet that he sometimes forgot his original intent, the promotion of republican households, and he simply glorified the suffering, devoted, bare-breasted mother. In *La Femme* he spent three delirious pages describing an Italian Renaissance painting that portrayed a young woman nursing a band of starving orphans. Rather than a praise of domesticity, Michelet here emphasized the near sensual rewards of public giving. In addition, he apparently forgot that this was a version of wet-nursing, which he, like Rousseau, condemned, and that it was something women could do quite successfully without men. For Michelet the painting captured "the intoxication of charity," which would be women's reward for their perpetual acts of sacrifice. [21]

But hierarchical domesticity was the ultimate goal. Near the end of the manual Michelet depicted his vision of perfect harmony: It is a cold, snowy winter Sunday; the family cozily gathers around the "flaming hearth where supper is warming." There is almost no sound, and "he, the man, takes advantage of this day to do what he likes. . . . [He reads.] He knows that she is behind him. She makes almost no noise, but does all that is necessary with a soft, undulating movement." She instructs the children with lessons drawn from nature; robins arriving on this winter day offer excellent examples of fraternity. In fact, one did not even have to listen to her exact words; simply her presence instructed. At the end of the day the children delight their father by singing the Marseillaise and a hymn to God. And over this patriotic apotheosis "she" blesses them all. [22]

Since the 1840s Michelet had viewed women not merely as symbols of the republic but as the means by which the republic would be made possible, a republic uniting the bourgeoisie and the "people." In his view, women, like the working class, had become alienated from the bourgeoisie, which had grown egotistical, cold, and cynical. Bourgeois men rarely married until their late thirties and then sought loveless matches of convenience with wealthy, spoiled women. Michelet was convinced that "in the second or third generation this bourgeoisie [would] be as feeble as [the] nobles were before the Revolution."[23] Miserable marriages were wreaking havoc with the birthrate and with masculine energy and political commitment. In the preface to *La Femme* he condemned modern novelists for their negative portraits of marriage, which he felt encouraged adultery among wives.[24] The alternative to such despair should be neither infidelity nor the denunciation of marriage. Rather, the unhappy bourgeois bachelors must find a woman of the "people" who could be educated and transformed to suit her husband's needs. "The woman you ought to marry . . . should be simple and loving, having not yet received any final definition. . . . I like her best poor, alone, with few family ties. Her educational level is a very secondary issue."[25] In fact, Michelet had observed that "the women of the people (who [were] not nearly as vulgar as the men . . .) listen[ed] to men [socially] above them with confidence. . . . [They expressed the] touching confidence of the people."[26]

Such marriages would in themselves constitue miniature republics in which alienation was overcome and roles appropriately assigned; in turn these households would produce properly reared republican citizens and future republican mothers. The republican exploration of gender, and this was especially the case for Michelet, always linked women and the working class. Michelet observed that working-class women were doubly exploited, increasing his concern and his desire for these women, whom he regarded as more malleable and in greater need of salvation. Furthermore, women's "natural" subordination mirrored the condition of the entire working class about which Michelet and all republicans were deeply anxious. In Michelet's vision, the seemingly insurmountable nineteenth-century problems of the state, class, and gender might all be resolved on the condition that women followed their proper biological destiny and allowed themselves to be defined by republican men. Woman would then be the "Sunday of man . . . his joy, his freedom, his celebration."[27]

During the intense debate on the woman question which occurred in the 1860s, a few courageous women challenged Michelet.[28] Critics, such as Jenny d'Héricourt, condemned his deep misogyny and exposed Michelet's fierce attacks on women despite his language, "sweet as honey" and full of "love and poetry."[29] Most men, however, perceived Michelet as a passionate defender of women. *L'Amour* and *La Femme* were extraordinarily popular, especially among their intended audience, the bourgeois students of Paris. Not surprisingly, Michelet's views of women and the family were echoed and reinforced in the works of Victor Hugo, who also was, and often continues to be, acclaimed as an advocate of woman's emancipation.

Hugo's influence on the nineteenth-century bourgeoisie was enormous.[30] During the 1850s this former royalist and member of the July Monarchy's Chamber of Peers declared himself the spiritual leader of republicanism. He claimed to be the inspired poet-seer who would direct the nation. At the time of Louis-Napoléon's coup (1851–52), a series of accidents and misunderstandings, as well as genuine principles, had placed Hugo in the predicament of political exile and a very new affiliation with republicanism.[31] He and his close associates made the most of this mildly uncomfortable situation. From his island exile in the English Channel he set himself up as the "Grand Proscrit," the morally and aesthetically superior alternative to the corrupt and mediocre Louis-Napoléon. He would guide the French toward the regeneration of the nation, state, and family. Although Hugo was only a recent convert to republicanism, his claim to inspire the movement was accepted by most republicans. His allegiance provided legitimation and stature to their opposition. After the collapse of the Second Empire and the establishment of the Third Republic, Hugo would be venerated as a republican secular saint.[32]

In 1862, after decades of creative labor, *Les Misérables* appeared.[33] Its appearance in imperial France was a major political and literary event.[34] Stories were told of Parisian artisans and students forming associations to purchase a copy to read aloud in their *cercles d'amitié*. The novel's circulation contributed to the opposition's electoral victories in 1863, which marked a further relaxing of the repressive regime of the Second Empire. *Les Misérables* was a "modern epic," intended to prepare a new future. In its pages Hugo pronounced his magnificent, sonorous, and endless words on the social question, republicanism, revolution, gender relations, the family, and the future of France. Two central and interrelated themes dominated this massive fiction: the horror and pointlessness of class war, and the urgent need to construct loving, healthy, "intact" families.

Hugo dramatically expressed an important shift in republicanism after 1851: class conflict, civil war, and armed insurrection on the barricades were increasingly seen as the greatest threat to emancipatory politics and republicanism. The ideals of solidarity and pacification were replacing those of conflict and militancy. Yet at the same time neither Hugo nor the republicans wanted to repudiate entirely the older, heroic revolutionary tradition. In a long digression set entirely outside the action of the novel, Hugo described his own experiences during the June Days of 1848 when he fought with the forces of "order," on the side of the new Second Republic, against the unemployed workers. He portrayed this episode with horror as the "Carmagnole defying the Marseillaise . . . [a] revolt of the people against itself." While denouncing the madness of the "mob," he also recognized the "grandeur and magnificence" of those who have suffered abject misery.[35]

This aside reinforced the clear message of the long dramatic sequence portraying the death of young republicans on the barricades, an episode central to the novel's narrative. Such confrontations must be stopped at all costs; Frenchmen must cease to battle one another.[36] The unnatural fratricide of the national family must be halted. On one level, Hugo's solution was to offer what was already becoming by the 1860s the social program of advanced republicans. "Encourage the rich and protect the poor . . . end the unjust exploitation of the weak by the strong . . . adjust workers' wages . . . introduce free and obligatory education . . . democratize property, not by abolishing it but by universalizing it, so that every citizen without exception is a property owner."[37] Radical republicans would continue to adhere to this program until at least 1914. Yet the novelist never assumed that such practical reforms to alleviate "misery" would alone be adequate.

Class war, while an awesome experience in Hugo's literary universe, was only one manifestation of a much more profound despair within French society. Strife permeated even the most intimate relations, particularly those between men and women. The problem lay in the intense experience of separation, dehumanization, and isolation created by the complex intersections of class, gender, politics, and individual identity. In some instances this experience was so devastating that the family itself became hopelessly corrupted and beyond all salvation. Then family relations multiplied degradation, viciousness, and death.[38] The family, however, might also be the source of overcoming this multiple despair. Such a family, centered around the same *femme simple* described by Michelet, would be the source of harmony, unity, and solidarity. The "natural," procreative, loving subordination of wives to husbands in the family was to be a model for all social relations and would also produce individuals capable of entering such relations. The authentic *femme simple* would instruct bourgeois men in the deeper values of life which lay outside the market and politics.

Les Misérables offered the hope of a better republican future for all of France, but only if such new, healthy, productive families could be established. The novel turned around the regenerative powers of the permanently childlike Cosette, the quintessential *femme simple*. She embodied the multiple metaphors of class and gender as the abandoned, illegitimate daughter of an *ouvrière* who had been exploited as a seamstress, prostitue, and textile worker. At a dramatic moment of gunfire on the barricades Hugo stopped the action and shifted the scene to Cosette's awakening in a distant, calm neighborhood. Hugo emphasized that "she knew nothing" of the armed conflict.[39] Her perpetual ignorance was constantly underscored and portrayed as a great strength. Oblivious to the barricades, Cosette savored the quiet of the household and her dreams of love; she opened her shutter to the bright sunlight and contemplated a nest of swallows. "The mother is there, spreading her wings over her brood; the father comes and goes, bringing food and kisses in his beak. . . . Cosette thinks of Marius as she watches these birds, this family, this male and this female, this mother and her little ones."[40]

Hugo's long, didactic novel ended with the marriage of Cosette and Marius, two orphans reconciled to their own origins and about to embark on the creation of a harmonious future. Cosette created family peace and by extension a larger social and political reconciliation. Her ability to end conflict had little to do with rational persuasion and much to do with her instinctive "feminine" qualities to promote love and harmony. Again her "ignorance" was stressed. While understanding little, she alone recognized and demonstrated that it was the banal acts of daily life, not political manifestos, which were truly significant. In the concluding epiphany of the novel she described a future family gathering set in a beautiful flowering garden where her husband and her guardian would eat the strawberries she had raised. "[And there] we'll all live in a republic where everyone will say 'tu.' "[41] Cosette was the ideal wife instinctively able to enlighten her husband without abandoning her subordinate role.[42] In *Les Misérables* Hugo, like Michelet, identified the success of the future republic as dependent upon the correspondence between the political and domestic realms. Class conflict, which posed one of the greatest dangers to a nascent republic, would be eliminated as class relations followed the new family model. Division would be transformed into a new harmony in which hierarchies would be accepted as reasonable and natural.

Hugo's impact on the generation of young men coming of age in the 1860s was enormous, greater even than that of Michelet. One member of this generation and future Radical politician, Camille Pelletan, stated that it was Hugo who inspired the students of the 1860s to be republicans and anti-Bonapartists.[43] By the end of the decade Hugo himself was consciously cultivating a following among those young men, who easily moved from literature to journalism to politics. He had long hoped to establish an influential political circle to implement his ideas. In May 1869 Hugo's two sons, Charles and François-Victor, established a political journal, *Le Rappel*, which soon became one of the major organs of early radicalism. They were joined on the editorial board by ardent republican journalists close to Hugo: Henri Rochefort, Paul Meurice, and Auguste Vacquerie. The last was the brother-in-law of Hugo's beloved eldest daughter, who had accidentally drowned in the 1840s. Soon after the establishment of the Third Republic the young Camille Pelletan, future Radical leader and minister, joined the group as a reporter, feature columnist, and eventually editor. In the late 1870s Edouard Lockroy, another future Radical deputy and minister, became an editor following the premature deaths of both François-Victor and Charles Hugo. In 1873 Lockroy married Alice Hugo, Charles' widow. Well into the 1880s the editorial board remained an intimate, family affair.

The very first issue carried an article by Victor Hugo addressed to the editors of *Le Rappel*, entitled "A mes fils." He urged them to maintain their fraternal unanimity and saluted them as "sons of the revolutionary changes of the nineteenth century." In his view these "journalist-poets" incarnated the essence of the century, which was "L'HOMME."[44] At the end of the article he promised as "a quiet old man" to write no more for their journal; not surprisingly Hugo failed to keep this promise. Through the 1870s he contributed articles and several political poems. Most important, in terms of building circulation, he permitted *Le Rappel* to serialize his latest works, *L'Homme qui rit* in 1869 and *Mes Fils* in 1874.

Hugo and the younger men whom he attracted to *Le Rappel* all endorsed the cult of domesticity so venerated in the "master's" fiction. They all accepted as natural the exclusively masculine worlds of the university, the editorial room, and the political arena. *Le Rappel* depended on the loyalty of the younger men to Hugo's patriarchal inspiration and on the ostensible camaraderie of all the "sons." Like all newspapers of the Left, *Le Rappel* always spoke of "universal suffrage" when it meant universal male suffrage. Sharing the accepted rhetoric of the day, "manliness" was frequently noted as a critically important, positive moral attribute. In the newspaper's columns republican politicians always spoke with an "*éloquence virile*" and expressed "*une foi virile*" in the Republic.[45] At the same time *Le Rappel*, again following its patron's direction, was sympathetic to the reemerging women's movement of the 1870s.

Perhaps because Hugo's commitment to Jacobin republicanism was never that rigorous, he was willing to recognize the need for expanding women's rights. Neither he nor his contemporaries were ever troubled by the contradictions between such support and his richly crafted portraits of women's subordination to men. In an oft-quoted eulogy for a utopian socialist in 1854, Hugo had proclaimed the nineteenth century the era of women's rights.[46] In the early years of the Third Republic he accepted the honorary presidency of La Ligue française pour le droit des femmes. Auguste Vacquerie, his close associate, also joined him as a proponent of the league. While the woman question never dominated the columns of *Le Rappel*, the movement was politely recognized. The earliest meetings of the Association pour le droit des femmes in 1869 were advertised in its back pages. During the first decade of its existence, one of the few articles to address women's issues appeared, significantly, in the midst of civil war, the Paris Commune. Auguste Vacquerie's lead story for 11 May 1871 was "Les Droits de la femme." In it he endorsed a proposal being debated in the English Parliament which called for women's suffrage. His article eloquently supported a concept of equality that would have no gender references. "All caste distinctions would be broken and the relations between the sexes would become equal, as between the classes. And then . . . we would have real equality of which we now have only a forgery . . . since we presently call equality a state of things in which one half of the human species is the servant of the other half."[47] At the same time, however, the article was a partisan attack on moderate republicans and Orléanists who idolized the English system but were appalled at the thought of women's suffrage. Ostensibly about women's rights, the article was as much an effort to expose the contradictions of the Radicals' political opponents. Similarly, during the 1870s and 1880s, when *Le Rappel* followed the efforts of fellow Radical republican Alfred Naquet to legalize divorce, the parliamentary debate was covered as much to gauge the growing Radical presence in the Chamber and the increasing success of anticlericalism than to report on women's rights. While the campaign for women's rights was recognized, the men of the *Rappel* circle always subordinated it to what were considered more important and pressing political issues. Like Hugo, their sympathy for the women's movement did not interfere with their implicit endorsement of domesticity and hierarchical gender relations.

The rhetoric and images of Michelet and Hugo which dominated republican political culture by the 1860s were disseminated by a wide circle of second- and third-rate writers, journalists, and politicians. One member of this group who merits greater attention was Eugène Pelletan. Like his much more accomplished and famous contemporaries, Pelletan joined the issues of political transformation, anti-Bonapartism, domesticity, and the education of women. Although largely forgotten by the early twentieth century, Eugène Pelletan was a widely read journalist, lecturer, and politician of the 1850s and 1860s who frequented the circles surrounding both Michelet and Hugo.[48] His election in 1863 to the republican opposition brought warm congratulations from the exiled Victor Hugo.[49] One police report characterized Pelletan as a *"mouton enragé."*[50] During the 1870s and 1880s he was venerated as one of the founders of the Third Republic—initially a member of the Government of National Defense, then elected to the National Assembly, and finally senator for the Bouches-du-Rhône.[51] Following the triumph of the republicans in the 1880s, he chaired the committee to erect a statue at Michelet's tomb. He was invited to the wedding of Alice Hugo and Edouard Lockroy, and he attended François-Victor Hugo's funeral in 1874. These connections gave his son, Camille, entrée to the offices of *Le Rappel*. More important, Eugène Pelletan shared Hugo's interest in the nascent women's movement. At a special Masonic meeting, *la fête de famille*, in February 1878, Pelletan forcefully reiterated his strong support for rigorous women's education, but he refrained from endorsing women's suffrage. Later that same year he attended the Congrès du droit des femmes, whose honorary presidents were Hugo and Vacquerie.[52] Like Michelet and Hugo, he intended to influence the new generation of university-trained young men.[53] His participation in these events of the early Third Republic were the logical conclusion of a career that had stressed the critical role of mothers in the creation of republicans and the republic. Complementing the images of domesticity, powerfully evoked by Michelet and Hugo, Pelletan emphasized the role of the mother as educator and transmitter of a particular moral vision.

That vision combined republicanism, liberal Protestantism, romantic sentiment, anticlericalism, an unshakable belief in progress, and support for the social order. As Katherine Auspitz demonstrated, such an outlook was promoted by the increasingly influential Ligue de l'enseignement through its moral standards demanding *"pur et dur"* republicans.[54] The family was the linchpin of this morality and central to the success of a republic, but it must be a reformed family, transformed by a new cooperative marriage. Like Michelet and Hugo, Pelletan too was profoundly disturbed by the miserable marriages he observed between bourgeois men and women. In the 1860s he was convinced that the "decline" of the family was linked to the public and private decadence of the Second Empire. The same year in which *Les Misérables* appeared, 1862, Eugène Pelletan published *La Nouvelle Babylone*. In it the Parisian opposition journalist offered a portrait of Louis-Napoléon's new Paris. He damned not only Haussmann's boulevards but implicitly the entire imperial society and state. Using the literary device of a naive but intelligent provincial visiting the capital after a thirty-year absence, Pelletan revealed a city in disarray (*boulversée*).[55] Apartments, buildings, gardens, and neighborhoods had been ripped apart; the material chaos was matched by spiritual discord in which "*la réligion de foyer*" had been totally disrupted.[56] The traditional veneration and interdependence of home, family, appropriate gender roles, and work had been replaced by new values of luxury and idleness. Wealthy, unproductive wives were parasites on the family, and their children could only grow up to be effeminate men, unfit mothers, and parasites on the state.[57] Pelletan concluded this moral itinerary by calling on his readers "to save the family" if they wanted "to save the fatherland, because a nation is only the family enlarged." What was needed was to "regenerate *men at home*."[58]

But Pelletan was not merely expressing a nostalgic yearning for a lost domesticity; he also proposed a new set of relations between husband and wife, a new respect for mothers, and a new emphasis on the education of women. Two years after *La Nouvelle Babylone* he wrote *La Charte au foyer*, selecting a political metaphor for his title. Arguing that equality was possible between the separate spheres of the domestic world and the public realm, Pelletan vigorously endorsed a reform of women's education. Women needed to have access to all forms of knowledge if they were to succeed in their "natural" duties as wives and mothers. At present boredom was creating frivolous women who were entirely estranged from their husbands. Most serious, they were ruining their sons, who became calculating egoists, bereft of "manly" virtues.[59] The following year Pelletan's exploration of the condition of women went much further. His 1865 work *La Famille: La Mère* was actually a survey of women's history from "the state of nature" to the present, including such topics as "Asian women, Athenian women, hétaera, medieval chivalry, and women during the Revolution." Not only were historical eras explored, but different stages of a woman's life history were analyzed: "the engaged young woman, mother, the separated woman." Again, failed marriages, linked to the moral and political decadence of the Second Empire, were a major concern. Now Pelletan went further and endorsed divorce as a necessary evil to combat the greater evil of incompatible couples.[60] Because he had difficulty throughout the survey in reconciling his belief in progress with the historical realities of women's continuing subordination, the final chapter on "women as citizens" was full of contradictions. On the one hand, Pelletan insisted that women shared with men the same essential quality of humanity, and therefore they must have access to all the rights and liberties inherent in humanness. On the other hand, he claimed that women could never truly have a profession; they could only master an "*état*," an occupation, something comparable to the weaving of classical antiquity. A few pages later, however, he admitted that once women worked for wages, they would have to be recognized as citizens. Implicit in this conclusion was the recognition that an exclusively domestic existence barred one from public life. But that public realm was also in need of reform. Significantly he stated, "The problem with politics is that it has been masculine. . . . There is a need for women's sentiments." While apparently promoting marriages in which wives and husbands would be genuine companions, Pelletan also seemed to fear the consequences of such a reordering of the domestic order and potentially the gender order. He ended ambiguously by calling for the education of women in order that "women may be what they ought to be."[61]

Despite, or perhaps because of, their contradictions these works were extremely popular and led to well-attended public lectures that in turn were published. In 1869 Pelletan, now a republican representative for the Seine, gave a lecture entitled "Woman in the Nineteenth Century" to a Paris audience. He covered his usual themes: domesticity and the equality of separate spheres, the importance of mothers in raising good citizens (i.e., republicans), and the pressing need to reform women's education. On this occasion he included in his critique the Civil Code, insisting that "women reason just like men" and therefore could not be treated as less than full adults.[62] Pelletan speculated on the future possibility of extending not only civil rights but also political rights to women. "She is part of society; I would not want to claim for her now *le droit de cité*, that is a question for the future, but I will say that she does not have the right to be disinterested in what happens in society."[63] Although Pelletan's audience certainly included women, his arguments were an effort to convince *men* of the urgent need to change educational institutions and women's civil status. Then, Pelletan claimed, a transformed woman would make possible more compatible relations between husband and wife, a more tranquil, more moral, and happier family, and the nurturing of more "manly" sons. Such families in turn would support the reform efforts toward a new, parliamentary republican regime that would itself lend further encouragement to harmonious domestic and social environments.

A new republic was established, but not as republican reformers of the Second Empire, like Eugène Pelletan, had imagined. The Third Republic was tentatively declared during the fall and spring of 1870–1871 in the midst of military defeat, invasion, and civil war. Its actual political and institutional foundation was protracted and precarious, not being complete until at least the early 1880s. Michelet's students, Hugo's young admirers, and the supporters of Eugène Pelletan were witnesses and participants in this process. Like their fathers, this new generation of republicans subordinated all issues to their primary concern, the establishment and preservation of the Republic. Even after the republican victories of the 1880s, some would remain uneasy about the regime's security until the First World War. Republicans persisted in the fear that class war would undermine the state and open the way for a monarchist restoration. Many republicans felt that the Paris Commune of 1871 had brought them perilously close to that danger. Through the 1870s and early 1880s they had two goals: to defend the weak Republic against monarchist threats and to heal the rift between various groups of authentic republicans. Needing to articulate a vision of the state, these young republicans inevitably turned to the metaphor of the family, which had traditionally served as a model for the body politic. They relied on the rich familial images and rhetoric that their fathers had shaped in the 1850s and 1860s.

Eugène Pelletan's son, Camille, gained his early journalistic experience as a reporter on the Hugos' paper, *Le Rappel*, covering the Commune. By 1880 he had joined forces with the leading Radical republican, Georges Clemenceau, to found a new paper, *La Justice*, and in 1881 he won a seat in the Chamber, joining Clemenceau on the far Left. Both from the columns of *La Justice* and in the Chamber, Pelletan and Clemenceau fought for the amnesty of former Communards now exiled or imprisoned. For this campaign Camille Pelletan wrote two historical studies, *Questions d'histoire: Le Comité central et la Commune* (1879) and *La Semaine de Mai* (1880). The first, serialized in *Le Rappel*, often recalled Hugo's fictional descriptions of rebellion and barricades. Like Hugo, the young Pelletan decried the unnatural destruction of civil war and its legacy of unending retribution. In Pelletan's view it was because of the "horrible cycle of blind repressions and violent uprisings" that nothing had lasted in France. "[Every] repression is powerless, because it forgets the sons of its victims. . . . The republic must put an end to this detestable chain reaction."[64] He evoked the image of the family, but now a monstrous one leading to the death of its members and threatening the Republic itself. This abnormal family was composed only of brothers bent on revenge, pledged to carry out an endless round of vendettas. Despite his sympathy for the Communards and the lack of much evidence, Pelletan included a description of *la pétroleuse*. In his account a poet "reportedly saw . . . an old woman in an outlandish, motley dress holding close to her breast a bottle filled with kerosene and caressing it with a tenderness that was both grotesque and sinister." [65] The unnaturalness of civil war transformed the family from the means to reproduce life into the means to perpetuate assassination; women, rather than being republican mothers nurturing their infant sons, became crones suckling destruction. Pelletan reminded his readers that civil wars were "deadly for the republic." [66] They were to be abhorred as a counternature. Amnesty would end this cycle and institute a new era of fraternal reconciliation.

References to family and gender were frequent in Pelletan's discussions of the 1870s and early 1880s, expressing the need for republican unity as the basis for the new regime. After the early 1880s, however, such rhetoric that linked the family and the state became less frequent. Legitimating foundation metaphors, centered around mothers and families, were no longer as urgently required as they had been during the uncertain first decade of the Third Republic. In practice most republicans accepted the flawed institutions of the Third Republic. Increasingly, they turned to a rhetoric championing the Republic as the legally established order. Republicans of all varieties were involved in parliamentary maneuvering to strengthen the existing state and their position within it. They did not want to encourage rhetorical allusions to its origins. Now they stressed instead the permanence and legality of the state whose foundation had been completed. Thus, by the late 1880s, Third Republic republicans gave less public attention to the woman question than their fathers had during the Second Empire.

In addition, those politicians who reached maturity in the 1880s and 1890s had come of age during a period of ever sharper yet increasingly problematic segregation between bourgeois men and women.[67] Political success inevitably reinforced this segregation; Camille Pelletan was a case in point. Student of Michelet, rapt admirer of Hugo, and his father's direct political protégé, Camille Pelletan was among the minority of Radical deputies who joined the Groupe parlementaire de defense des droits de la femme.[68] In his personal life, he flamboyantly rejected Michelet's dictum that republican bachelors must marry and create republican families. Camille lived in a "free union" for thirty years and, at least according to gossip, did not demand monogamy from his companion.[69] His highly unorthodox domestic life must have been a bitter disappointment to his moralistic father. Years after his father's death, Camille Pelletan did marry at the age of 54 to a much younger woman, a former *institutrice*. There were no children from either union. Despite the apparently happy relations with companion and wife, Camille Pelletan could not imagine women as genuine partners. Being excluded from the world of politics, they remained outside the most important concerns of republican men. Like that of most of his peers, Camille Pelletan's education was shaped by the lycée and the men of his family. The masculinism of this early formation was further reinforced by the university and the bohemian circle of poets that Camille frequented as a young man.[70] As he matured and became increasingly involved in politics, his milieu was that of editorial rooms, Masonic lodges, and the Chamber of Deputies. These exclusively male environments were charged with that masculine ideology of honor, courage, and performance which Robert Nye described.[71] Significantly, in his memoirs written at the end of his life in 1913, Pelletan continued to puzzle over an old comrade of his student bohemian days, Léon Valade, who liked to spend time with women. "He adored women, not at all with a robust, conquering physical passion . . . but with a sort of curious tenderness for everything about them and for all those complications of feminine nature. He preferred their company, scrutinizing their fleeting impressions, exploring their most superficial moods, and deciphering their most secret impressions."[72] An interest in women, other than a "conquering physical passion," was incomprehensible and in itself disturbingly feminine. Camille Pelletan was by no means exceptional. Variations of this aggressively masculine lifestyle could be found among leading Radical republicans. After 1880 it was heightened by the mounting sense of crisis which surrounded the gender identity of many bourgeois men.[73] For some this led to a growing incomprehension and reduced sympathy for the woman question, for others to a deep antipathy and misogyny.

By the 1890s these republican politicians, who lived personal and professional lives largely segregated from women, could not avoid addressing a new set of political and social problems connected with women's actual experiences. With continuing republican electoral successes, these men were increasingly called on to construct and implement republican legislation affecting the lives of French women and men. It had been relatively easy to use woman and the family as part of a rhetorical repertoire portraying the benefits of a future, harmonious republic; now, in the Third Republic, republican politicians had to respond to concrete issues of women's reproductive, productive, and civic lives. Three related conditions—women working outside the home, male industrial workers, and women's demands for civil and political rights—revealed the tensions, contradictions, and limits of republican ideology. These conditions challenged assumptions of the republican nineteenth-century belief system, while they pressured republican politicians to formulate effective policies. Republicans were forced to ask: What should be the appropriate relation between the state and women workers, who were, in reality, not citizens? Could men whose working situations permitted few options for individual independence really function as citizens? Could women and men whose lives were regulated by the factory ever establish republican families? Were working mothers the cause of the declining French birthrate? If working women could be biological mothers, could they be republican ones? Could women be citizens; could the much vaunted republican universal suffrage be genuinely universal?

These questions created considerable uneasiness among the most ardent supporters of republicanism, the Radicals. These politicians were loosely joined by opposition to clericalism and Bonapartism and by support for a variety of programs to create what they considered a democratic state and society. The Radicals claimed no enemies to their left and by 1893 were entering electoral and parliamentary alliances with socialists. In 1901 they organized a formal Radical party that from 1902 on experienced a steady series of electoral victories, enabling them to soon dominate both the Chamber and the Senate. The Radicals were key actors in the process of restructuring the relations of the state to both female and male workers, to women as a group, and to the family. They are the critical group of politicians in our analysis of gender and ideology, not simply because of their numbers in parliament but also because they insisted that they alone were authentic republicans. Their dedication to this highly gendered ideology led them to a series of impasses. Most significant was the tension between a commitment to individual rights and the need to enforce social obligations on the larger republican community, the nation. This tension intruded in all areas of social policy but was especially acute when Radicals sought to respond to the circumstances of working women. The complexity of their response was further heightened by republican ideology that had consistently denied women the status of individual and citizen. Given this ideological context, we can ask: Was it possible for republicans to fashion policies congruent with both their ideology and women's needs? Further, could Radicals even identify those needs given their ideology, their masculine environment, and, most important, the complexities of women's diverse situations? The social realities of women encompassed that of the bourgeoisie, the working class, and the peasantry; women included a probable majority who were deeply religious Catholics, as well as Protestant, Jewish and nonreligious minorities.

The Radicals brought to the dilemmas of working-class women complex ideological assumptions that linked economic and sexual exploitation, which identified the *ouvrière* with subordination both abhorrent and yet natural. Furthermore, the questions raised by women working outside the home, particularly in factories, became entangled with two other major debates at the end of the nineteenth century—the population issue and state intervention in the economy. The concerns of midcentury had grown into a crescendo of alarm as the French birthrate continued to fall.[74] Women's participation in production could not be separated from their role in the reproductive process. Politicians of both the Right and the Left called on the state to act in defense of the most fundamental "national resource." In addition to the argument that women's unique condition as mothers required special protection, reformers also noted that since women were considered legal minors, the state had a further responsibility to care for their welfare.[75] These arguments legitimated a series of gender-specific laws that not only regulated women's working conditions but also intervened in circumstances surrounding pregnancy, birth, and child care.[76] One Radical social theorist justified the 1892 limitation of adult women's working day in the following terms: "If women who worked to excess would only injure themselves, it might be permissible to argue that the legislator should not intervene; but this is not the case. The woman injures the child she might produce. Without regulation of female labor, society will soon be menaced by a bastardization of the race."[77]

Such gender-specific legislation was enacted because it used the rhetoric of domesticity and natalism, it strengthened gender segregation in the labor market and the factory, and it did *not* protect men.[78] Nonetheless there were liberal theorists and politicians who viewed any form of state intervention as a threat to laissez-faire principles. Some reformers did in fact dare to extend the argument of the state's obligation to protect the weak to male workers as well. This then linked the issue of working women's conditions to the issue of the extent to which the state could legitimately intervene in labor conditions, imposing social obligations. By the late nineteenth century, republicans participated in the general theoretical critique of liberalism. Republicans and especially Radicals particularly questioned those liberal assumptions limiting the state and its powers.

This distancing from liberalism was expressed in the theory of *solidarité*, most closely associated with Léon Bourgeois. He was a contemporary of Camille Pelletan and like him a founder of the Radical party. Bourgeois was much less dramatic than Pelletan, more comfortable with government and

party bureaucracies, and identified as one of the more moderate and concil-
iatory Radicals. Whereas Pelletan was a strong supporter of the principle of
reform, Bourgeois participated more directly in the committee work that
constructed actual legislation. Bourgeois intended his theory of *solidarité*
to provide a new set of principles for Radicals, enabling them to tran-
scend liberal individualism *and* refute socialist class conflict. *All* members
of society were tied by bonds of reciprocal indebtedness; the republican
state was to guarantee that this reciprocity would be acknowledged. Bourgeois's theory in practice endorsed a mild slate of social reforms, especially
insurance programs.

Despite its moderation *solidarité* did propose new functions for the
state; it is not surprising, then, that at the heart of Bourgeois's theory should
stand once again an image of the family. Along with the dominant medical
metaphor of the healing physician, the family was often the metaphor used
by solidarists to represent the state. According to Bourgeois, the family was
the original network of mutual relations of dependence. Without following
its full implications, Bourgeois came very close to revealing the gender bias
of liberal individualism and liberal contract theory. Behind the sacrosanct
individual of both liberal and republican theories stood others who had
been neglected and excluded from political consideration, the members of
the individual's family, the women and the children.[79] Addressing republican youth at the Sorbonne in May 1897, Bourgeois proclaimed, "Solitary
man does not exist; man in the state of nature is already associated with
another. . . . The origins of *solidarité* are the family and the fatherland."[80]
This assertion implicitly questioned fundamental republican assumptions
about individual rights and the citizen. However, Bourgeois had little interest in pursuing these larger issues. He viewed *solidarité* in practical political
terms as the means to legitimate social reform legislation, not as a critique
of republican individualism. Not surprisingly, Bourgeois was prominent
among those politicans who identified the declining birthrate as one of
France's most serious problems. Labor legislation, including the ten-hour
working day, all had "the higher goal to insure the vigor and the future
of the race, by organizing social hygiene."[81] Bourgeois campaigned for
both gender-specific and universal labor reforms principally as a means to
protect the working-class family and by extension the "fatherland."

When not equating himself with the healing physician, Bourgeois's
favorite metaphor was "*le bon père de famille.*" Minister of labor in the
brief Poincaré government of 1912, Bourgeois reminded the Senate, "We
are the guardians of our nation's finances, but we are also the guardians

of social peace. We are required to administer the national fortune wisely, like good fathers of the family . . . , but we are also required like good fathers of the family which we head to see that no child can say that they don't have their fair share." [82] In Bourgeois's view a "fair share" for French working women was a series of insurance and protective laws that would better enable them to fulfill their obligations as mothers and wives. *Solidarité* could reduce the consequences of unjust social inequalities, but it had no intention of disturbing the results of what were regarded as natural inequalities. Bourgeois listed these as "differences in sex, age, race, physical force, intelligence and will." [83]

While *solidarité* with its emphasis on domesticity, social hygiene, and gender inequality was ill equipped to support universal protective labor legislation, some Radical politicians continued to link gender-specific protective labor legislation with legislation covering all adult workers. A few of the most advanced Radicals, like Pelletan, were willing to admit that, despite the existence of the republican state, working-class men, like women, were denied meaningful equality. Pelletan insisted that universal labor legislation was necessary in order that *men* might have greater economic security and therefore be better able to fulfill their responsibilities as citizens. [84] In the early twentieth century, however, many Radicals came to fear that by enacting such universal labor legislation they would indeed be admitting what Marxist leader Jules Guesde had proclaimed: "To vote a protective labor law, is to recognize social classes. . . . You will affirm that there is an oppressed and exploited class." [85] Rather than risk a legal recognition of class and an admission of inequality among citizens, those Radicals committed to improving workers' conditions often relied on gender-specific legislation. Most Radicals found it easier to recognize the subordination of working women and extend some legal protection, especially to mothers, than to acknowledge that working-class men could not easily exercise their freedom. In addition, limited protection for women could establish precedents. These then might possibly be gradually expanded to protect all workers. At the same time, however, most Radical politicians were reluctant to view women in the same way as men, primarily as members of the work force. Women remained above all mothers.

The debate on legislation to limit the length of the working day, for example, contained the range of these different arguments. On the one hand, the 1900 law reducing some men's working day to ten hours by 1904 was supported by many simply to make the gender-specific legislation of 1892 more efficient. On the other hand, there were both supporters and opponents of the law who viewed it as a step toward a ten-hour working day for all French workers. In practice it did not significantly improve working conditions for either men or women in the textile industry, where it was most commonly applied.[86]

Republican rhetoric that had long associated the Republic with a harmonious but hierarchical family, centered around the nurturing *femme simple*, made it difficult for Radical politicians to view working women as anything other than mothers. The Radical leader Bourgeois was quite content to promote gender-specific labor legislation as a means to increase birthrates, protect motherhood, and defend the fatherland. Many Radicals, never the most cohesive of political groups, simply continued to use whatever argument and rhetoric seemed least controversial. Most, therefore, voted for the gender-specific legislation, and their often vacillating support for universal legislation was usually couched in the rhetoric of social peace and natalism. This strategy avoided difficult ideological issues about genuine equality which might consider the conditions of both working-class men and women. The debates on labor legislation immediately prior to the First World War raised—but could not resolve—the issues of the relations between gender, class, and citizen. Certainly the republican rhetoric forged during the second half of the nineteenth century could not easily provide answers to this debate.

At the same time that politicians succeeded in securing some gender-specific labor legislation by arguing the special case of women as mothers, as a vital national resource, or as persons with limited legal protection, the growing French women's movement was demanding greater civic equality. Paradoxically these women in presenting their claim to full citizenship appealed to republican ideology. Since the beginning of the Third Republic, middle-class, republican women had been organizing to demand the extension of civil and political rights. They were deeply committed to the Republic and assumed its establishment would necessarily increase the participation of women in public and political life.[87] This was not the case; greater civil rights were won only slowly over several decades, and suffrage was denied for the entire history of the Third Republic. This resistance indicated the strength of gender differences in republican ideology, the diversity of republican politicians' responses to women's emancipation, and the range of women's attitudes toward the Republic. Some gains were made: divorce became legal in 1884, although not by mutual consent; in 1893 single and separated women were accorded full legal status; women could be witnesses in law courts after 1897; and in 1907 married women gained control over their own wages. Slowly Eugène Pelletan's call to reform the Civil Code and recognize women as full legal adults was being realized. Education, which Eugène Pelletan and many others had identified as critical in the 1860s, was also being extended to girls and young women. The Ferry laws of 1881 and 1882 legislated that free, secular, and obligatory primary education be available to boys and girls; public secondary education was established for girls in 1880. The republican politicians who promoted this expansion were very explicit, however, that the goal of educating girls was to ensure a new generation of "republican mothers." In most towns educational institutions were segregated. The state-authorized primary curricula differed sharply for the two sexes, and the girls' secondary schools did not prepare their students for the baccalaureate exam, necessary for admission into the university.[88] Although the republican educational reforms closely mirrored the ideological commitment to both equality and gender hierarchy, they did create new careers for women with the possibility of upward social mobility. Between 1876 and 1906 the number of women teachers quadrupled, and by 1906 almost all public primary school teachers were women.[89] Among republican schoolteachers were to be found advocates for the further extension of women's civil and political rights, especially the vote. Yet republican and Radical politicians continued to view them as civic versions of "republican mothers" who offered a distinct, female instruction for their pupils. At the same time, however, the administration tended to ignore the particular needs of women teachers.[90]

The expansion of state-organized education, and especially female education, was bound up with the conflict between the Third Republic and the Catholic Church. One motive in creating state secondary schools for girls was to reduce the number of convent-educated bourgeois women. Female education was an aspect of the clerical question in which women and their deepest allegiances were constantly being examined. Certainly within the bourgeoisie the most common expression of alienation between men and women was sharply different attitudes toward the church. Most bourgeois women from Catholic families continued to practice their religion, often with increasing fervor as the century progressed.[91] Bourgeois men, on the other hand, were in many cases indifferent or, among those who identified with the Republic and Freemasonry, actively anticlerical. Republican women, while organized, were a definite minority. This sharp difference in religious preference, which often reflected even more intimate barriers between many bourgeois men and women, became a bitterly debated public question as the clerical issue intensified in the first decade of the twentieth century.

Anti-Dreyfusards, nationalists, clericals, and the traditional monarchist Right mobilized bourgeois women into an antirepublican political force despite their disenfranchisement.[92] Catholic women's commitment to the church and a religiously dominated culture, coupled with their social and political isolation from republican politics, easily convinced some among them of the need to defend actively their beliefs and lifestyles against the attacks of the anticlericals.[93] For these mostly affluent women, joining together in national organizations such as the Ligue des femmes françaises and La Ligue patriotique des françaises, antirepublicanism became a women's cause. During the 1902 legislative election La Ligue des femmes françaises distributed powerful campaign literature. In the Allier they appealed to "Jacques Bonhomme" not to be duped by wealthy Freemasons. In the Vendée they called on "Mothers, French women, Christians, and Vendéennes to pray, to fight and to influence their husbands and sons for the army and the liberty of the Church, in the name of the blood of [their] ancestors. Long live God, freedom and France." In Lyons La Ligue des femmes françaises produced a striking color poster of Jeanne d'Arc accompanied by a song recounting the heroism of the virgin who had repelled the barbarians and saved France.[94]

Republican women did respond to this effort to identify antirepublicanism as a women's cause. Trade union women in Marseilles—match makers, laundry workers, fish sellers, factory workers, and office workers—demonstrated to condemn the Dames de la patrie française. They were denounced as "reactionary, clerical, aristocratic and capitalist." The female trade unionists urged "their men" to vote socialist. It is significant, however, that this counterdemonstration was organized by socialists, not republicans, and that the left-wing view of women's relation to civic life was the mirror image of that of the Right. Women should influence "their men" to do the right thing. Finally, it is of note that this instance of republican women's activity is the only such incident in the police reports on the 1902 electoral campaign, whereas there are regular entries on the well-organized activities of the Ligue des femmes françaises.[95]

It is hardly surprising that the discussion of women's political allegiances should become part of the debate surrounding women's suffrage. Republican feminist organizations, which had adopted suffrage as their central demand, called on the Radical party to make its commitment to universal suffrage a reality. However, influential parliamentary leaders, Georges Clemenceau and Emile Combes, for example, as well as sections of the Radical party's rank and file remained adamant opponents of women's suffrage. Typically the largest group of Radical deputies shifted their positions depending on political circumstances. The ostensible reason that most Radicals offered for postponing or denying full political equality was defense of the Republic against the onslaught of clerically controlled women. This was hardly a logical argument for those who were dedicated to "the sovereignty of universal suffrage," but the reality of many women's continued commitment to the church and the prominent position of women in stridently clerical and antirepublican organizations supplied justifications for the Radicals' hesitation and resistance.

This purported republican defense was tied to the Radicals' fear that any change in the system might threaten their recently established prominence. Many among them recognized no distinction between their own electoral victories and the survival of the Republic. Defense against the clerical danger also served as a rationalization for some Radicals' deeper misogyny, which could not imagine women acting in the public arena. While republican ideology had always claimed that women must be emancipated from the priests, it had not imagined them as citizens.

Women's suffrage leaders petitioned Radical congresses beginning with the first in 1901. Each time the congress, which excluded women, easily defeated motions to endorse women's suffrage. Not until 1907 did the party program include a statement on women. In that year, at the height of its political power, the Radical party pledged to endorse "the gradual extension of the rights of women," who, the party stated, should be legally protected in all the circumstances of their lives. "Communal, departmental and national assistance ought to be provided for pregnant and poor women; the legislated rest of six weeks before and after giving birth should include women in small workshops, stores and in offices."[96] Gender-specific protection for mothers was easier to promise than the vote. With thunderous silence the Radicals ignored the question of votes for women.

Antifeminists, however, did not constitute the entire party; it also included the leading parliamentary spokesmen for suffrage, such as Ferdinand Buisson and Justin Godart. Ferdinand Buisson, a prominent Radical, member of the important Chamber Committee on Universal Suffrage, was a staunch supporter of women's struggle for political equality. Like Camille Pelletan and Léon Bourgeois, Buisson was of that generation that had reached maturity just as the Third Republic was established. He had been a leader among republican educational reformers, served as president of the Ligue des droits de l'homme, functioned as an important force in the Radical party, and was a highly respected member of the liberal Protestant community. In 1906 the bill on the municipal vote for women was sent to the Committee on Universal Suffrage; finally, after three years, Buisson reported favorably to the committee; in 1911 his report was published as *Le Vote des femmes* and widely read. Despite this support the Chamber failed even to debate the bill during the 1910–14 session.[97]

Buisson's argument in support of women's suffrage reflected the difficulties encountered when republican ideology was used to promote the political emancipation of women. Not surprisingly, Buisson's discussion was littered with contradictions and tensions similar to those found in Eugène Pelletan's 1865 study of women's past, present, and future. Like Pelletan, Buisson's republicanism was supported by a staunch belief in progress, rationalism, and a Protestant-inspired morality.[98] He too had difficulty in adjusting an ideology of equality, separate spheres, and gender hierarchy to demands for women's political rights. In *Le Vote des femmes* Buisson sought to present women's suffrage as another inevitable step in the march of human progress, fulfilling the rationalist vision of "the natural rights of all human beings."[99] The actual political struggle for women's rights had begun with the French Revolution, according to Buisson. It seemed obvious to him that the Third Republic, heir of the Great Revolution, would inevitably extend political and legal equality to women. He proudly pointed out that steps in this direction had already been taken in the realm of republican educational reforms. "Elementary schools," he claimed, "have familiarized the nation with the idea of seeing children of the two sexes being treated with perfect equality. . . . In the *lycée* the female staff is subject to the same conditions, to the same manner of recruitment, the same exams and same inspection as the male staff."[100] Buisson predicted that women's rights would continue to evolve naturally, until they would eventually include the right to vote in municipal elections and even some day in national elections.

While he outlined this hoped-for progressive evolutionary development, Buisson was aware that it was at variance with historical facts and with contemporary French conditions. After surveying the advances of women's suffrage in other nations, he concluded with considerable dismay, "It is France that is backward. . . . We will soon be alone, or as good as alone, with Spain and Turkey."[101] Buisson knew full well that the lycée curriculum for girls differed from that for boys and did not prepare them to enter the university. Nor were female and male teachers, or students, treated the same. And no matter how energetically he sought to link women's rights and suffrage to the Revolution, he was too honest not to admit that in prerevolutionary France there had been "numerous, strange examples of the right to vote being given to women." Buisson's discomfort was palpable as he had to concede that the Revolution deprived some women of rights they had had during the *ancien régime*. Further, he also had to grant that the Jacobin revolutionaries treated women who claimed their rights with "extreme harshness and a most unjust disdain." [102] The conflict between the revolutionary women's emancipatory demands and the Jacobin's exclusionary practice placed the origins of the modern women's movement and the origins of modern French republicanism in an antagonistic relation to each other. Buisson's argument for evolutionary, inevitable progress lost much of its persuasiveness. Despite all his good will and commitment to women's suffrage, Buisson could not simply incorporate the struggle for women's rights into the heritage of the Revolution and the republican formulation of equality and progress.

Throughout the nineteenth century the contradictions within republican ideology had been apparent. Perceptive observers recognized the tension between the ideal of political equality extended to all citizens and the demand that women occupy a separate domestic sphere. Even those republicans most sympathetic to women, such as Eugène Pelletan, imperiously relegated them to the home. Despite all the talk of separate but equal spheres, there could be no question that in the republican vision the domestic world was subordinate, although vitally necessary, to the public realm of politics. A few republicans feared that such contradictions might endanger the legitimacy of republicanism itself. In the middle of the century Jenny d'Héricourt had demanded women's emancipation on the grounds of republican egalitarian principles. She warned moralists such as Michelet that failure to award women these universal rights would undermine all claims to equality. "Take care! disciple of liberty, you have not the right to think and to wish in my place. I have, like you, an intellect and a free will, to which you are bound, by your principles, to pay sovereign respect. Now I forbid you to speak for any woman. . . . Take care gentlemen! Our rights have the same foundation as yours: in denying the former, you deny the latter in principle." [103] Not a few republicans were uncomfortable with their ideology that attempted to encompass both male political equality and a subordinate female domesticity. The ideological dissonance became especially pronounced as they had to confront concrete issues that dealt with women's lives and as they had to respond to women's demands for political rights.

Yet their belief system offered few possibilities for fundamental adjustment. Some Radicals, like Léon Bourgeois, employed a rhetoric that presented the state as a benevolent patriarch. This emphasis on the enforcement of social responsibility proved a successful method to enact gender-specific legislation. The state would direct working women's lives in the absence, or inadequacy, of fathers and husbands. Bourgeois's image of the Radical politician as *"bon père de famille"* carried distant echoes of the patriarchal royal state. But there were limits to republican paternalism; political equality and individual liberty were the essence of a republican identity and had to remain paramount in its ideology and rhetoric. In a similar fashion, one might say that republicans never went far enough with their cult of domesticity. The republican version of domesticity was never able to compete successfully with the more powerful Catholic version. Despite all the republicans' quasi-mythical references to fecundity, spirituality, and nature, they could never match the appeal of the much older and more internally consistent Catholic cult of mother and child. Michelet had been quite clear that in his domestic idyl the organizing power of the church would be dethroned in favor of the republican husband's authority. Eugène Pelletan and Ferdinand Buisson, with fewer erotic undercurrents, were equally concerned to reduce the church's influence on women and to offer an alternative morality for marriage and the family. For many French women, however, the secularized myth had little appeal.

Prior to the First World War, French women gained a few advances in the area of civil rights. Here too even the limited gains were problematic, since from its inception the republican meaning of individual and citizen had always meant men, and there has never been any attempt to alter this fundamental assumption. For the large group of working women, some received protection through gender-specific labor legislation that many politicians had accepted only because of women's maternal functions. There is considerable evidence that most working women resented these laws and that they did little to improve their lives.[104] This limited and disappointing legislative result was not surprising considering the contradictions and tensions within republican ideology. Although it offered relatively few improvements in response to women's political, social, and economic needs, this contradictory ideology did function remarkably well in the state and society of the Third Republic. It certainly remained intact until at least the interwar period. The republican cult of domesticity provided rhetoric and symbols through which erstwhile political opponents could communicate and agree on fundamental social institutions.[105] The universal acceptance among all politicians of separate spheres supported the masculine world of

the Chamber of Deputies. The idealization of wife and especially mother
was an intriguing point of consensus and competition between republicans
and clericals, which merits more attention.

Most important, the central tension between political equality and a
gendered hierarchy provided a dramatic illustration of the "inevitable" co-
existence between equality and inequality. It demonstrated the "natural"
impossibility of complete equality. In the powerful writings of Michelet
and Hugo, gender and class constantly reflected and stood for each other.
The organization of harmonious gender relations in the family was to be
a model for class relations and vice versa. When considering the state, the
family, and society, republicans found the hierarchical ordering of gender
the most accessible and powerful medium to express their desire for harmony, security, and the end of conflict without imagining any fundamental
transformation of social structures. At the same time, however, republicans, and particularly Radicals, were never simply satisfied with a defense
of the political or social status quo; to do so would undermine their identity
as republicans. Their desire for stability, including the stability of traditional gender relations, was constantly disrupted by their continuing allegiance to political equality. The very concept of "republican motherhood"
embodied this perpetual dissonance.

Three

Divorce and the Republican Family

THERESA MCBRIDE

UPON HIS RETIREMENT from public life, Alfred Naquet wrote to a friend that in the course of thirty years in politics as a founder of the Third Republic his most concrete achievement was the passage of the 1884 law allowing divorce, the Naquet law. Naquet maintained that the reform of marriage was the centerpiece of republican social policy: "Divorce is a step taken along the road to freedom."[1] Naquet's faith in the liberating aspect of divorce and in its contribution to the social good was not universally shared at the turn of the century when he wrote this revealing letter. Naquet's commitment to freedom in human relationships remained strong, but many moderate and conservative republicans had come to believe that divorce merely added to the "crisis" in the French family.

The question of divorce differs from other social legislation in the early Third Republic, such as protective labor legislation or programs to promote childbearing and child rearing, in a number of ways. The reform of marriage was, by the nature of French law, a national policy, governed by the Civil Code. It could never have been an experimental reform, as were many labor policies, tested in a particular enterprise or inspired by local initiative. Nor was the divorce issue as directly connected to reproduction as were many labor policies and the reforms to improve maternal and infant health, yet pronatalism did emerge as an issue in the Third Republic's debate about divorce, and both sides to the debate suggested that children and the future of the French family were their concern. More than any other social policy, divorce was the one most emblematic of republicanism, and it had been a part of the republican agenda since the Revolution.

Marriage reform became identified with republicanism when the revolutionary National Assembly transformed marriage into a civil contract in

1792 and passed the first divorce law. The goal of the revolutionaries was to secure individual liberty and democratize the family and to substitute the state's authority for that of the church. They empowered the individual to form and dissolve contracts and offered a level of freedom never before experienced by placing the responsibility for the arbitration of family disputes in the hands of the family councils ("*conseils de famille*"). But in 1804 the Napoleonic Code reversed the revolutionary trend toward democratization and reinforced the authority of the father within the family. In effect, the law defined the limit of the state's authority at the threshold of the home, restraining itself from further interference in the domestic sphere which might weaken the father's authority. But the Civil Code also extended the state's power by establishing uniform national laws and supplanting local traditions and regional custom on property disposition, inheritance, and marriage contracts.

The Civil Code moderated individual rights by insisting upon a man's responsibility for his family but recognized only the male as a truly free, self-determining individual. A woman's place was inscribed within the family, and what "rights" she enjoyed derived from her relationship to the head of the family. The Civil Code defined the mutual responsibilities of husband and wife; these were reciprocal, if not equitable. If the husband failed to support and treat his wife with respect, he violated the basis of the contract, just as the wife did if she failed to reside with her husband or to remain faithful to him. By thus tying individual rights to the family or to the social good, the code helped to set the terms of the debate about marriage in the nineteenth century as a fundamental question of social interest. The revolutionary tradition, which emphasized the right to make or dissolve contracts as an essential privilege of citizenship, was the tradition to which Alfred Naquet belonged. It was these two political traditions that would clash in the debate over reinstating divorce.

The Father of Divorce

Alfred Joseph Naquet was born into a bourgeois Jewish family in Carpentras in the Vaucluse in 1834, and his evolution as a political thinker is rooted in that personal history. Naquet was a second-generation republican, like Camille Pelletan and Georges Clemenceau. Raised by a father who was a republican and a freethinker, Naquet developed an early dislike for Napoleon III and the Second Empire. Naquet was also a nonobservant Jew whose atheism was as much a part of his personality as his republicanism; he was a secularist and a scientific positivist. Naquet married Estelle Combanelle, a Catholic, in 1862 in a civil ceremony without religious ritual, for the civil character of marriage was to Naquet and other republicans an indisputable mark of their republicanism. Naquet acquired a medical degree at age 25, completed a doctoral thesis in chemistry in 1865, and occupied a number of teaching posts until 1867. Appointed at that time to the Faculty of Medicine in Paris, Naquet filled his free time with radical politics.[2] But during what would become a long career in politics, he maintained an interest in science and a positivist approach to social issues.

In 1867 Naquet helped to organize an international congress on peace in Geneva at which he denounced the Napoleonic influence on European politics and thereby insulted Emperor Napoleon III. As a result, Naquet was targeted as a dissident and was indicted for his participation in a secret political society, the Ligue de la paix et de la liberté, which he had helped to organize. Condemned to prison for fifteen months, Naquet profited from the opportunity to continue writing. He was confined to a prison hospital because of ill health, and it was here that he wrote his vehement denunciation of marriage, *Religion, Property, Family* (1869).

It was also at this time that Naquet's own marriage began to fall apart. In the early years of their union, Estelle Naquet had accepted her husband's ideas about religion. None of their three children were baptized at birth; two died in infancy and were buried without any religious ceremony in 1865 and 1867. But after the death of their second child and with her husband in prison, Madame Naquet returned to her faith and decided to raise their surviving son as a Catholic. Unable to tolerate this situation, Naquet separated from his wife when he emerged from prison. Despite his abhorrence of religious education, Naquet permitted his son to be raised by his wife, insisting that he recognized her rights to the child, whom she "had brought into the world" and "helped survive by the most assiduous care."[3] Naquet was thus suggesting that a woman had a special claim to her children which her husband could not match, an assertion he would repeat in the divorce debate. Naquet remained married to his wife for thirty years, professing the greatest esteem for her, and never made use of the law associated with his name. It was only after Estelle died in 1903 that Naquet married Odile Signoir, his housekeeper. Naquet always denied that he had campaigned for divorce out of self-interest, and however much his own marriage was a failure, it cannot fully explain his lifelong commitment to the reform of marriage as an instrument for social change. To the end of his life Naquet continued to believe that the reconstruction of the family was "the departure point for the future reformation of humanity."[4]

The ideological manifesto contained in *Religion, Property, Family* began with a philosophical attack on the existence of God, proceeded through an analysis of the evils and inequities of the system of private property, and concluded with a denunciation of marriage as "an institution essentially tyrannical, in its essence an attack on freedom."[5] Influenced while still a student by the writings of Charles Fourier and by the Saint-Simonian critique of marriage and traditional morality, Naquet echoed many of the principles of these utopian socialists in his book. Although he later adjusted his political positions to suit the situation, he remained convinced that marriage was, as Charles Fourier had written, the "tomb of women's liberty."[6] Not surprisingly, *Religion, Property, Family* plunged Naquet again into legal trouble when it was judged by a Parisian court to be an outrage to public morality.[7] For this, Naquet was condemned to suffer four months' imprisonment, to be fined, and to lose his civil rights for life. He managed to escape to Spain, evaded the prison sentence and waited out the wrath of the emperor until he could return to France in November 1869 under an amnesty for opponents of the empire. Naquet resumed his scientific work through collaboration on a chemical dictionary and the *Grand dictionnaire universel* and continued to write political articles for opposition newspapers such as *La Marseillaise* and *Le Rappel*.

When the Second Empire fell and the Emperor Napoleon III surrendered to the Prussian army at Sedan in September 1870, Naquet immediately joined the Government of National Defense formed to replace the imperial government. He was subsequently elected to the Chamber of Deputies in February 1871 to represent the department of the Vaucluse as a member of the far left Union républicaine, led by Léon Gambetta. His first actions were to introduce legislation to ensure unrestricted freedom of speech and of association, a bill to restore freedom of the press and a proposal to allow divorce. While none of these bills received legislative approval in the 1870s, Naquet's proposed law on the freedom of the press led eventually to the important measure of 29 July 1881 establishing press freedom, and he personally led the campaign for divorce until its achievement in 1884. In the 1870s Naquet was an eloquent opponent of President MacMahon's "moral order" policies and of the president's attempt to turn the Republic in a rightist direction. Few would last so long or remain so active in the struggle to found a democratic republic as Alfred Naquet, who served in the Chamber of Deputies between 1871 and 1884 and in the Senate from 1884 to 1889, returning to the Chamber for four more years until his retirement.

Naquet's first attempt in 1876 to introduce divorce into the French Third Republic was a proposal that closely resembled the revolutionary legislation of 20 September 1792. The bill would have permitted divorce by mutual consent (a kind of no-fault divorce) and on a variety of specific grounds, including incompatibility. Significantly curtailed by the Civil Code of 1804, divorce had been outlawed completely during the Restoration by the Bonald law of 8 May 1816.[8] Alfred Naquet shared the motives of the revolutionary legislators, which were articulated in the 1792 law's preface: "The right to divorce is a consequence of individual liberty. An engagement which could not be dissolved would be equivalent to the loss of that liberty."[9] He echoed the legislators of 1792 when he evoked the right of each individual to love and to be free of the constraint of an unbreakable contract.[10] But Naquet's 1876 proposal was never even discussed; the legislative session was interrupted by the attempted coup d'état of 16 May 1877 of MacMahon. Naquet himself admitted that there was little widespread support for such a radical measure at the time, and only he, Léon Richer, and Émile Acollas made divorce a campaign issue in the subsequent election.[11] It took two more legislative attempts by Naquet in 1878 and 1881 before he was successful in achieving the much more limited law on divorce of 27 July 1884.

Naquet remained in the Chamber representing the Vaucluse from 1871 until 1884, when he entered the Senate to lead the campaign for divorce there. During his tenure in the Chamber, Naquet promoted a leftist republican agenda ranging from unrestricted freedom of the press and of association (important for the formation of unions) to increased restrictions on religious congregations; he also initiated measures to promote a graduated income tax and to provide accident insurance for working minors. In lobbying for such legislative initiatives, Naquet was allied first with the far Left and later, in the early 1880s, with the moderate republicans known as Opportunists, before returning to the far Left. Although he called himself a socialist, Naquet distrusted authoritarian collectivism and had more in common with the utopian socialism of the Saint-Simonians and Charles Fourier than with the Marxian socialists. Naquet only joined the Socialist party after leaving parliament and then out of admiration for the humanistic socialism of Jean Jaurès.[12] Naquet was in essence a Jacobin egalitarian, his inspiration was the egalitarianism of the Revolution of 1789, and his greatest legislative achievement—the divorce law—represented the fulfillment of the Revolution's promise of individual liberty.

A devoted republican who called the Republic "our only salvation," Naquet was nonetheless often at odds with other republicans.[13] For ex-

ample, Naquet's ideas for the constitution of the new republic differed
from those of the preeminent leader of the republicans, Léon Gambetta.
The two fell out in 1875 over the acceptance of the constitutional laws, because Naquet preferred a presidential system like that in the United States
rather than a weaker parliamentary regime. He would later blame his split
with Gambetta on his advocacy of divorce, but it clearly resulted both from
personality conflicts and from broader political differences.[14] Even while
supporting the Opportunist governments of the early 1880s, Naquet was
outspoken in his criticism of their leaders for their lapses, such as in 1881
when he denounced Jules Ferry's imperialist policy in Tunisia because the
National Assembly had not been consulted prior to the invasion.[15] After
retirement, Naquet admitted that his political reputation had been blem-
ished by his changing alliances: "I fought Gambetta and I was reconciled
to him; I was both the friend and the adversary of Ferry; I followed and
then abandoned General Boulanger."[16] However inconsistent about political parties, Naquet was clear about two major elements of his political
faith. One was a fundamental belief in human freedom, which helps to
explain his struggle to make the Third Republic more democratic, evident
in the paradox of his support for General Boulanger in the late 1880s. The
other characteristic of Naquet's political faith was an abiding commitment
to radical social reform, beginning with divorce.

In 1881 Naquet undertook to edit a journal called *L'Independant*, a title
that might describe his entire political career. His coeditor at *L'Independant* was Paul Strauss, then approaching 30 and not yet a member of the
Parisian municipal council, while Naquet himself was in his late 40s with a
decade of national service behind him.[17] The partnership in the newspaper
was brief, but Strauss would follow Naquet's lead in devoting himself to
social questions and particularly to the plight of mothers and children,
entering the Senate just as Naquet was ending his political career, and
authoring the comprehensive law on child welfare of 1904 and legislation
to create a national policy on maternity leaves in 1913, the Strauss law,
among other measures.

The ultimate success of the 1884 divorce bill demonstrates not only
Naquet's persistence but also the rising influence of far left republicans
such as Clovis Hughes (socialist, Bouches-du-Rhône) and Camille Pelletan, who, like Paul Strauss, were of a different political generation than
Naquet and who shared a solidarist political philosophy that differed from
Naquet's mix of Saint-Simonian social critique and Jacobin egalitarianism. Naquet saw the achievement of a divorce law as the completion of the

revolutionary agenda, whereas other republicans were already beginning to question traditional republican assumptions about unrestricted liberty, laying the groundwork for the solidarism of the 1890s. Naquet's success was not ideological; his survival as a politician was most obviously due to his political flexibility—or opportunism—and to his capacity to form a coalition between the far Left and the moderates whose support was crucial to the divorce bill.

In the end, the Naquet law of 1884 was a compromise measure based on the Civil Code, rather than one resembling the more liberal law of September 1792 for which Naquet had hoped. The Naquet law allowed divorce only for four specific grounds: adultery by the wife, adultery by the husband, cruelty or serious insult (*"sévices et injures"*), and the conviction and imprisonment of one of the spouses for a serious crime. Divorce by mutual consent and divorce for incompatibility were not reintroduced in 1884 and did not reappear in French law until 1975. "None of us want a return to the law of 1792," insisted Louis de Marcère (center Left, Nord), the sponsor of Naquet's proposal in both the Chamber and the Senate, implying that he rejected totally the radicalism of 1792.[18] After a long and contentious debate, the majority in the National Assembly accepted a revival of the Napoleonic Code but dropped the distinction between male and female adultery which had been a fundamental aspect of the code's approach to divorce and which continued to be part of the Civil Code's grounds for legal separation.[19] This was the most important way in which the Naquet law diverged from the Napoleonic Code of 1804, and the controversy over it suggests the republicans' ambivalence toward allowing greater female autonomy through divorce.

Shortly after the divorce bill's passage in 1884, Naquet again broke ranks with the republican leadership, became increasingly critical of the elitism of the Republic, and involved himself in a new campaign to shape a more popular government. He alienated his former political allies during his involvement with General Georges Boulanger (1886–89), who was viewed as a significant threat to the survival of the Third Republic.[20] Other far left republicans such as Camille Pelletan supported Boulanger for a time at the beginning, but it was Naquet who became Boulanger's closest political advisor, drafted his constitutional program, and stayed with Boulanger until the end.[21] When Boulanger committed suicide to avoid legal prosecution for his violation of electoral laws, Naquet found himself politically isolated and the sole Boulangist in the Senate. The scandal of Boulangism did not end Naquet's political career, however; he survived another decade and was reelected to the Chamber as a representative from Paris between 1893 and 1897. Implicated in the corruption of the Panama Canal affair, as were a number of leading republicans, Naquet again evaded imprisonment by leaving the country for London. He was acquitted of charges of corruption in March 1898 and returned to France but retired from public life.[22] He died in Paris on 12 November 1916, survived by his son and his second wife.

Divorce as Social Policy

Between the 1880s and the beginning of the First World War in 1914, the republican majority passed a series of laws that laid out the broad outlines of a social policy. Why the Naquet law became an element of that policy is not easily explained, for as Naquet admitted, "few reforms in France provoked such a lively opposition."[23] The success of Naquet's bill in 1884 after eight years of intense lobbying resulted from four factors: the identification of divorce as an essential privilege of personal freedom and therefore central to republicanism itself; the strength of anticlericalism among the republicans, who saw divorce as a way of undercutting the Catholic Church's influence over private life and public authority; the influence of the far left republicans, many of whom shared Naquet's radical critique of the family and French society; and the belief that a crisis had developed in French family life, which convinced many moderate and conservative republicans that the institution of marriage needed to be reformed.

The reform of marriage was central to the revolutionary heritage of the republicans. Naquet insisted that divorce was a fundamental aspect of personal freedom. "Divorce will have the same effect in the family that political liberty has in the country," he argued; "it will be a component of order in the family, as political liberty is the element of order in the nation."[24] Its proponents insisted that divorce lay at the core of the republican agenda.[25] I have argued previously that Naquet and his colleagues were successful in transforming the vote on the divorce law into a referendum on the Republic. A vote for divorce became a vote for individual liberty; a vote against it, an affirmation of clericalism and monarchy.[26]

This equation of republicanism and divorce was made clear in the parliamentary debate. Advocates of divorce charged that their opponents were part of a clerical and monarchist plot to subvert the legacy of the Revolution, emphasizing that the suppression of divorce had been passed by the clerical and monarchist Chamber of 1816. Naquet charged that the Bonald law to suppress divorce had been "the first assault of the clerical forces upon the modern democratic spirit."[27] The Naquet law thus became a component in the republicans' attack on clericalism and the "moral order" policy of President MacMahon and the rightists. It would be hard to overestimate the impact of anticlericalism in the struggle to secularize the state, which has been called France's "last religious war."[28] The anticlerical republicans implemented a program of secularization in education and imposed controls on religious congregations, as well as reestablishing divorce and reaffirming the secular character of marriage. In response, the foes of divorce denounced Naquet's bill as "a grave attack on Christian civilization," and Naquet was vilified in the anti-Semitic press because of his Jewish background.[29]

As we shall see, the emphasis on the freedom of personal contracts as a foundational element of republicanism did not mean that the republican elite embraced the idea that individual happiness and self-fulfillment were the primary goals of human life even at the sacrifice of duty to the family and society. They endorsed free choice for men—reluctantly in some cases—because they believed that men enjoyed this right as a privilege of republican citizenship. But the right to dissolve an unhappy marriage was much more equivocally granted to women, who remained defined by their duties in the family and who did not enjoy the full benefits of such citizenship. In the end, the advocates of the Naquet law had to convince their opponents that they had no intention of granting to women the same right to seek self-fulfillment through romantic relationships.

Crisis in the French Family

The public debate sparked by the campaign for divorce not only made the Naquet law one of the most controversial of the Third Republic's social policies but also lends the issue a great importance to the political history of the Third Republic, for it was in the divorce debate that political opinion seemed to coalesce in defining a "crisis" in the French family. It was not just the far Left and the feminists who were demanding the reform of marriage laws by the mid-1880s. By this time a consensus was developing across the political spectrum that there were serious problems, especially within the working-class family, which demanded immediate solutions. Rightists often argued that divorce would be counterproductive, weakening even further the fragile family structure, but they were forced to agree that marriages were breaking down even without legal divorce. Many moderate republicans and even some on the far Left had difficulty reconciling divorce with their goal of improving family life. To all of them Naquet insisted that divorce would not destroy marriage and that he wanted (despite what he had written in 1869) to preserve the institution of marriage: "I want to strengthen it, to solidify it, and I believe that divorce, far from weakening it, is the means by which to solidify it, to strengthen it."[30] Writers Paul and Victor Margueritte became tireless campaigners for the position that allowing easy access to divorce would reduce the number of "concubines" and "bastards." "Far from destroying the family," they argued, "divorce will moralize it."[31]

For Naquet and the Margueritte brothers, one of the factors that undermined stable family life was the legal inequality of women. The Civil Code of 1804 had made community property normative, so that except in that minority of marriages in which a written marriage contract specified the disposition of the separate property each spouse brought to the marriage, the husband had full use of all property that had been his wife's as well as any income or property acquired during the marriage.[32] In working-class relationships where substantial property was not involved, a woman was even less capable of legally claiming any income as her own or forcing a man to support his children. Women's legal incapacity was so widely recognized in the Third Republic that both sides in the debate over divorce raised the issue of greater legal protection for women. Louis Legrand (Opportunist republican from the Nord), a strong critic of divorce, complained that the community property system sacrificed a woman's interests entirely to her husband's administration.[33] There was considerable agreement about the problems created by this legal situation, but what the republicans did not agree on was that the solution could come only from the full civil emancipation of women, and they settled instead for allowing divorce.

The far left republicans focused on the plight of the working woman who was unable to support her family on the wages of poverty and was too often victimized by an alcoholic and abusive husband. In the parliamentary debates, Marcel Barthe (far left republican, Basses-Pyrénées) sketched the image of the working-class woman with a child in her arms who awaited her husband at the workshop door every payday; she waited there to urge him to return home so that his wages would not be wasted on alcohol at the pub.[34] From forty years of experience as a lawyer Barthe knew that such a woman had little legal protection against her husband's irresponsibility, and he argued that she could hardly be expected to provide a healthy and stable environment for her children in such circumstances. With inadequate earning power and no legal rights over the family's property nor claim to her husband's wages, a woman was bound to be victimized by an unscrupulous or abusive man. Like Naquet, Barthe was a Fourierist, but he opposed Naquet on divorce precisely because of his convictions. Calling the Naquet law divorce for the rich, Barthe argued that the Napoleonic Code on which it was based was too preoccupied with property and alimony to solve the problems of working-class women.[35] Barthe concluded that divorce would be worse for these women than their present situation. He asked his colleagues how a poor woman could survive alone, separated from her husband, unable to earn an adequate wage of her own.[36]

By the 1880s the evidence was mounting that women needed better protection than the law could provide; it was clear that the reform of marriage and separation laws was overdue. Dr. Edouard Toulouse, who worked in a hospital for mentally ill women in the poor Parisian suburb of Villejuif, described how poor women were mistreated or abandoned by their husbands and ended up in a terrible state.[37] Physician Michel Dussac produced a "medical-legal" study of separation cases in 1878 which supplied a weight of medical evidence that many wives were justified in leaving their husbands. The gruesome details of Dussac's study document a variety of sexual abuse and physical violence as well as the effects on women's health of sexually transmitted diseases contracted from their husbands.[38] It was not just among the working poor that the ravages of physical and sexual abuse were taking their toll on family life. Personal testimonies of the ways in which husbands abused their power over their spouses became part of the debate over the divorce law, and none were more compelling than the letters from bourgeois women sent to legislators during the parliamentary debates and those that were collected and published by a journalist about 1901.[39] One woman complained that she had been unable to prove grounds for separation from her husband even though he had been consistently unfaithful to her. The jury found him "a perfectly honest man" because he had refused to sleep with her for five years and therefore had not infected her with the venereal disease he had contracted as a result of his sexual liaisons.[40] Another bourgeois woman began the legal process for separation, but when her husband learned about it, he had committed her to an insane asylum. Her conclusion was that it was "much easier for a husband to commit his wife than for her to obtain a divorce."[41] The personal evidence confirms what the medical reformers claimed—that many women were physically and psychologically endangered by their legal powerlessness.

Criminologists in this period were also developing the theory that crime had its roots in family dysfunction. Juvenile delinquency showed a marked increase in this era, and criminologist Louis Albanel's study attempted to demonstrate that a major cause of the problem was that half of such juveniles were living in single-parent households or in households in which the parents were not married.[42] Other criminological studies pointed out that violent crimes against people occurred most often within the family.[43] Describing what he believed was a rising tide of female criminality, appeals court judge Louis Proal argued that women's adulterous proclivities were a major factor. Proal noted, as did other criminologists and jurists, that the penal code allowed a husband to kill his unfaithful wife with impunity if he discovered her with a lover "*en flagrant délit*" but that civil law denied him the possibility of divorcing his wife for her adultery, so that "crimes of passion" were actually encouraged by French law.[44] Proal argued that there had been an increase in female adultery and denounced new women's fashions, novels and the popular theater, which featured fictional stories of romance and illicit sexual relationships. Proal connected female adultery to the breakdown of the family and to the increase in violent crimes.[45] Yet Proal also deduced from the criminal statistics that marriage had a moralizing influence because single people committed more crimes than married ones, and he argued for strengthening the family as a means of reducing crime.[46] Such "scientific evidence," which attempted to link crime to sexual transgressions, particularly those by women, supplied arguments for both sides of the divorce debate.

The heightened concern about declining sexual morality among the middle and upper classes, rising crime and the prevalence of broken families among the working classes convinced many that the reform of marriage was essential. Even those opposed to divorce argued that the process of legal separation did not adequately preserve the integrity of marriage or protect the women who sought 90 percent of the separations.[47] Senator Jules Simon, a centrist republican who was among the most eloquent and influential of the opponents of divorce, attempted to convince his colleagues of the need to reform legal separation while eloquently defending indissoluble marriage.[48] Deputy Louis Legrand argued similarly that the indissolubility of marriage protected women better than a situation in which divorce was available. Legrand seemed to echo Louis de Bonald's often quoted analogy between marriage and civil society in which Bonald denounced the revolutionary divorce law for creating "a veritable domestic democracy."[49] Bonald shrank from democracy both in the family and in the state, arguing that it would be dangerous to allow the wife whom he called "the weaker part" to rebel against her husband's legitimate marital authority. Louis Legrand, on the other hand, took for granted the liberalization of political society but came to the similar conclusion on divorce that "in a democratic society, it is better to protect the weak than the strong. . . ."[50] For this reason, Legrand joined Jules Simon in voting to prohibit divorce but like Simon argued that the legal separation process should be reformed to provide greater protection to women via the courts.[51]

Jules Simon also insisted that women themselves wanted the protection of indissoluble marriage and that they did not desire divorce. Simon supported his point by reading aloud letters that had been written to him by women. He read one letter that he insisted touched him so deeply that he could scarcely bear to read it aloud. If divorce were possible, the unhappy woman had written to Simon, "what would be my position? divorced against my will, without a name or my husband . . . [yet he] is able to marry a fallen woman who could legally bear his name."[52] Edouard Allou, who was appointed a life senator after a distinguished legal career (conservative republican, Haute-Vienne), called the indissolubility of marriage a "brake" or obstacle to protect "the poor woman."[53] Yet the "brake" was to both protect and restrict women, for what Allou feared more than leaving women without this protection was that they might not be "restrained" from their natural impulse to passion. Unlike Simon, Allou believed that separation was a greater evil than divorce because a woman was able to keep the right to use her husband's name "in order to compromise him in new adventures." Allou concluded, "There is nothing more cruel in the world than this situation."[54] A woman needed to be protected from her own natural weakness and not just from the exploitive male in order to prevent the destruction of her family's honor.

Among the other motives that figured in the divorce debate was the national obsession with France's slow population growth. During the parliamentary debates, Deputy Louis Guillot (far left, Isère) opposed reestablishing divorce for this reason, interjecting, "We are the last nation from the point of view of population!"[55] One critic of divorce insisted that divorce undermined the commitment to the marriage and that marriage would "no longer be considered as a union destined to produce children for the creation of a family, but only as an accidental affair of money, material consideration, or of pleasure."[56] But advocates of divorce such as Senator Joseph Eymard-Duvernay (conservative republican, Isère) argued instead that society had an interest in divorce precisely because of the population issue. Divorce would allow an infertile couple to dissolve their marriage, remarry, and begin producing children.[57] According to Eymard-Duvernay, "society would thank" couples who remarried and subsequently had children. Advocates of divorce cited statistics showing that childless couples were more likely to divorce, although these did not necessarily prove the point they wished to make, that better marriages could produce more children. And despite such populationist arguments in the debate and probably because the male parliamentarians were squeamish about discussing the male responsibility for procreation, impotence was not inserted among the grounds for divorce in the final version of the Naquet law.[58] It is impossible to gauge precisely how significant the populationist sentiment was to the success of the Naquet law, but it appears to have played only a minor part. On the other hand, Eymard-Duvernay's personal support was very important to the law's passage, for his was the deciding vote on the legislative committee that recommended the Naquet bill to the full Senate.[59]

Naquet, who had argued from the beginning that unhappy marriages could only contribute to the decline of the French birthrate, was himself no pronatalist. To the contrary, Naquet noted the hypocrisy of decrying the poverty of the working-class family and simultaneously denouncing the practice of birth control.[60] Naquet was less concerned with the birthrate than with the total reform of the institution of marriage, for he believed that the low birthrate was simply one symptom of a greater social problem.[61] Bourgeois marriage was based on material interest, in Naquet's view, and this led to the delay of marriage and to the frequenting of prostitutes by young men. This practice lowered "the moral level of the population" and exposed "almost all men" to venereal diseases spread by prostitutes, which exercised "a funereal influence on the race" and caused its "degeneration."[62]

A Vision of the Family

Although many commented on what they believed to be a "crisis" in the French family, few republican politicians offered such a coherent vision of its nature and causes as did Alfred Naquet. Naquet called the mother rather than the father the "pivot" of the family.[63] He even suggested that children should bear the mother's name because only maternity and not paternity could be established for certain.[64] Naquet argued that the reality of mothers working outside the home for inadequate wages and of the widespread prostitution of young women who were unable to earn a liveli-

hood on their own could not be ignored.[65] Suggesting a radical solution
to the plight of working women and poor mothers who could not survive
without male support, Naquet insisted that the best way to provide poor
families with some economic security and to protect children from abuse
and abandonment was a program of government assistance paid directly
to each mother according to the number of children she had.[66]

Other republicans emphasized that the family was the proper context
for the education and nurturing of children but were concerned that family
authority not be undermined because it was essential to the integrity of
French society. Pursuing Naquet's plan seemed likely to turn the whole
theory of French family law on its head, for the legal rights and responsibilities of men were defined in relationship to the father's authority—the
"*puissance paternelle.*" The question of how to provide support and protection for women raising families while not undermining paternal authority
was at the heart of a number of debates about social policy. In arguing
for divorce in the Senate, Edouard Millaud (leftist republican, Bouches-
du-Rhône) specifically tied the issue of divorce to the pending legislation
to extend the government's regulation of abandoned children and to include "morally abandoned" children within the state's authority, which
was finally passed in 1889. In urging that similar principles be applied to
the question of divorce, Millaud recognized that both pieces of legislation
challenged the omnipotence of the father within the family, but he argued
that such legislation would serve to remind both men and women of their
parental responsibilities. Millaud argued that divorce would be a protection against husbands "who brutalize those whom they should love" and
might help to reform "bad mothers." [67]

But other legislators were less optimistic that children could be saved
from victimization by divorce. Some legislators seemed more concerned
about the competition for control of the children or the inheritance of
property.[68] One legislator wondered how the children of divorce could be
well treated if submitted to the authority of a "stranger" (stepfather).[69]
Another questioned whether it was possible for a second husband to have
any feeling for the children of his "rival" (the first husband).[70] "Do you
really think some man is going to support these children of another man?"
asked Jules Simon of his colleagues in the Senate; "how can one count on
the benevolence of a divorced man?" [71] Opponents of divorce argued that
children would suffer most from divorce.

It was the inveterate critic of marriage Alfred Naquet who defended
the affective ties within the family and maintained throughout the de-

bate that the family would not be threatened by divorce. He responded sharply to the critics of the divorce bill and attacked their image of "a mass of children handed over to the far-from-tender mercies of step-mothers and step-fathers, and thus deprived of the healthful education of the true family circle."[72] Naquet argued that a natural attachment militated against the abuse of one's children or spouse; "this love of family is powerful in the human heart."[73] Poor women were not to blame for the problems of working-class families; rather, it was they who were victimized by a system that rendered them unable to provide for themselves or for their children. "Bad husbands, in far larger numbers than bad wives, shirked their conjugal and paternal duties [and] . . . as matters now stand in France, a woman cannot live by her own labor. If by rare chance she succeeds in supporting herself she must have no children, and there must be no 'dead season' [women workers such as seamstresses were particularly susceptible to periods of unemployment]. This is a hard and unpalatable truth," insisted Naquet, "which cannot be erased by the fine dissertations of philosophers and moralists. Prostitution or an adulterous liaison is the only means by which she can keep the wolf from the door."[74] Thus, Naquet simultaneously focused attention on the cruel social reality of working-class families and attempted to make divorce palatable to those republicans who took for granted that the patriarchal family structure must be preserved.

Naquet believed that to criticize the working classes' morality and family values was to apply an inappropriate moral standard to their social reality. It was true that many more working-class couples separated or divorced, Naquet argued, but the upper classes committed adultery with impunity and thus had no need for divorce. Novelist Émile Zola described adultery as the inevitable feature of bourgeois marriage (something with which he was personally acquainted, as he maintained separate households for his wife and mistress), because bourgeois women were married off to serve the family's economic interest rather than for love.[75] Among the lower classes, Naquet insisted, there was less "dissimulation."[76]

In emphasizing the role of the woman as the "pivot" of the working-class family, Naquet was admitting the reality and acceptability of single-parent households. Like Paul Strauss, who authored the law on maternity leaves, Naquet was not concerned with illegitimacy as a moral issue. Naquet pointed out the hypocrisy of penalizing women alone for the evils of illegitimate births, abortion, and infanticide. One of the major causes that led desperate women to commit abortion or infanticide was their seduction and abandonment by lovers who were immune from legal prosecution because of the legal prohibition on suits to establish paternity. The other major cause was economic. Naquet equated abortion with infanticide— the killing of human life—but he argued for greater legal tolerance for women who sought out abortionists, because he blamed the economic system rather than the women who committed such acts.[77] "Out of the poverty and disrepute in which unmarried mothers are held, women have begun to lose the maternal instinct."[78] That Naquet's view was becoming more common by the 1880s is evident from the sympathy with which male juries treated women accused of infanticide, a capital crime, and by the infrequent prosecution of abortion.[79] Naquet personally believed that social evils such as prostitution, abortion, and infanticide would disappear when legal marriage was suppressed and "freedom [was] restored to love," but he refrained from stating this unpopular position during the debate over the divorce bill.[80]

Sexual Freedom and Divorce

In the 1880s, as the divorce debate entered its final phase, Senator René Béranger, a former lawyer from Lyons, formulated a different critique of sexual freedom and the social crisis whose themes crossed those of the divorce debate. Béranger launched a direct challenge to male sexual irresponsibility in his campaign for *"recherche de la paternité"* to allow paternity suits under French law. The right to establish paternity legally was allowed under the Civil Code only in cases of rape, but Béranger's reform would have permitted any unmarried mother to seek economic support from the father of her child. Béranger's proposal was rejected overwhelmingly in 1883, but it was revived and finally became law in 1912.

Male adultery remained a well-accepted prerogative in the masculinist culture of the Third Republic. Georges Clemenceau, a rising political star among the Radicals, was a notorious adulterer, having open affairs with other women in the 1880s including a liaison with actress Suzanne Reichenberg (who later took up with General Georges Boulanger). Clemenceau kept his American-born wife Mary Plummer and their three children in the countryside with his mother. Yet despite his own lapses from marital fidelity, Clemenceau abruptly divorced his wife when he discovered that she too had taken a lover.[81] Feminist Hubertine Auclert tried to make a political issue of this kind of hypocrisy in the debate over divorce by publicizing the adultery of a member of the Senate who was an opponent of divorce, but she was unsuccessful in promoting critical self-reflection among the political leadership.[82] Bourgeois and aristocratic men could practice adultery with impunity, while the indissoluble bond of matrimony kept their wives from similar temptations. An errant wife could be punished for her adultery by separation, leaving her husband in control of her property and the legal father of any children born to her even after they separated. Before the Naquet law, both the civil law and the penal code treated male and female adultery differently; a man's adultery was considered grounds for separation only when committed in the conjugal domicile, making it harder for a wronged wife to prove her case. Moreover, the penal code prescribed a jail sentence for a woman convicted of adultery (the penalty prescribed was three months to two years), whereas a man was merely fined.[83]

The controversy over making men more accountable for their sexual misconduct is reflected in the long debate about adultery in conjunction with the divorce bill.[84] In its final form, the Naquet law resolved the adultery issue in two ways. A narrow parliamentary majority approved equalizing the position of men and women so that either a husband or wife could sue for a divorce on the grounds of adultery.[85] This represented a major change in the legal treatment of the double standard, although it did not transform cultural attitudes. Senator Edmond de Pressensé, who argued eloquently for equalizing the treatment of men and women in regard to adultery, dismissed the idea that a respectable woman would seek a divorce solely on the basis of her husband's infidelity, calling a woman who did "neither truly a mother nor a wife." [86] Secondly, the parliamentary majority also made certain that the law restricted the errant spouse from marrying his or her lover if the suit for divorce was based on adultery (the guilty spouse could not marry the lover when the lover was named as co-respondent). The restriction of remarriage of the adulterous spouse proved to be essential to the passage of the Naquet law.[87] Hence, the supporters of divorce dissociated the law from any suggestion that they were promoting female autonomy and attempted to reassure their opponents that divorce would be a protection for the virtuous woman.

Feminist Republicans and Republican Feminists

Although women's roles and women's nature were very much at issue in the divorce debate, women had little opportunity to speak for themselves. Not only were women unable to vote or serve in the National Assembly, women could not serve on juries in this period nor as legal witnesses (until 1897), and no women were admitted to the French bar before 1901.[88] By custom, women reporters were excluded from the journalists' gallery in the Chamber of Deputies. Only once was the issue of women's suffrage interjected explicitly into the divorce debate; a speaker ridiculed the implication that women could express their own interests when he interrupted, "A plebiscite by women?"—to which the Chamber responded with laughter.[89] Both advocates and opponents of divorce asserted that they represented the true interests of women and could speak on behalf of women.[90]

Naquet insisted that the liberalization of divorce was in the interest of women.[91] His claim to understand those interests was based on the fact that he was one of only a handful of men in the National Assembly in the 1870s who could be considered women's rights advocates. Among these was his friend Léon Richer, founder of France's first feminist movement and an early campaigner for marriage law reform. But Naquet disappointed many feminists in not advocating women's suffrage.[92] He was skeptical that women could be trusted to participate in republican politics because women were more religious than men and he feared they would be influenced by Catholic principles contrary to republicanism.[93] Moreover, Naquet's own account of his political campaigns emphasizes the resistance he encountered among women outside Paris to the idea of divorce, thus raising doubts about how well he articulated the interests of women.[94]

Naquet supported the extension of women's civil rights, but he did not claim that women and men were equal in all things. He argued for greater legal rights for women precisely because of woman's unique role and presumed special qualities as mothers. Woman was the "biological analogue" of the male—equal in rights because she was biologically and morally different.[95] "The woman is therefore not inferior to the man considered overall," he reasoned; "if she is inferior to him on several points, she makes up for this inferiority by her superiority of the same order."[96] He suggested that, by contrast, his opponents preferred to treat French women as American law had treated slaves before their emancipation.[97] Although he disappointed feminists over his lack of support for women's right to participate in the political debate themselves, Naquet made explicit what was clearly an unexamined subtext in the debate—that the male legislators could be inspired by the plight of poor and abused women yet were reluctant to challenge their own privileged position.

Feminists themselves were as divided over the issue of divorce as were the republicans, and most rejected easy divorce as dangerous to women's interests.[98] The success of the divorce law nonetheless reflected both the influence of the feminists who had made marriage law reform part of their agenda since the early nineteenth century and the fact that liberal feminists had staunchly supported the Third Republic. Leading feminists supported Naquet's campaign for divorce, hoping that the issue would place the broader question of women's legal emancipation on the national political agenda, although in this too they were disappointed.[99]

The Role of the State

Unlike many of the social reformers discussed in this volume, Naquet was not a partisan of *l'etat providence*, or the welfare state. Inspired by a mixture of Fourierist socialism, Jacobin egalitarianism, and anarchism, he was skeptical of political solutions that extended the state's authority over private life.[100] About 1890 he wrote: "I am, for my part, profoundly a Socialist. Social inequality and injustice are revolting to me. . . . But I have the certitude, no less profound, that Collectivism [*sic*] would aggravate, rather than mitigate, the evils from which we suffer; that the solution . . . should only be sought in the action of natural laws and of the normal machinery of society, [with] legislative reforms hardly ever interfering, except in the manner of oil intended to lubricate the State machine." [101]

In the debate over divorce, the role of the state emerged as a significant issue, for the Naquet law would inevitably extend the authority of the legal system over private life. Naquet distrusted the courts—those "absolute omnipotent tribunals" [102]—and was reluctant to entrust judges with discretionary authority in divorce cases. As he commented after the law was passed, "It is certain that judges are human and that in matters of separation and divorce, as in all other matters, their decisions derive to a certain degree from their intimate feelings." [103] Rather than allow too much freedom for judicial interpretation, he tried to formulate a set of procedures which minimized the arbitrariness of individual judgment and equalized the treatment of individuals in the courts. Although he would have preferred divorce by mutual consent or divorce on the grounds of incompatibility to provide individuals with greater control over the decision to dissolve their own marriages, Naquet settled for a law that at least ensured that divorce would be widely available.[104]

Because of the existence in France of a system of legal assistance, reestablishing divorce opened the floodgate to marital dissolutions. A system of legal assistance (Bureau d'assistance judiciaire), authorized on 22 January 1851, allowed citizens to seek exemption from court and lawyers' fees for demonstrated need. Domestic disputes such as separations and suits for maintenance constitued the bulk (60%) of the cases tried under this system. With the cost of a simple divorce or separation about five hundred francs, this measure meant that separations had been far more accessible to the lower classes in France than in any of its European neighbors.[105] Charles Desmaze, writing in 1881, argued that legal assistance made separations too easy; he suggested that the situation had been better when women kept quiet and reconciled with their husbands even when they had been beaten.[106] Jacques Bertillon, the demographer who supplied much of the statistical data cited by legislators in the divorce debate, concluded that there had been a significant increase in separations as a result of "assistance judiciaire."[107] Hence, critics feared that under the system of legal assistance, family breakdowns would multiply if divorce were reinstated. This prompted the pragmatic argument by one legislator that enacting divorce without abolishing the system of legal assistance would bankrupt the state, for the costs would be too high.[108] Senator Gustave de Lamarzelle (rightist, Morbihan), another opponent of divorce, was quick to criticize the fact that poor couples flooded the Bureau d'assistance judiciaire with requests and, he insisted, did not even attempt to provide concrete grounds for the dissolution of their marriages, assuming that stating their incompatibility was sufficient. To Lamarzelle, the system of legal assistance provided much too easy an access to divorce, and he argued that divorce institutionalized the right to adultery.[109]

The debate over divorce also betrayed a deeper concern about the state's role in the family. Leftist republican Marcel Barthe spoke of the "annihilation" of the family—the family would be suppressed and "the state [would] substitute itself for the father and the mother."[110] Senator Louis La Caze (conservative republican, Basses-Pyrénées) passionately stated his belief in the preservation of the family's autonomy: "A year ago I spoke on the issue of the tenure of judges, today it is the matter of another magistracy: the magistracy of parents, the magistracy of the father. Sirs, you must respect that!"[111] Several years after the implementation of the Naquet law, another critic wrote, "The State, having become the almost universal father of the family, substitutes its own agents."[112]

Opponents of divorce and some of its less enthusiastic supporters generally viewed positively the granting of greater authority over marriage to the judiciary because they believed that the judiciary would be able to prevent the widespread dissolution of marriages. Baron Gui Lafond de Saint-Mür (rightist senator, Corrèze) preferred the process established by the Naquet law in which local courts and judges had a role in adjudicating family disputes contrary to the assumption of the 1792 law that the couple themselves and their families should determine when the marriage was irretrievably broken. The Naquet law avoided the excesses of easy divorce in Lafond's eyes, while asserting the state's legitimate interest in the family.[113] The divorce law also seemed to promise an end to the scandalous abuses of the separation process in which judges were too lenient or false testimony could be easily manufactured.[114] In one famous case, the wife of Clovis Hughes, a socialist deputy from Marseilles, found herself falsely named by a paid private investigator assisting in a separation case. She took her revenge on the investigator who had supplied perjured testimony by shooting him; she was tried for murder but was promptly acquitted by a sympathetic jury whose members were probably equally appalled at the scandal of manufactured evidence in such cases.[115] Her husband subsequently became one of the leading advocates of divorce by mutual consent because mutual consent would have eliminated the need to supply evidence of specific grounds in order to obtain a divorce.

In the final debate on the Naquet law, crucial political support was provided by the government of Jules Ferry. The minister of justice, Félix Martin-Feuillée, voiced this support, noting the rising number of separations being granted by the courts and concluding that "men are not angels."[116] Martin-Feuillée's support of the Naquet law was thus more pragmatic than that of Prime Minister Jules Ferry, who acquiesced as long as the bill did not include divorce by mutual consent, which would mean easier divorce. Ferry warned that marriage was "not a game," it was "a question of moral life or death."[117] Like other republicans, Ferry and Martin-Feuillée concluded that bad marriages were the state's business, because the state had to be concerned with procreation and the care of children and because family breakdowns were increasing even without legal divorce.

For the reformers and legislators of the Third Republic, marriage and divorce were considered in the broader context of a "crisis" in the French family. During the early Third Republic a general family policy was articulated which encompassed education, labor legislation, maternity leave, and assistance to single mothers, as well as simplified marriage laws and the reestablishment of divorce. Like the other social policies described in this volume, the issue of divorce focused anxieties about changing women's roles, alcoholism, adolescent delinquency, prostitution, low birthrates, and high infant mortality. Despite a hypocritical tolerance of the extramarital liaisons of middle- and upper-class men and the stigmatizing of the lower-class family as less cohesive, the debate over divorce emphasized the importance and integrity of family life and the need to balance individual rights against the needs of the family and of society. Unfairly criticizing his leftist colleagues for their support of divorce, Senator La Caze insisted: "We have labored for a century to establish a society of rights, but today we renounce constituting a society of responsibilities." [118] Republicans who supported the Naquet law were equally concerned with the survival of the French family and the integrity of French society.

A majority of republicans agreed upon the final version of the Naquet law because of its moderation and because they recognized the legitimate role of the Third Republic in family life. The republicans in general rallied to the call to defend the Third Republic against the power of the church and to fulfill the promise of freedom and the legacy of the Revolution. Leftists generally voted for the Naquet law even while hoping for further changes to transform society, and Naquet himself was satisfied with the law only as a first step, even as he continued to work toward reducing the state's control over private life. Meanwhile, the republican elite was reassured that the Naquet law would not in itself seriously challenge the patriarchal family. Because of its moderation, the Naquet law served as the basis for French divorce until 1975. At the same time, the law made possible sweeping changes in French family life; thereafter men and women would be treated more equally in determining fault for the breakdown of a marriage, and greater legal protection would be afforded to women in abusive marriages. While controversy over the effects of the Naquet law continued to mark the political debates of the Third Republic, Naquet remained hopeful that the law could contribute to creating a society in which men and women would be equal—a world in which each man and each woman was "at the same time a shareholder as well as a worker." [119]

Four

The Right to Life

Paul Strauss and the Politics of Motherhood

RACHEL G. FUCHS

POLITICIANS, government officials, social hygienists, and moral reformers of the early Third Republic focused their attention on familial issues, specifically on mothers and infants. They wrote of an infant's right to life (*droit de vivre*) and made child protection and saving the children a national concern. Unlike the contemporary "right-to-life" movement in the United States, French politicians and reformers of one hundred years ago did not primarily concern themselves with condemning abortion.[1] Rather, French reformers believed that an infant, once born, had a right to life, and a Republican government owed that infant protection so it could exercise that right. Furthermore, many politicians believed that it was the state's responsibility and obligation to provide insurance and welfare to assure the healthy survival of children. The relatively uncontroversial idea of saving babies' lives became the linchpin of the social welfare programs developing in late nineteenth-century France. Like most other welfare and social insurance reforms of that era, those designed to protect infants began on a municipal and departmental level, before the passage of national legislation.

Among the leading political figures, Paul Strauss was one of the most persistent, taking the initiative in actively pursuing policies to preserve infant lives by aiding and protecting the mothers. He held public office, first municipal and then national, for fifty-seven years—from 1883 to 1940. Through an examination of his ideas, programs, and policies we can perhaps come to a better understanding of the development of social welfare programs in France, the shift from optional charity to obligatory welfare

as analyzed by François Ewald, Henri Hatzfeld, and others, and the reform politics of Third Republic France as clarified by Sanford Elwitt and
Judith Stone.[2] Strauss was so central to the politics of social reform that
Émile Zola, in his didactic novel *Fécondité*, modeled the good Dr. Bou-
tan after Strauss. Strauss, the consummate consensus politician of energy,
tact, and compromise, also received support for his legislative and philanthropic projects from such notables as Alexandre Dumas *fils*, Madame
Marie Curie, and Madame Anatole France.[3]

Paul Strauss's preoccupation with the behavior of women and saving
children's lives resulted from his overriding concern with issues of hygiene
and health, his real humanitarian interests in preventing infant mortality,
his close association with the medical profession, and his French nationalism. His brand of nationalism was not right-wing but a form of French
patriotism and loyalty to the ideals of the Third Republic. Above all, Strauss
was part of a larger national concern with France's stagnant population
growth, or depopulation, especially in the light of a unified and growing Germany, whose politicians also expressed keen awareness of relative
demographic issues.[4]

In front of the full house of the German Reichstag, one German politician responded to a request for new increases in the military budget
with the following words: " 'We do not need to make such sacrifices; the
French lose a battalion each year.' " In quoting his German counterpart in
1891, Jules Simon, a prominent French politician and associate of Strauss's,
added that France lost a battalion because it let "the infants of the poor
die." "We let 180,000 infants perish each year. Does France have 180,000
too many that we can allow such assassinations?"[5] With this statement
Simon added his voice to that of Strauss and of numerous French politicians—of all political persuasions—who decried the high infant mortality
and exhorted politicians and mothers to take action to combat the depopulation of France and avoid being economically and militarily vanquished
by Germany. On a national scale, the politics of motherhood, and Strauss's
activities, became intertwined with the rhetoric of depopulation, of nationalism, and of national defense.

In their polemics and propaganda, politicians and reformers fought
the war against depopulation using a proliferation of military metaphors.
Mothers became the primary vehicles in the French army to combat national depopulation. Urging increased natality was the role of the moralists
and religious conservatives. Working toward decreasing mortality was the
realm of the doctors and practical politicians, such as Strauss. A low natality combined with a high infant mortality in France led many politicians

in the 1890s to believe that their country would again be vanquished by Germany. Again using military language, one demographic study claimed that France lost one army corps a year to preventable infant disease and death.[6] To stop this drain on France's "armed strength," the study advised the state to fund baby health clinics, to encourage mothers to nurse their babies themselves, and to fight premature return to work after childbirth.

The medical profession, especially pediatrics, increased in expertise and power and thereby provided new weapons in the arsenal of political intervention in motherhood and child rearing. Not only did doctors now know how to save infant lives with pasteurization of milk and control of communicable infectious diseases, but doctors became political and held seats in the national, and especially the municipal, governments. Doctors were programmatic legislators, engaged in a "sanitary crusade" to change the environment; they worked with other legislators, such as Strauss, to accomplish some of their goals.[7] Although not a physician himself, Strauss was elected to the Academy of Medicine in 1909 for his legislative and public relations work toward improving the health and hygiene of the working people of Paris.

Populationists, including doctors, extolled the virtues of motherhood.[8] The politics of motherhood became that of reconciling the desire for more babies, and for those babies to live longer, with the fear of social revolution in the cities.[9] The long depression of the 1880s further exacerbated the social and economic problems in the major metropolis and increased the fear of working-class unrest—especially among the new, and poorest, arrivals in Paris. Programs to save the children while "moralizing" the mothers were an apparent answer. Strauss and his cohort viewed the defense of the family and the social order as one of the functions of the state and emphasized the key role of the housewife/mother in generating and maintaining the spirit of family life in a strong and growing nation.[10]

Initiative and support for maternal welfare legislation, impelled by the concern for depopulation, came from the center "solidarity" coalition and from those involved in local politics. Solidarism united such seemingly disparate groups as "the growing corps of state experts, university-based social theorists, [and] reforming Catholics" with Protestant and Freemasonic activists and anticlerical reformers.[11] Indeed, Jacques Léonard underscores the reciprocity between *"humanisme médical"* and Freemasonry; Paul Strauss had been an active Freemason.[12] Protestants such as Henri Monod, Charles Gide, and Camille Rabaud wrote strongly against the vanity, pride, and love of luxury leading to voluntary family limitation among the bourgeoisie. They believed that the main way to increase population was by sacrificing individual interests to the general interests and that the state must encourage parents to have several children.[13] The language of the politicians, however, did not center on the mothers but rather emphasized the needs of the babies and the national urgency in "saving the children." Protecting infants was the most uncontroversial means to combat depopulation, and the politics of motherhood called for using the mothers as vehicles by which infants would be aided and France not lose that battalion per year.

Paul Strauss, a solidarist, intricately involved in journalism and in local politics, perfectly fits the type of Radical republican social reformer in both ideology and professional experience. He was born in the small rural town of Ronchamps in the Haute-Saône in 1852 of a Jewish, part Alsatian family of modest means: his uncle was a rabbi in Belfort and his father a cloth merchant originally from Alsace. After attending the Collège de Lure in the Haute-Saône, he pursued his further education in Paris. There he received his civic education by reading the opposition papers, *Le Reveil, La Marseillaise,* and *Le Rappel.* In 1870, at the age of 18, he enlisted in the national guard of his hometown and later in a battalion of the Haute-Saône to fight the Prussians.[14] During the crisis of 16 May 1877 his published republican, anticlerical ideas led to his condemnation and subsequent exile to Belgium. When he returned to Paris in 1881, he defended Gambetta's politics and was elected vice president of the Association of Republican Journalists. In 1887, at the age of 35, he married 18-year-old Renée Bernard, the sister of the writer and future Dreyfusard Tristan Bernard. She died in 1933 at the age of 64.[15] He died at his country villa in Hendaye, near the Spanish border, ten years later, in 1942, at the age of 90. Renée Bernard Strauss was rarely at his side, was rarely acknowledged, and seldom appeared on the rosters of charities Strauss supported, as did the names of other politicians' wives.

The Strausses remained childless. One can only speculate if his childlessness contributed to his ardent desire to save infant lives. Renée Bernard Strauss sensitively displayed a tenderness to children in a book she wrote about weak and sickly working-class children who were cured at public assistance's seaside sanatorium in Hendaye, and she had accompanied her husband on his visit there in 1912.[16] Moreover, in 1917 Paul Strauss was part of a committee that believed that those who had none or few infants should aid the families having many children.[17] There is no evidence that the Strausses aided poor children or adopted any after the 1923 adoption law. If the couple wanted children but was infertile, that wish might have contributed to Strauss's sense of French degeneracy. Ironically, many of the politicians concerned with depopulation had few or no children. Like Strauss, René Viviani and Aristide Briand were childless; Paul Leroy-Beaulieu had one child, and one of the most outspoken pronatalists, Jacques Bertillon, had only two children. The politicians' small family size underscores the possibility that bourgeois politicians wanted to protect working-class babies for cannon fodder.

Professionally, Strauss pursued a career as a journalist and publicist, writing for a number of papers, most notably for *Le Radical* and *Le Voltaire*, and working as editor in chief of *L'Independant* from January to June 1881, during the time it was managed by Alfred Naquet.[18] After leaving *L'Independant*, he wrote again for *Le Voltaire*, where he collaborated with politicians such as Raymond Poincaré. During his days as a journalist, he made the personal and political connections, with Naquet, Léon Gambetta, Jules Ferry, Eugène Spuller, Auguste Scheurer-Kestner, Joseph Reinach, René Waldeck-Rousseau, and others, which were to serve him during his later professional life. Indeed, contemporary historian Pierre Birnbaum refers to Strauss, Naquet, and Camille Pelletan as "Gambettistes," ideologically akin in their ideals of a republic in which all men are emancipated French citizens without regard to religion. Collectively they formed the *nouvelles couches* (newly important social groups), constructing the Republic.[19] As a young man of 26, in 1878 Strauss was a socialist, but one who believed that a republican democracy was the ideal form of government. He wrote in opposition to monarchy and clerical domination. The clerical influence, he asserted, was hostile to liberty, hostile to the emancipation of man, and incompatible with modern society. By 1881 he dropped his overt socialism.

Strauss's concept of liberty, however, like that of his republican cohort, applied to men.[20] His discourse and programs ignored, or denied, women's right to liberty. Strauss reiterated that the form of government based on universal (male) suffrage, in which the "Rights of Man" would be exercised by the vote, was the one that could best alleviate human suffering. Throughout his career his language permitted state intervention in women's lives—in the name of protection, if not in the pursuit of liberty. As early as 1878 he was calling for immediate social reforms to remedy suffering, misery, ignorance, and physical as well as moral maladies.[21] He never wavered from these views.

In 1883, after election to his first public office, the municipal council of

Paris, Strauss discontinued his extensive work as a newspaper journalist and turned his attention to writing books that continued to publicize his populationist social reform platform. He wrote prolifically, though repetitively. From 1892 to 1913 he authored eight books on improving hygiene and child rearing among the working classes in Paris as a means of combating depopulation, and in 1897 he founded *La Revue philanthropique*, a journal devoted to publicizing and popularizing the mutuality of private secular philanthropy and public assistance. In stating the objectives of the *Revue*, Strauss wrote that his editorial policy would be impartial but would endeavor to be altruistic rather than egotistical in the humanitarian task of alleviating misery and combating disease. Patrons of this new journal included such eminent solidarist and Radical politicians as Léon Bourgeois, Émile Cheysson, Henri Monod, Jules Siegfried, and Théophile Roussel. Until 1934 Strauss contributed regular editorials and "Bulletins" about reform proposals before the legislature.[22]

Strauss served as municipal councilman from the working-class Rochechouart neighborhood in Paris from 1883 through 1897. On the municipal council, he chaired the budget committee and served as president of the commission on municipal assistance and president of the commission on milk; he also participated in numerous committees and subcommittees devoted to improving the health and hygiene of Parisians.[23] In these positions he initiated or supported new hospitals for children, the distribution of free sterilized milk to newborns, the sanitary improvement of streets and housing, programs of aid to single mothers to encourage them to keep and nurse their babies, refuge-workshops for homeless pregnant women, and convalescent homes for women after childbirth. From 1887 through 1897, he was an active member of the departmental general council of the Seine. On this council he devoted his energies to questions of public assistance for children and their mothers. For example, he chaired the commission on *enfants assistés* from 1887 to 1897. He demonstrated fiscal conservatism while at the same time advocating measures to protect the health and lives of infants. He reconciled these disparate goals by calling on secular philanthropy to work with public assistance. Strauss's interest in the children was unflagging, and he often repeated that the future was "in the children, the little martyrs."[24]

In 1897 Strauss was elected to the Senate, where he served until he lost in the election of 1936. When he assumed office, he articulated that the "depopulation of France ha[d] become one of the most important concerns of a legislator."[25] As a solidarist member of the Left Radicals, he promoted health, hygiene, and public welfare programs that were both republican and laic. He particularly advocated solidarity on issues of social hygiene and frequently referred to the "fundamental pact of *solidarité sanitaire.*"[26] In addition, Strauss chaired or served on many committees devoted to protecting the health of women and children. From 1888 until 1914 he played an active role on the national Conseil supérieur de l'assistance publique, and in 1902 Premier Waldeck-Rousseau appointed him to chair the subcommittee on infant mortality of the extraparliamentary committee on depopulation. Strauss's most prominent role was as minister of hygiene, assistance, and social welfare (Prévoyance sociale) in the cabinet of Raymond Poincaré from 1922 to 1924. The societies to which he belonged and the committees on which he served indicate his long and abiding interest in social hygiene as a means of combating depopulation, even though in his political ideology he moved from the socialism of his younger years to the more right-of-center nationalism of Georges Clemenceau and Poincaré during his later life.[27]

During his entire life, Strauss worked toward achieving two goals: improving public hygiene and preventing infant mortality. He launched a *croisade sanitaire*, or crusade for modern hygiene and sanitation in housing (including uncontaminated water), streets, sewers, private dwellings, and public institutions, to prevent the spread of contagious diseases, such as tuberculosis. More persistently, he strove to reduce infant mortality by program formulation, implementation, and reformulation on a local level. After the First World War, Strauss expressed concern with the low birthrate and sought to remedy it by opposing birth control and contraceptive propaganda.[28]

With military metaphors permeating his language, by 1901 Strauss had outlined his comprehensive program to reduce the "national peril of depopulation" from infant mortality. He charged patriots and philanthropists to cooperate in this "battle for national defense."[29] To Strauss, it was not important whether charity, benevolence, philanthropy, public welfare, or state socialism sponsored the programs; infants had the right to life, and their parents were not to put any obstacle in the way of that right.[30] This consideration of infant lives, not primarily the well-being of the mothers, marked Strauss's propaganda and policies.

Unlike the socialists, who firmly believed in the unique state responsibility for the poor, and also unlike traditional Catholics, who argued in favor of religious private charity, Strauss believed in a mixture of public welfare and private benevolence. Stemming from his solidarist belief that the French society was "a vast family," and because he was unable to secure enough public funds for his programs, Strauss encouraged private, secular philanthropy to establish institutions for mothers and children and to cooperate with government agencies. As a consensus politician he needed to appease his critics on the right and enlist their support, so he encouraged some of the favorite charities of those critics.[31] He declared that the commune, the department, and the state were all responsible for public welfare and that government agencies should cooperate with private benevolence. This cooperative process served to establish more facilities while it saved the government money and appeased his critics on the right. It was also strictly in keeping with solidarists' vision of a society consisting of associative action, based on the idea of the family as the elemental social unit.[32]

Neither Strauss, who was strongly anticlerical, nor other politicians, such as Gustave Dron, supported any religious charity. In Strauss's concept of public assistance and private philanthropy, a person's individual religious preference made little difference, as long as he or she did not try to make religion a criterion for giving aid. "The fundamental condition of public and private assistance is that it be generous, disinterested, free from ulterior motive and pure of all corruption. Once these conditions have been met, the fighters for the same cause have the right to differ in opinion on political, religious, philosophic, and economic problems; they ignore their differences when they meet . . . in order to assert the necessity of the task of assistance and to describe the methods of application."[33]

In pleading for secular philanthropy and cooperation between private charity and governmental welfare, Strauss maintained, "It is by assistance to mothers of newborns, relief during pregnancy, refuge-workshops for pregnant women, childbirth in which the anonymity of the mother is protected, convalescent homes, aid for maternal nursing, protection of working women, infant day care facilities, free pediatric centers, and by yet other means, that the odious misdeeds against children, that infant mortality, can and must be necessarily and victoriously battled."[34] He believed that solidarity and the common responsibility of "altruists" strengthened the battle against pauperism and infant mortality and that altruism and human fraternity were at the basis of civilization.[35] He assured his readers, particularly the traditional Catholics, that although public welfare in France was becoming a "sacred debt," private charity would not disappear because the poverty of the society was so great.[36] In answer to the socialists, Strauss, as well as Dron and Waddington, repeated that hygiene was "not a struggle of classes" but was "on a neutral ground for humanity and love of country." [37]

Municipal and Departmental Programs

From 1883 to 1897 Strauss oversaw social policy formulation, implementation, and reformulation on a local and departmental level. He had profound political and fiscal influence on programs of aid to unwed mothers when he served as chair of the commission on *enfants assistés* of the general council of the department of the Seine. These programs all fell under the rubric of the programs for *enfants assistés*, thus underscoring the centrality of the children. When initiated in Paris in 1875, the programs were to provide for "children born outside of marriage so that the mothers could better keep and care for their babies" and were called "aid to unwed mothers to prevent abandonment." Those children aided were the "infants whom their mothers, despite their meager resources, agreed to keep and to raise." [38] Strauss and others understood that babies who were not abandoned would have a greater likelihood of survival than the abandoned infants. After 1885, public officials, with Strauss in the forefront, shifted their concern from child abandonment to maternal breast-feeding as a means of enhancing the survival of the infants. Accordingly, departmental officials changed the name of the programs to "aid for maternal infant feeding."

Strauss reiterated to the director of public assistance and fellow members of the general council of the Seine that the protection of infants was "the keystone of the entire social edifice"; no question was "more serious, no obligation more pressing for a generous democracy." [39] Strauss reminded his audience, many of whom referred to the programs of aid to unwed mothers as "a subsidy for debauchery," that the programs of aid were "in the interest of the child" and that the mother was "the paid wetnurse of her infant." [40] Welfare programs were designed to aid the infants through providing for the mothers' physical well-being and by "moralizing" her. An elaborate hierarchy of *dames visiteuses* and inspectors were to "*contrôle*" for the mother's morality and hygiene so she could best nurse her infant. [41] Strauss and public assistance officials demonstrated no notion of family privacy for poor mothers. In their viewpoint, the women were not citizens, and the children belonged to the state as much as to the mothers. [42] Motherhood had become a national duty.

As chair of this committee on *enfants assistés*, Strauss heard complaints from program inspectors that the mothers received insufficient monthly allotments and for too short a duration. Moreover, by policy, mothers who breast-fed their infants themselves received 10 francs more per month than mothers who bottle-fed their babies. The inspectors argued that the women who bottle-fed should not be financially penalized, since their failure to nurse resulted not from lack of maternal love for their infants but rather from the misery of their material condition. The inspectors, closer to the women and their daily lives, presented their case in terms of the women's needs. Strauss countered by stressing the infants' needs and by asking the director of public assistance and the general council of the Seine for more money.[43]

Except for an occasional visit to a hospital or infant care facility, Strauss never visited any of the welfare recipients. He always argued in favor of maternal nursing and advocated assistance that would encourage mothers to nurse their babies, regardless of the undernourished condition of the women and their need to work outside the home. The estimated minimum cost of living for a woman alone in Paris was 850 francs a year; at 20 francs per month from public assistance, a mother received only 240 francs per year. She could not support herself and her infant on that income, nor could she nurse her infant if she worked outside the home. She could get by if she shared her living quarters with a sister, mother, or other companion, as did several women on welfare in Paris.[44] Strauss urged mothers to work at home in the needle trades during the times that they were not nursing their babies or when their babies slept. Perhaps because he was childless, he exhibited little comprehension of babies' demands or the demands of work on the mothers. He insisted on maternal breast-feeding because it would more likely decrease infant mortality than would bottle-feeding. Strauss argued that a mother who nursed her infant devoted most of her time to her baby whereas the mother who raised her infant with a bottle would entrust the infant to a parent or a neighbor and thus engage in a "lucrative occupation."[45] He agreed, however, to request an increase in monthly allotments from 15 to 20 francs for mothers who were in the "absolute physical impossibility of nursing their infants."[46] Strauss told his inspectors that insufficient funds made it impossible to give more money to the mothers or to give it for longer periods of time.[47]

At first glance it appears that Strauss offered more rhetoric than substance, using the idea of saving children's lives as an overt agenda for more obscure political purposes. Though he appeared to drag his feet on authorizing more funds, he had no authority to appropriate money. Indeed, each year he tried to obtain more funding from his superiors. Couching his argument in humanitarian, nationalistic, and financial terms, he stated that aid for maternal nursing not only prevented abandonment and saved infant lives but also produced healthier citizens and, most important, saved the department money in the long run. He calculated that the programs of aid to maternal nursing—even if the amount and duration of aid would be increased—were cheaper than providing for the abandoned infants.[48]

Henri Peyron, the director of public assistance, countered that increasing and prolonging aid to the mothers would "weigh heavily on departmental finances." In response, Strauss demonstrated the techniques of negotiated compromise. He stated that prolongation of aid would pertain only to "cases absolutely necessary to the life of the infant."[49] He later argued that ending assistance prematurely would amount to an inhumane and improvident act, resulting in abandonment and infant deaths.[50] Strauss finally triumphed in this power struggle, for in 1892 he demanded and received limited authority in decisions on the disposition and allocation of money.[51]

Some moralists expressed outrage that programs of aid for maternal nursing helped support single mothers and thereby endorsed vice. They expressed astonishment that a married mother, by the sole fact that she was married, was often deprived of aid from public assistance. Moreover, she received less from her local welfare bureau than did a single mother from public assistance; and a single mother did not have such "irreproachable conduct" as the married women had. Strauss insisted that the criterion for aid had to remain the danger of infant abandonment (and death), a risk far greater for the offspring of single mothers. The single mother was poorer and was herself abandoned and unprotected.[52] For Strauss and other political reformers of late nineteenth-century France, the "moral model of behavior as motivated by ethical and cultural imperatives was increasingly replaced by the medical model."[53] Doctors and public officials could save infant lives; they could not force a change in morality. As a result, "moral exhortations . . . began to appear obsolete. In their place emerged a scientific and medicalized discourse."[54]

Both the moralists who wanted aid to married women and the potential welfare recipients themselves prevailed in policy reformulation beginning in 1885. The practice of excluding married and cohabiting women resulted not simply from insufficient funding but more significantly from official understanding that married women were less likely to abandon their infants. Women knew, however, that priority was given to single mothers. Therefore, when they expected the inspectors, they quite likely sent the men out of their rooms; others had little incentive to marry. Inspectors and *dames visiteuses*, moreover, frequently ignored the marital status or cohabiting arrangements of the women receiving aid. Policy implementation led to policy reformulation, taking into account the actual survival strategies of the women. Starting in 1887, Strauss and others on his committee reformulated policy in line with its actual implementation and accepted some married or cohabiting women into the program, provided they were truly in poverty.[55] Strauss correctly noted that legitimate infants were also exposed to the possibility of abandonment and that the "deprivation of maternal care was the principal cause of infant mortality."[56] Policy changed because he and others recognized the women's reality and the precarious lives of their babies.

Ironically, while sponsoring and implementing programs of aid to mothers to prevent abandonment, Strauss also supported regulations that made abandonment easier. Starting in 1885 (the same year in which married women were included in the program for maternal nursing), the general council of the department of the Seine lifted the requirement that a mother had to provide a name and birth certificate for a child she intended to abandon. Henceforth, a mother could deposit her child at the Hospice des enfants assistés at any hour of the day or night and with total anonymity. While appearing to contradict the programs to prevent abandonment, this policy actually served the goal of saving infant lives. Easy child abandonment was designed to prevent abortion and infanticide.[57]

The puericulture movement, first appearing in 1865 to encompass a broad scale of programs to teach women how to raise healthy babies, received strong endorsement from Strauss. Educating mothers became the key to nineteenth-century scientific child care as well as to the acculturation of working-class women to bourgeois methods of child rearing. This involved helping the mothers breast-feed whenever possible. Although maintaining the superiority of mother's milk, Strauss and others permitted the medically instructed use of properly sterilized milk, bottles, and nipples as alternatives. Strauss eventually determined that all needy children, regardless of their mother's marital status, should be eligible for some programs of aid. He proposed that free baby clinics and convalescent homes for new mothers be available to needy married women, although priority should be given to single mothers. Strauss helped provide municipal financing for his good friend and collaborator Dr. Pierre Budin, who instituted free sterilized milk dispensaries and well-baby clinics where infants had to be medically examined and weighed each time a mother sought milk.

Strauss was a powerful force behind the creation and inspection of municipal *crèches*, or inexpensive infant day-care facilities, as an extension of aid for maternal nursing and to prevent infanticide.[58] He also urged municipal subventions and inspection of private infant day-care facilities. The facilities served as a further means to educate mothers and encourage them to continue breast-feeding both at home and at the facility. Doctors there weighed infants each week and guided mothers in measuring the progress of their infants. The practice, however, often failed to meet the ideals. These facilities numbered too few to make significant inroads, and they often were situated far from the mother's work. Strauss also promoted *pouponnières* in Paris. These institutions were similar to the *crèches*, but working women could leave their babies there for several weeks at a time. These babies would be fed by an unwed mother in residence there. The unwed mother would nurse her own baby and then feed the baby of another woman with her "extra" milk. This second nursing would be supplemented by bottle-feeding with sterilized milk. This would, in Strauss's view, save two babies: that of the unwed mother, who might have abandoned it, and that of the working mother, who either might have abandoned her baby or provided insufficient care. *Pouponnières*, however, only arose in the late 1890s and never became popular; only a handful existed in the Paris region.

Strauss enjoyed great success in achieving cooperation between private philanthropy and public programs at the local and departmental level. For example, he worked with the private, laic Société philanthropique in 1894 for the establishment of a refuge-workshop, the Asile Michelet, for homeless, pregnant women in their last month of pregnancy. Upon his initiative the municipal council of Paris gave a subvention to this private charity for running the shelter. He argued that such shelters "prevent[ed] thoughts of infanticide and abortion and safeguard[ed] the health of the little ones, who even before birth suffer[ed] from the disastrous effects of their mothers' misery."[59] For similar ends, Strauss secured the financial and programmatic cooperation between the municipal government and the private charities initiated by his close friend and collaborator Marie Béquet de Vienne to provide shelter for pregnant and postpartum women. It was also through his initiative that the municipal government received a legacy from former Second Republic leader Ledru-Rollin's widow, which was used to open a convalescent home for postpartum women and their babies.

National Programs

From the time he entered the Senate in 1897, Strauss urged the national adoption of many of the programs he had been instituting and directing on a local level since 1883. In doing so he continued to stress the themes of depopulation and infant mortality, reiterating that the protection of mothers and infants was "of such high importance" that it belonged "in first place among the concerns of governments and legislators." The "evil of depopulation" was growing worse.[60]

Strauss exhorted the national government to follow the lead of the department of the Seine and establish a variety of programs of maternal assistance. He strongly advocated the protection of women during pregnancy to prevent stillbirths resulting from physical exhaustion and economic deprivation. This protection would take the form of paid maternity leaves from work during the last four to six weeks of pregnancy and the establishment of maternity homes, or shelters, in which destitute and homeless pregnant women could live and work until their babies were born. He proposed that maternity hospitals and midwives offer free (and if necessary, secret) childbirth for the women. Strauss did, however, want to reduce the role of midwives, whom he accused of being abortionists or "angel makers." He also called for convalescent homes for destitute mothers in which they would receive education and guidance in child rearing while they were recovering from childbirth. Strauss persistently argued that financial assistance, education, and guidance be given to mothers in the form of paid maternity leaves, monetary allocations to encourage them to keep and nurse their infants, free consultations with pediatricians on infant care, and dispensaries of free sterilized milk at which doctors would dispense advice along with medical care. Each time a mother came for milk to the dispensaries established in Paris, she had to bring her "control card" measuring the infant's weight to prove to the doctor that she was properly feeding her child; Strauss urged similar practices throughout France. In the true spirit of social insurance against misfortune or poverty, Strauss wanted industries and the state to support mutual assistance programs for the expenses of childbirth and maternity leaves. Furthermore, he wished to avail mothers of infant day-care centers that provided sterilized milk, medical care for the babies, and education in infant hygiene. Finally, Strauss recommended that other departments follow the lead of the Seine and make abandonment easy and anonymous for the mother as a way of preventing abortion and infanticide.

According to Article 340 of the Napoleonic Civil Code, fathers of illegitimate children legally bore no responsibility for either the child or the
mother. Strauss advocated changing the law to enable mothers to find the
fathers of out-of-wedlock children and make them accept some responsibility for child support. Strauss shared with others the belief that if the
law allowed *recherche de la paternité* (paternity searches for fathers of out-
of-wedlock children), it would be a means of combating infant mortality,
since if the father were held responsible for child support, fewer children
would be killed—either directly by infanticide or indirectly by abandonment.[61] He may also have believed that paternity searches would spare the
government some expense in supporting single mothers and their children.
But, in the utilitarian family of Strauss and similar reformers of the late
nineteenth century, the fathers were really not there. Poor men were not
providers of child care. The single mothers had only the patriarchy of the
state as male providers.

In addition, Strauss concerned himself on a national level with con-
taminated water, overcrowded and dilapidated housing, the inadequately
implemented law of 1893 on free medical care for the poor, the lack of a pension plan for the aged poor, the terrible scourge of tuberculosis among the
general population, and lack of rest for pregnant and parturient mothers—
all as causes of depopulation. These social ills resulted in premature and
weak infants prone to diarrhea, rampant infectious diseases (such as tuberculosis), and death. The state should prevent such social ills, Strauss argued,
with better housing, sanatoriums for tuberculosis patients, new hygienic
methods of child rearing, weeks of rest for pregnant and new mothers, and
maternal nursing—in general, national obligatory social welfare reforms
so that France would not lose its "numerical strength" and allow "itself to
be increasingly surpassed by younger and more fruitful nations."[62] The responsibility for three major legislative acts belongs to Strauss. He worked
toward the passage of the 1904 law on *enfants assistés*, the 1906 law to
provide low-income housing, and the 1913 law on maternity leaves.[63]

The 1904 law on *enfants assistés* is striking in its replication of the programs that had evolved in the city of Paris and the department of the Seine.
Almost one hundred years had passed since the enactment of the 1811
national law pertaining to *enfants assistés*, and that law operated more in
the breach than in the promise. Each department had ignored different aspects of the law and passed its own regulations. The national legislation
of 1867 on finances for programs of *enfants assistés*, the Roussel law of
1874 to protect infants with a wet nurse, and the Roussel law of 1889 to

protect abused and mistreated children were just pieces of a bigger puzzle: how to resolve the problem of caring for children in need.[64] To Théophile Roussel and Paul Strauss, the nation sorely needed comprehensive, non-contradictory legislation. Throughout the 1890s both Roussel and Strauss worked tirelessly for new national legislation that would assist children in need, including the children of impoverished mothers. In their arguments they continued to invoke the specter of depopulation in addition to the relatively uncontroversial idea of saving children's lives. Roussel died in 1903, leaving Strauss, the floor leader in the Senate, as final author of this important law.

By 1898, ten years after the initial proposal of a new law for *enfants assistés*, the bill was virtually complete, having undergone several revisions in the Senate and the Chamber of Deputies. It then took six years of Strauss's propaganda and politicking, by means of books and speeches, to obtain its passage through both houses. Legislators based their opposition on questions of finances, on the alleged relative morality of married and single mothers, on aversion to child abandonment, and on the different roles of government and private philanthropy.

Children protected by the 1904 law were those in temporary shelters, the abandoned, those who were mistreated or "morally abandoned," the infants with a wet nurse, and poor orphans. Article 3 stipulated that "infants whose mother could not feed and raise them because of lack of resources be accorded temporary assistance with a goal to prevent abandonment." The politicians left marital status unspecified. Article 7 further stipulated that assistance be accorded to children of widows, divorced women, or women abandoned by their husbands. It did not specify that children of married women living with their husbands or women in consensual unions be denied assistance; nor did it specify that they were entitled to such assistance.[65] Legislators, unable to agree on such details, left them up to local option or to a series of regulations.

Strauss needed support wherever he could get it, for he even met opposition within his own political interest group and among the members of the Conseil supérieur de l'assistance publique.[66] Jules Siegfried and Paul Strauss clashed over two crucial proposed articles for the law of 1904: that of secret, open admissions to the foundling hospital for women who sought to abandon their children, and aid to unwed mothers for maternal nursing and to prevent abandonment. In a heated discussion, Strauss bragged that this dual program in the department of the Seine had succeeded in reducing the number of abandoned children.[67] Siegfried's priority was to reduce illegitimate births, and he condemned Strauss's system for promoting their increase. Strauss then tersely replied, "What is important to me is that I arrive at a decrease in the number of infanticides." Siegfried retorted that with Strauss's system, women would "no longer see it necessary to marry" and that permitting paternity searches was a "surer means to decrease the number of abandonments and infanticides." Although Siegfried agreed with Strauss in the desirability of allowing single mothers legally to pursue the putative father for child support, Siegfried's opposition to free, easy, and anonymous child abandonment prevented Strauss from getting that provision into the law.[68]

But Siegfried and Strauss did see eye to eye on the other side of the latter's agenda, that of affordable hygienic housing for the urban poor. The 1906 law on low-income housing repeats on a national level what Strauss suggested as the 125 regulations to implement the Paris regulations of 1902 on sanitation and public hygiene. He called for cleanliness of public and private streets and alleys; improved sewerage; cleanliness in the buildings that border the public and private roads; heating, drinkable water, elimination of refuse, and lighting in buildings; cleanliness of all locations storing or selling food or food supplies; and prevention of contagious diseases through hygiene. Doctors and scientists were to enforce these measures through regular inspection, and the committee that drew up the regulations consisted of four doctors as well as city officials.[69]

Almost as soon as Strauss entered the Senate in 1897, he introduced a bill for paid maternity leaves. From 1899 to 1913 he exerted his considerable influence in securing paid maternity leaves for women and enabling them to have the rest he believed they needed during their last month of pregnancy. Before he entered national government, the closest Strauss came to advocating rest for pregnant women was to suggest that public hospitals and private charities admit women during their last month of pregnancy. By 1893 public hospitals in Paris, such as the major maternity hospital, La Maternité, and its new wing, Baudelocque, had to admit women seeking to spend their last month of pregnancy there. This hospital policy reflected the implementation of the law of 1893 on free medical care.[70] Almost no women, however, came to the hospital before delivery. Strauss did facilitate the opening of a few municipal and philanthropic homes for unwed mothers in Paris.[71] It took the national legislation of 1913 on maternity leaves for him to realize his goal that women should have several weeks of rest before and immediately after childbirth. He desired legislation specifically to prevent infant deaths and congenital birth defects as a result of premature births occasioned by pregnant women standing up at difficult jobs until they delivered their babies. Strauss viewed legislation for maternity leaves as an extension both of labor legislation and of his 1904 legislation for *enfants assistés*. He asserted that the latter law had considerably improved national, municipal, and departmental welfare for women and children, but it was necessary to do more. In his campaign for passage of the 1913 bill, he enlisted the support of the medical profession and of secular, private charities; with their help, he prepared public opinion for protection of maternity.

In urging the passage of the maternity legislation, Strauss cited medical experts, such as Dr. Adolphe Pinard, who argued that women be spared the necessity of heavy work starting in their seventh month of pregnancy and that one month of rest was necessary for the mother both before and after birth. Pinard, who had once opposed Strauss but now served his cause, chastised his associate for saying that maternity leaves were a patriotic move. Pinard argued that there was more to the issue than patriotism; it was simply a question of humanity. Pinard said that four weeks of rest was just a beginning. He had seen too many infants come into the world after only seven months of gestation because women worked too long, often standing.[72] Strauss stressed the urgency of passage of the 1913 legislation to save the lives of women and infants and the "future of the race."[73]

After 1914, Paul Strauss's tenacious perseverance in battling depopulation only became more intense and pronatalist. In 1917 and 1930 he worked to expand the law of 1913 on paid maternity leaves. He also worked on the law of 1913–14 on assistance to families with many children (*familles nombreuses*) and supported amendments in 1922, 1924, 1926, and 1931 increasing the scope of that law. He urged further allocations to women in childbirth, bonuses for breast-feeding, and bonuses for having children (*primes de natalité*) in 1918, 1921, 1930, and 1932. His pronatalism, evidenced by his legislative opposition to contraception and abortion, began in the first two decades of the twentieth century when he lent his name to proposals to convict more people of performing abortions. In 1919 his pronatalism led him to support the law prohibiting the dissemination of information on contraception and abortion enacted in July 1920. Yet he did not believe that abortions were the reason for the low natality in France; rather, it was voluntary sterility.

No matter what the issue or program, at every possible occasion Paul Strauss urged a vigorous system of inspection and governmental control of the agencies of private and public welfare. He argued for teams of doctors, scientists, and other trained people to go into state-supported public and private institutions, as well as women's homes, to make sure they were hygienic. He also encouraged bourgeois women to serve as either paid or volunteer social workers, as inspectors, and as teachers of working-class women about proper hygiene and child rearing. The system of aid for maternal nursing which Strauss so meticulously designed and implemented in the department of the Seine had a system of inspection, but he thought it lacked adequate funding and personnel. That inspectors visited each aid recipient only once a year and *dames visiteuses* inspected each aid recipient only monthly was, Strauss argued, insufficient.

Strauss's private rhetoric calling for an effective system of mandatory inspection as part of laws and regulations was even stronger than his public. In private sessions of the Conseil supérieur de l'assistance publique in 1897 he strongly suggested the enactment of regulations enabling doctors to inspect the public and private *crèches* regularly.[74] He further insisted that inspection of l'assistance publique's programs not devolve on the already overburdened inspectors of the programs for *enfants assistés* and called for a new inspectorate and one doctor per *crèche*. In these meetings he often locked horns with members of the council of a different political persuasion who did not consider themselves "*étatists*" and who did not want so much state intrusion in the family. He also disagreed with Henri Monod, who as director of l'assistance et l'hygiène publique, refused to approach parliament for more appropriations and personnel.[75] When unable to get his way, however, Strauss compromised as long as the health and lives of babies were not endangered.[76]

Paul Strauss did not hesitate to involve the state in the private realm of the family on any issue even remotely involving the lives of poor children.[77] In families with no father, the state, through its inspectors, became the patriarch by having the authority to provide assistance to the women and children, if the women did as the male bureaucrats requested. Inherent in Strauss's programs and ideology was the concept that the children really belonged to the state and were the nation's insurance for the future. Since indigent mothers, by themselves and without assistance, could not ensure the lives of their babies, the male bureaucrats and inspectors—often themselves childless—were to provide the patriarchal authority and support for them.

Paul Strauss was a man with a mission—saving babies' lives—and he worked toward realizing that mission through a variety of general improvements in health and hygiene. His programs were part of the larger French concern with social hygiene, induced by the rise in expertise and political prominence of the medical profession since the 1860s. Strauss served on committees and commissions with doctors and used their expertise and influence in the passage of his bills. With Dr. Pierre Budin he initiated and established the influential Ligue contre la mortalité infantile in 1902. He also worked with one of Budin's students, Dr. Henri de Rothschild, who established philanthropies and charities furthering Strauss's (and his own) goals. The equally prominent doctor-politician Théophile Roussel also counted among Strauss's friends and associates. In 1935 Strauss stated one of his dreams: an indissoluble and confident union between *accoucheurs* and pediatricians in their common attachment to educating women in infant and child care for the protection *"des berceaux populaires."* [78] To some extent, Strauss was the political spokesman for physicians and their views. New developments in medicine and hygiene and the growth of the medical profession as lobbyists and legislators led to the ability to do something about filth and disease bred from crowded and overburdened cities.

The depression of the 1880s made the urban poor more visible. Strauss may have considered them a threat to law and order in the cities, thus feeling a need to do something about them. New arrivals in Paris and the unemployed generally lived in crowded, unsafe, unhygienic shacks at the edge of the city where alcoholism, tuberculosis, and a likelihood of early death plagued them. Although he lived in a wealthy western arrondissement of the city, Strauss may have been distressed by the sight of poor mothers with hungry babies living and begging on the streets. Their plight may have inspired compassion and a sense of solidarity for the nation's well-being. Furthermore, changing attitudes toward children, regarding them as the most vulnerable of the poor, may have inspired Strauss and other politicians to design programs and institutions to protect them.

Positivism and anticlericalism became the buzzwords among doctors and politicians of the Third Republic, including Paul Strauss.[79] They sought to undermine the combined influence of the church and the monarchy in order to establish the secular Republic. From 1815 to 1870 assistance to the poor, for the most part, was in the hands of private religious charity. Those charities often proselytized, thereby bending people's minds away from a secular Republic. Republican officials (secular by definition) wished to mold the minds of the poor to republican sentiment. They also wanted to undercut the power of the church; they therefore created their own welfare programs and reduced subventions to church charities. Combining anticlericalism with the positivist belief that social ills could be remedied led to a spate of reforms.

The writings of Paul Strauss (as well as those of other solidarists) are replete with references to the French Revolution of 1789–93. As early as 1878 he discussed the "Rights of Man" in arguing for universal (male) suffrage, and in 1888, along with Camille Pelletan, he was one of the organizing members of La Société pour les droits de l'homme et du citoyen. Reflecting the philosophical juxtaposition of the right to freedom and the right to life, he stated, "The French Revolution has abolished social orders and classes, it has proclaimed equality among all the citizens. But has it eliminated misery and ignorance, these two cancers in the social body?"[80] He often repeated the maxims of 1793: "Every French citizen has a right to existence. . . . Public assistance is a sacred debt; society owes subsistence to its unfortunate citizens."[81] Given the discourse on the rights of man and on the right to life, it comes as no surprise that the Congrès international d'assistance met in Paris in 1889 and that a corpus of national social welfare legislation ensued from 1889 to 1893, with other legislation to follow after years of intense debate over wording and fine points.

Strauss stated that he was supported and strengthened not only by the "*force médicale*" but also by the "*force féminine*." His relationships with women, however, left an opaque record. Aside from dedicating his book *Fondateurs de la République* to his wife, he never mentioned her in any of his speeches or books. He pointed out, however, how essential activist women were to the protection of poor mothers and children, and he often publicly thanked Olga Veil-Picard and Marie Béquet de Vienne, two philanthropic women with whom he worked closely. They furthered his causes by providing both money and time to found institutions for poor, homeless, pregnant or postpartum women and their children.[82] The skill with which these women ran their organizations prompted Strauss to endorse the admission of women to the administrative commissions of the Bureaux de bienfaisance. He argued that women had administered private organizations with such marvelous results that they should be allowed to administer some public institutions.[83] Yet he remained reluctant to admit women to administrative roles in l'assistance publique. He supported much of the legislation that the feminist congresses advocated, and the 1908 Congrès national des droits civils et du suffrage des femmes listed Paul Strauss as a member of the Comité d'honneur.[84] When feminists and senators later hotly debated the issue of a single mother's right to seek the father of her out-of-wedlock child for child support, Strauss's intervention was "eloquent and energetic." In the Senate debates of November 1912, just before passage of the law permitting paternity searches, he forcefully, but unsuccessfully, argued against the excessive fine and imprisonment that the bill imposed on women who brought a putative father to court "in bad faith." Furthermore, he urged the same protection for women against extortion in *recherche de la maternité* (maternity searches), which the law offered to the putative fathers in paternity searches. He ended his Senate speech on these issues expressing his "ardent desire to protect *les enfants naturels* and to come to the assistance of seduced girls and abandoned women."[85]

Perhaps Strauss's early ideological socialism explains his long-abiding interest in improving the conditions of the working classes through hygiene and saving the children; it also may have firmly rooted him in the potential and power of the state. Later his solidarism led to his conviction that the state had to take responsibility for the children, for the good of the greater French community. He had always been patriotic, and when nationalism called for preventing depopulation, he was in the forefront— whether it was by saving babies' lives before the First World War or through his pronatalist policies in the 1920s. In his obsession with depopulation, in the name of humanity and patriotism, Strauss resembled many contemporary politicians from various backgrounds and political persuasions. His programs and ideologies echoed the principles of *solidarité*—a moral imperative to social reform in which each member of society was indebted to all others. As he wrote, "the national collectivity [had] the right and the duty to exercise . . . suitable protection, and enforce coercion if people fail[ed] to recognize the rules of hygiene."[86]

While securing the health of and economic relief for their children, Strauss's ideas and programs infringed on the liberty of the mothers. Medical surveillance and education of the mothers in any of these programs involved moralization and some degree of social control by requiring a form of acceptable behavior as a condition for aid.[87] Women who sought relief were deprived of freedom of choice about how to rear their child. If they wanted assistance, they had to comply outwardly with the advice of the inspectors and doctors. But the individual liberty of poor women was not an issue to Strauss when the health of their babies, as future French citizens, was concerned.

In explaining the development of the "provident state," François Ewald correctly assessed the shift from the ideal of laissez-faire liberty to the emphasis on saving lives, and the transformation of organized relief from optional benevolence to obligatory responsibility of the state for insurance and welfare. Strauss articulated that shift in attitudes from the sacredness of individual liberty to the idea of the obligation and welfare of the state. In 1901 he criticized the idea of individual liberty by writing, "The economists praise, at every turn, optional relief and private charity; that is to say a regime which permits the community to allow the aged, the infirm, those without work and without lodging to die of hunger; in this gentle country where the octogenarians are compelled to beg on the streets . . . the liberty to be destitute is the last word of their doctrine, the conclusion of their philosophy." Despite these doctrinaire economists, he continued, parliament had passed the law of free medical assistance and would pass other laws founded on the principle of the "obligation" of the state. Strauss stressed obligation and responsibility of all levels of society for compulsory public welfare to provide relief and also to prevent poverty and mortality.[88] Prevention of poverty and death became the important tenet of late-nineteenth-century welfare ideology and programs. These programs began with the unassailable doctrine of saving infant lives, so strongly and repetitively advocated by Strauss and echoed throughout the Senate chambers.

The state, with Paul Strauss in a leadership position, regulated women's bodies because they were pregnant or new mothers. Strauss was not outwardly concerned with the sexuality of poor women. Rather, he seemed indifferent toward women's sexual morality. Strauss illustrates a new view of the family in late-nineteenth-century France; the two-parent nuclear family was no longer the only acceptable mode. The single-parent household of mother and children was now acceptable and made possible through limited public welfare. This was a radical change from the first three-fourths of the nineteenth century.

Strauss's activities exemplify the interrelationship of public policy, designed by relatively rich men, and the private lives of poor women. Although his ideology and programs involved teams of doctors, inspectors, and *dames visiteuses* attempting to educate poor women and supervise their mothering practices, the women themselves exerted pressure on the government. In a way, poor mothers helped set the agenda by persisting in their marital and child-rearing habits. Cohabitation was a fact of life in nineteenth-century Paris. This is not to say that poor women did not want to marry; many did but had insufficient economic or social clout to enforce a marriage. Depopulation and the desire to save infant lives were so overwhelming that politicians modified the old moralists' code condemning nonmarital sexual activity. If they wanted to save infant lives, the politicians had to recognize and work with poor women's lifestyles. Strauss realized this and urged a proliferation of programs for single as well as married poor mothers. Practicing proper modern hygiene under medical precepts became the new morality. The social reform movements of Strauss saved infants lives and also made their mothers' lives somewhat easier. The republican state, represented by Paul Strauss and public assistance, excluded impoverished mothers from its concept of individual liberty because the child's welfare was paramount; it defined the republican motherhood for the poor, and that was in service of producing healthy babies for the nation.

Five

Setting the Standards

Labor and Family Reformers

MARY LYNN STEWART

STATE INTERVENTION in the labor market, as in the family, began with children. The child labor laws of 1841 and 1874 established maximum hours for the employment of children and prohibited children and female minors in underground mines and other egregiously dangerous work sites. An 1892 act included adult women, albeit with a daily limit of eleven hours versus ten hours for children. Another article forbad the employment of women, adolescent girls, and children at night. In 1900, an amendment set a single ten-hour limit and extended it to men working "in the same places as the protected population."[1] This glance at the history of hours standards suggests a progression in coverage from children, to women, to men. Typically, labor historians dismiss the gendered regulations as mere precedents to the universal regulations of 1919.[2] But neglecting gendered standards avoids explaining *why* legislatures restricted women's work before men's, leaving an impression that intervention in the female labor market was a natural antecedent to intervention in the male labor market. Confusing gender-specific with universal labor legislation misses differences in their purposes and rationales. This essay redresses these misconceptions by examining the intentions and arguments of Richard Waddington and Gustave Dron, two legislators who shaped the 1892 and 1900 laws.

Neither of these legislators first broached hours standards. In 1879 a social democrat and former worker, Martin Nadaud, deposited a universal ten-hour bill in the Chamber of Deputies. The same year a moderate republican employer, Jean-Louis Villain, introduced a bill to ban women's night labor. The Chamber appointed a committee to consider and consolidate the two bills. Over the next two decades, seven other committees redrafted hours bills. Although Nadaud sat on a few of the early committees, he did not play a decisive role in revising these bills or convincing the Chamber to pass consolidated versions of them. Nor did any other social democrat or socialist of modest background sway the moderate, middle-class legislatures of the 1880s and 1890s.

Bourgeois republican majorities passed the 1892 and 1900 acts. Forty percent of the deputies approving crucial articles had legal training; a third were in other liberal professions. Less than a tenth of the recorded votes came from the "interested" parties, mainly industrialists. The essential support for sex-specific regulations came from moderate and Radical republicans (36% and 19% of the vote). Almost a fifth of the voters were conservative; just over a quarter were Radical socialists and socialists.[3] The eight labor committees charged with revising labor bills between 1880 and 1900 reflected this eclectic mix. Lawyers filled one-quarter to one-half of the seats on any particular committee; manufacturers formed the second largest occupational group. Working-class representation on these committees never reached 15 percent. Politically, Opportunists predominated, followed by Radical republicans; the Left never held more than a quarter of the seats.[4]

Despite their social respectability and political moderation, these committees confronted tenacious legislative opposition to state intervention in the workplace. Debate dragged on for thirteen years because of laissez-faire liberal objections to interference in the "natural laws" of economics.[5] Nevertheless, hours standards moved through the legislature faster than a bill to compensate victims of industrial accidents introduced the same year (1879) but not enacted until 1898. Hours standards encountered less opposition because Opportunist governments eliminated men from the article defining coverage. Eliminating men reduced protests about interference in workers' right to contract their labor. Only a handful of strict liberals such as Yves Guyot contended that adult women were free to contract their labor, and only one of Guyot's amendments to exclude women passed in the Chamber of Deputies. After this, the committee developed a justification about facilitating women's role in bearing and rearing children. Later Guyot amendments garnered only thirty votes.[6]

As the debate shifted from men to women, it switched from class confrontations about rights to gender consensus on protecting the national interest in population growth and social stability. Instead of speaking about production and competition, reformers talked about reproduction and de-population, degeneration and the working-class family. Promises of lower infant mortality and better child care, and hence of more and healthier young men for the military draft, appealed to nationalists preoccupied with revenge; rhetoric about the housewife as a guarantor of family cohesion attracted Social Catholics and moderate republicans concerned about social order, and oratory about the "superior interests" of babies, husbands, and families was agreeable to politicians of all political persuasions. Even socialists devised a dualistic argument for universal and "special" (feminine) regulations. Once they introduced the subject of women, they replaced the language of individual rights to leisure with talk about maternal duties.[7] If their speeches echoed Proudhonian notions of the mother as the moral center of the family, they also repeated bourgeois themes of republican motherhood formulated in the 1860s and 1870s.[8]

Richard Waddington and Gustave Dron mobilized this multiparty, cross-class coalition. A member of labor committees from 1880 to 1891, Waddington shepherded four bills through the Chamber of Deputies. He was well positioned to persuade the moderate republicans who controlled the Chamber in the 1880s. Although Richard sat on the center Left, his brother William was an Opportunist minister and even premier in 1879. Richard spoke with authority on economic matters as director of a cotton firm. Elected with a crop of Radicals in the 1889 election, Dr. Dron promptly entered the labor committee. He overcame opposition to the night-work clause, using scientific evidence to sway the solidarist chambers of the 1890s. Though Waddington and Dron wanted universal hours standards, they constructed cases for gendered regulations which convinced majorities in both chambers. Why did these bourgeois men sponsor labor reform? Did they adopt gendered regulations as a political concession? Or did gender-specific restrictions address broader social concerns?

Political allegiance and ideology partly account for Waddington's and Dron's involvement in labor reform. As candidates of coalitions of Opportunist and Radical republicans, Waddington and Dron presented themselves to electors as alternatives to socialism and clerical reaction. Their platforms had cross-class planks such as tariff protection and secular education. Both deputies used the term "*l'état providence*," which a newspaper that supported Waddington defined as a state that "offers all citizens the means to ameliorate their conditions by their own means." Both spoke of solidarity or the responsibility of society toward its weaker members.[9] Generally, they understood weakness as a lack of control over working conditions. In the case of working women, they included exhaustion due to the double burden of jobs and housework. They were not particularly prone to bourgeois prejudices about women's nature. Waddington resorted to gender stereotypes primarily to explain why women worked longer hours: "Woman is more disposed to be patient, to suffer; she is less egotistic than man." Dr. Dron only indirectly alluded to women's alleged physical frailty.[10]

There were generational and sociopolitical differences. Coming of age as a republican during the Second Empire, Waddington shared his generation's concerns about republican defense. Electoral manifestos stressed lay education, because he was a Protestant with Catholic opponents in the 1880s. As a prominent member of the Rouennais elite, Waddington courted local merchants and manufacturers with protectionism.[11] Campaign posters offered only vague promises to promote "any practical measures that [would] ameliorate the situation and assure the independence of workers." When he made a specific commitment to labor regulation in 1891, he lost his bid for the Chamber as Opportunists defected to a splinter candidate. However, he soon won the first of several elections to the Senate.[12]

Born eighteen years later than Waddington, in 1856, Dron entered the national political arena at the end of the era of republican defense. To fight a formidable Catholic opponent, the local textile manufacturer Barrois, Opportunists and Radicals in Tourcoing, in the Nord, formed La Solidarité républicaine laïque et sociale. In 1889 the league endorsed Dron, a Radical not aligned to General Boulanger. Tourcoing was one of the few industrial cities to escape the Boulangist sweep that year. Dron built his base among workers, the most numerous group in his industrial town, and Radical segments of the petty bourgeoisie. He directly addressed workers, whose "hard existence" he knew. In 1893 and 1898, he broke with Opportunists and negotiated with the French Workers party to withdraw its candidate. Together with Paul Lafargue and local communists, he campaigned against the Social Catholic mixed (employer-worker) unions known as Notre Dame de l'usine. Electoral propaganda listed his efforts to win the ten-hour day and workers' compensation.[13] While other industrial cities in the Nord elected socialists, Tourcoing returned Dron.[14]

A survey of Waddington's and Dron's speeches and reports in the Chamber and in legislative committees suggests that they were not single-issue ideologues. Rather, they were program-oriented politicians who enjoyed solving problems and who followed through on legislative initiatives.[15] For instance, Waddington insisted upon a special corps of work inspectors, instead of relying on the police. He accepted women inspectors because they learned more in feminine workshops.[16] As chair of the committee overseeing implementation of the law for two decades, he lobbied for rationalization of the law and the inspection service.[17] In the Chamber, Dron tried for more than a decade to improve the law and the inspectorate, though he preferred extending coverage and enhancing enforcement powers.[18]

The economic environment of their constituencies helps explain their devotion to factory regulations. Like most deputies voting for labor bills, Waddington and Dron represented departments with industrializing or fully industrial economies.[19] Familiarity with industrial production was definitely a component in voting patterns. Of course ministers from industrial districts successfully defeated universal regulations in cabinet, and senators from industrial districts expunged women from a Chamber bill in 1882, delaying even gender-specific standards for a decade.[20] Clearly, contact with industry is an insufficient explanation for dedication to labor reform.

Familiarity with women in industry influenced Waddington's and Dron's conversion to gender-specific standards. Both resided in departments with high proportions of the female labor force in manufacturing. Nearly half the operatives in Waddington's cotton mills and one-third of the hands in the woollen mills of Tourcoing were women. Given a paucity of information about women's working conditions, personal knowledge added to their authority in debates. But representing departments with industries dependent on a female labor force hardly guaranteed sponsorship of feminine standards. Deputies from departments with the highest proportions of women in manufacturing—the Loire and the Vosges—led the opposition to gender-specific bills.[21] Manufacturers in these two departments were desperate for cheap but dependable (i.e., female) labor. Unlike the Seine-Maritime, the Loire had many marginal firms in highly competitive industries; unlike the Nord, the Vosges had to contend with labor shortages. It was exposure to feminine sectors without cutthroat competition or acute labor shortages which was conducive to advocacy of gender-specific hours standards.

The two reformers' occupations and philanthropic activities best elucidate their commitment to labor reform. Through different occupations, they had acquired a long-term perspective on labor and social problems. The key to their conversion to gendered standards can be found in their local philanthropic programs. Both practiced personal charity and administered public assistance programs for working-class babies; both observed working women's dual burden of paid labor and unpaid child care; both perceived a relationship between production and reproduction and between public and private affairs.

Practical knowledge of industrial production motivated Waddington. In forty-nine years as director of the cotton firm founded by his English grandfather, he expanded business by 50 percent, until the four factories in Saint-Remy-sur-Avre in the Eure-et-Loir produced 2,250,000 kilos of thread and 8,300,000 meters of fabric. In 1889 the firm employed 1,234 workers and paid 1,023,878 francs in wages. Not quite half the labor force were women, who received just over half the men's wages. The principal explanation for the wage gap was the sex-typing of jobs, specifically assigning women to lower-paying jobs.[22]

Unlike other Norman and northern mill owners, Waddington was an enlightened employer.[23] He offered an unusual mix of child care, mutual savings, and company-financed insurance plans. His child-care facilities differed from the *crèches* and kindergartens run by Catholic ladies in the Nord insofar as they were attached to factories and operated by Protestant ladies. Although his mutual savings schemes resembled the "social economy" (mixed employer-worker) approach of Catholic employers, his insurance schemes prefigured social security.[24] The annual cost of his social programs multiplied from 15,000 francs in 1875 to 94,000 francs in 1909.[25]

Like the Protestant mill owners of Alsace-Lorraine at midcentury, the Waddingtons began with company housing and child care. As early as 1872, Richard built a free *crèche* that cared for fifty-nine babies in 1889. A mother could leave her infant or toddler (2 weeks to 3 years old) with three staff members under the direction of nine ladies in the Waddington family. Twice a day mothers could breast-feed; they also received free milk to take home at night. These sensible yet unusual provisions allowed mothers to feed babies without excessive interruption of their work or sleep. In 1874, Richard added a kindergarten that served ninety-two 3- to 7-year-olds in 1889. Two licensed teachers supervised and taught gender-typed subjects—that is, the girls learned sewing. Concierges picked the children up and delivered them back to the factory. A doctor visited twice a week. Waddington senior had offered courses in the factories. In 1877, Richard required and paid for all his workers' children to attend communal primary schools. After the compulsory primary education acts of 1881, he provided free school supplies.

Since 1824 the company had subsidized mutual saving schemes. Members of the mutual aid societies received medical attention, drugs, and an indemnity when they were sick or having a difficult pregnancy. A 1905 investigation concluded that Waddington's factories were the only ones in France offering "organized protection for pregnant women." By the end of the century, Richard offered maternity insurance to provide benefits for a mandatory three-week leave—one of only 150 maternity insurance schemes for working women in 1905.[26]

Other benefits foreshadowed social insurance schemes. In 1878 Richard introduced pensions that supported eighty-two retired workers *before* the state had a pension plan. Thirteen years before the workers' compensation act, he financed accident insurance. He paid unemployment insurance. Other fully funded schemes included pay while on military duty (1877), relief in kind during winter slowdowns (1895), and, for distraction, a band (1897), square, and kiosk (1903). Finally, he built public baths (1907). In short, Richard disregarded laissez-faire and welfare state distinctions between private and public functions.

As another facet of Richard's mingling of family and firm affairs, social events were given that included workers. In 1892, twelve hundred workers attended the company's centennial dinner, which doubled as a wedding dance for his eldest son. Richard's speech affirmed that the "chief characteristic" of the company was "solidarity" between bosses and workers. His brother Evelyn spoke of "fathers and sons, raised in the midst of [the] workers, and living the same life." "We have absolute confidence in them and they know they can be sure of us." Reporters commented on the fraternization of bosses and workers at a "truly democratic demonstration." While there was fraternization, it was hardly democratic. For instance, teachers sent attendance cards to management, who fined workers whose children were absent two weeks without excuse and fired parents if truancy persisted. The Waddingtons were prepared to impose child-rearing as well as work standards on their labor force.

A system of care from the cradle to the grave stabilizes the labor force. Over a quarter of the labor force spent more than thirty years in Waddington's employ; nearly another quarter stayed in the plants sixteen to thirty years. As a third-generation industrialist, Waddington had developed a long time line in his dealings with labor. With a fully financed firm producing specialized products—and hence immune to intense competition—he could afford industrial experiments.[27] He went beyond the better-known enlightened employers who improved working conditions through industrial corporatism or employer-employee schemes. Neither the Protestant Dolfuss nor the Social Catholic Leon Harmel voluntarily lowered hours or promoted state intervention.[28] In contrast, Waddington resembles the third-generation industrialists in England and the United States who could afford benevolence and regarded the state as an agent to generalize private initiative.[29] He had been educated in England, had family ties there and in America, and had read about industrial experiments abroad.[30]

Limiting his municipal ambitions to his "suburban fief" of Darnétal (a community of sixty-seven hundred), Waddington played an important role regionally and departmentally. As a forty-two-year member of the Rouen Chamber of Commerce and as a general councillor of the department of the Seine-Maritime, Waddington stressed nonpartisan commercial issues such as transportation networks and tariff protection.[31] Yet, when labor regulations became a departmental issue, he defended them with a combination of industrial paternalism and practical politics. Factories destroyed "affectionate paternal relations between workers and bosses" and rendered "some supervision necessary to stop abuses." Moreover, he introduced a motion for relief to "morally abandoned" children and supported assistance to abandoned babies and subsidies to maternity hospitals. To justify these programs, he referred to the new medical imperative of assuring the survival of children, with no reference to the old moral qualifications about the marital status of the mothers.[32] His justification resembles Paul Strauss's rationale for more extensive programs in the Paris municipal council about the same time.[33]

Le Petit Rouennais, which supported Waddington, elaborated on his position. Critical of the "disdainful indifference" of orthodox (laissez-faire) economists, the editors contended that the state had a "supervisory role" to protect the weak and to position workers to contract freely. Worried about the advance of socialism among workers in a democracy, *Le Petit Rouennais* encouraged "the directors of society" to "settle accounts" with protective labor laws and joint employer-employee ventures. To distinguish its stance from Social Catholicism, the newspaper condemned "socialists of the chapel" for trying to "discipline" workers by dominating mixed unions such as Notre Dame de l'usine. Conversely, it applauded the "moralizing" character of municipal socialism, notably programs for orphans, the infirm, and the aged. It commended workers' hygiene congresses, especially resolutions for prenatal care.[34]

Waddington's industrial success inspired his acceptance of universal labor standards. In the 1880 labor committee, he argued for ten hours for all industrial workers. He maintained that technological advances made longer days economically unnecessary and ethically unacceptable. His political roles as intermediary between the Center and the moderate Left

and as a spokesman for industrialists account for his legislative devia-
tions. When the government opted for eleven hours for industrial women,
Waddington concurred, contending that France could only afford partial
measures, given international competition. In the mid-1880s, he reverted
to his original position, claiming that tariffs would protect French industry
from international competition. The majority on the committee rejected
universal standards on the grounds of men's right to work. Like other
reformers, Waddington consoled himself with the idea of "indirect regulation," or the assumption that employers would have to coordinate the
schedules of men and women.[35]

Experience in mixed-sex industry did not imply accurate predictions
about the effect of gendered restrictions. Waddington did not understand
that sex-typed jobs allowed employers to evade the generalization of short
time by organizing separate, single-sex shifts. He underestimated the in-
genuity of industrialists who created relay shifts of women to prepare the
raw materials and finish the products of men working twelve-hour days—
which meant that some women spent more time at the workplace, even if
they spent less time working.

Experiments with short time helped Waddington make optimistic fore-
casts about its effect on productivity. Citing examples from his own factories, he demonstrated that shorter days would not reduce output, because
workers would be less tired and factory owners would install more efficient
technology. Industrial spokesmen in the Chamber responded with long ex-
positions of liberal economic tenets. In addition to making dire predictions
about loss of jobs, wages, and profits, they objected that few industrialists
could afford new technology because few owned long-established, fully
financed firms, as Waddington did.[36] Socialists were more likely to adopt
(and amplify) Waddington's arguments about sustaining productivity by
improving efficiency.[37]

When critics in the Chamber asked why factory operatives needed protection, since machines did the heavy work, Waddington described the
speed, regularity, and intensity of mechanized labor. But another industrialist, Villain, diverted any discussion of the nature of factory work by
noting that "labor-saving" technology drew women into factories, that
pregnant operatives standing fourteen hours a day had difficult deliveries,
and that their small, sickly babies, when grown, increased the rejection
rate in the military draft.[38] Moderate and Radical republicans preferred
lofty pronouncements about women's reproductive role to mundane information about their productive work. Aside from one other brief exchange,

this was the only discussion of the pace and routine of paid labor in the debates on women's workday. The paucity of detail suggests that working conditions were not the significant issue.

Waddington himself had a social agenda that transcended the workplace. The Waddingtons were evangelical Protestants who believed in an ethic of individual and familial obligations to the poor, including improving behavior in a brotherly or sisterly manner.[39] Unlike northern Catholic businessmen, Protestant businessmen remained personally involved in charity. A commemorative brochure published after Richard's death paid homage to his "constant solicitude" toward his philanthropic endeavors. His pastor praised Richard's concern about "victims of social disorganization."[40] He did not challenge Richard's interference in working-class life.

In Rouen, where "every bourgeois had his own poor," the Catholic Church monopolized the established charities. Accordingly, Protestants and Freemasons had founded competitive charities.[41] In 1869, Richard replaced his father in the prestigious Société des amis des pauvres; as a member of this society he read detailed reports about needy and deserving Protestant families. Richard also contributed to and participated in state-subsidized social services. From 1869 to 1879 and again at the end of his life, he sat on the Darnétal Welfare Bureau. Even in the hiatus, he personally interceded for impoverished individuals.[42]

The Waddington women took considerable interest in infant charities. From 1856 to 1899, first Richard's mother and then his wife were members of the Société des dames protestantes, which visited indigent Protestant mothers in Rouen, provided clothing, and urged single mothers to wed and to baptize their children. These women had an intimate knowledge of the families they visited. They had few bourgeois illusions about the possibilities of full-time housewife-mothers or domestic bliss among the working poor. Richard was the major benefactor of the Société des dames de la maternité, which distributed layettes and food vouchers to sixty indigent mothers in Darnétal. Under his wife Mary's presidency (1886–99), the society applied for and received state subsidies. Like Richard, Mary emphasized healthy births and breast-feeding rather than marrying and moralizing the poor.[43] Concern about infant survival (and their future labor force) transcended their commitment to a patriarchal family or the Protestant religion.

Clearly, Waddington's interest in labor reform derived less from the narrow focus on production one might expect of an industrialist than from a broader perspective on the connections between reproduction and production and between maternal assistance, infant survival, and sociopolitical goals. He was not just a financially secure manufacturer. Educated at the Woolwich Artillery School in England, he fought in the Franco-Prussian War and wrote many volumes of military and diplomatic history.[44] If he could conceive of company programs for child care and social security to stabilize his workforce, he could imagine legal standards promoting population growth and family life and hence promising enough healthy and stable men for the military draft. His company's system of child care and social security ignored laissez-faire assumptions about the separation of the workplace and the home and about women's place; his political program of labor regulations to encourage social reproduction for military preparedness crisscrossed the artificial boundary between public and private spheres.

Waddington emphasized pronatalist, patriotic, and political reasons in his reports to the Chamber. Brief references to women's health gave way to extensive passages about improving women's working conditions to ensure healthier babies, which would ultimately lower the number of young men in industrial districts who were not fit for the army. Given his interest in and long-term outlook on military matters, this argument seems sincere. Never asserting that working women should be full-time housewives, he assumed that they had to combine reproductive and productive work. No doubt his labor requirements and involvement in outdoor relief contributed to this realistic, if demanding, conception of working women's role. Conversely, contentions that relieving women of one hour's paid labor a day would improve housekeeping, and that would keep working-class men away from bars and socialist meetings, were surely borrowed from Social Catholic rhetoric, presumably to attract conservatives.[45]

Republican and conservative deputies developed the argument that long days threatened women's maternal and housewifely role. Although some Radical republicans challenged the liberal claim that workers were free to dispose of their labor, the core of their case for gender-specific legislation was the preservation of a domestic family. When liberals objected that restricting women's work infringed on their liberty, republicans responded that women were not citizens and ceased to have civil rights upon marriage. Radicals were prepared to have women do wage work in "their natural sphere," the home, but moderates denied that they were even writing labor laws, as opposed to laws to fortify "the family" and safeguard society. Like Social Catholics, they presented sex-specific regulations as a means of policing working-class men by keeping them off the streets and out of trouble.[46]

Waddington had outlined and other republicans had filled in a justification for gender-based standards that transcended orthodox laissez-faire dogmas about the labor market. Assumptions about women's reproductive role and anxieties about depopulation and demoralization were so entrenched that sponsors of gendered standards did not have to show any correlation between mothers' paid work and infant mortality or to substantiate contentions that working women were poor housewives or claims that poor housekeeping drove men into socialism![47]

When an international recession crippled Parisian luxury trades in the early 1880s, concern extended to smaller workplaces. Along with several other deputies who sat on labor committees, Waddington was appointed to the Spuller Commission; in its meetings he heard gloomy testimony from representatives of luxury trades.[48] Evidence of a crisis convinced Waddington and others on the labor committee to include small workshops in the hours bill. This provision occasioned lengthy negotiations with the Senate, where Catholics and liberals would not countenance any surveillance of the "sacred" family, "violation of private residences," or restriction of parental authority as the "natural protectors of children." They only agreed to inspection of family workshops containing "a steam engine or mechanized motor" or classified as a "dangerous or unhealthy establishment" after speeches insisting that fathers did not have the right to maim or poison their children or blow up their homes.[49] Exempting most family workshops left an estimated 1,199,196 female workers without legal protection.[50] But the exemption respected, if it blurred, the line between private and public responsibilities and preserved the loose profamily alliance.

Familiarity with industrialists' problems left Waddington open to lobbying. By the time the labor committee discussed the night-work clauses, lobbies had persuaded him to exempt continuously fired plants and to allow sixty to ninety days of overtime in seasonal trades. In a protectionist vein, he claimed that ending overtime in the Parisian luxury trades would "fatally endanger" the prosperity of an important export sector. He also made gender-stereotyped statements about occupations that could "only be confided to the delicate hands of women" and overtly profit- and productivity-oriented remarks about women being "irreplaceable" on the night shifts of sugar refineries and glass factories because they were cheaper than men but more reliable than boys.[51] By catering to industries dependent on cheap female labor, he perpetuated job ghettos.

Waddington's concessions to industrial interests did not silence their opposition or spare him their hostility. Representatives of industrial societies testified against regulation before every legislative committee; industrial associations deluged committee members with pamphlets and letters. After a decade of debate, many were prepared to tolerate gender restrictions.[52] Others were suspicious. In the late 1880s, *Le Temps* reported that few industrialists were "duped" by Waddington's focus on "beings worthy of solicitude: women and children." They considered him a traitor, "a Machiavelli without knowing it."[53] As implementation of the laws moderated his position on ten hours, former opponents treated him as a "reasonable" reformer.[54] After 1900, he seconded industrialists' demands for a "flexible" application of standards and reiterated earlier concerns about France being ahead of its competitors in legislating standards. Although he played an important role in the Senate ratification of the international convention on women's and children's night work in 1911, he now paid more attention to military preparedness.[55]

Dron's socioeconomic and philanthropic perspective on industry was different. His origins and occupation were humbler than those of most deputies, which explains his identification with labor and social issues. His medical training accounts for his scientific conception of these issues. Unlike Waddington's factory villages, the industrial town of Tourcoing had no tradition of personal, familial, or firm philanthropy; at most a few benevolent families subsidized charities run by nuns. Whereas Waddington emphasized private charities but accepted state subsidies and supervision, Dron felt that private charities were too closely associated with individual donors, and hence too confessional and ephemeral, to be more than "auxiliaries, not substitutes" for public assistance.[56] In this industrial wasteland, Dron built municipal social services that exceeded Waddington's private programs. Yet, like Waddington, he personally intervened for individuals receiving assistance.[57]

Dron was among a minority of the 358 physician-legislators of the early Third Republic which Jack Ellis has profiled. Like 30 percent of them, he was born into a petty bourgeois family and pursued upward mobility by education; he also took the minority route of a college, rather than a lycée, a provincial medical faculty, and a specialization in ophthalmology. Medical training left many physicians of the Pasteur era with concerns about physical survival; it also sapped their faith. In Dron's case, medicine convinced him of "the necessity to protect life, even before birth," and of the need for laicization of the health, welfare, and education systems. Following a familiar path, Dron returned to his native town, where he built up a practice before entering municipal politics. But he deviated from the norm for physician-legislators in setting up his practice in an industrial town. He was also one of the few physician-legislators to champion labor standards and one of only 31 percent to vote for ten hours.[58]

House calls made Dron popular as "the doctor of the poor, the humble and the disinherited." His practice brought him into contact with the six local Catholic charities, all of which avoided state subsidies and supervision.[59] Since they accepted city funds, they were subject to municipal monitoring.

Dron dedicated himself to municipal health and welfare. In 1883 he made a good political marriage, to Marie Leloir, niece of the head of the local Radical faction and adjoint to the mayor of Tourcoing. Within a year, he was elected to city council, which appointed him to the Hospices Commission that supervised a hospital, orphanage, and old-age home. After becoming vice president of the commission in 1891 (and after local outbreaks of smallpox and diphtheria), Dron doubled the size of the hospital by adding a maternity wing, contagious diseases pavilions, and public baths and gardens. A fiscal conservative, like Strauss, he defended the expense in terms of economic efficiency, saying, "It is wise to protect the entire population from the dangers that can issue from one morbid case. This is especially true in industrial cities like ours, where the labor and skill of humble workers . . . constitute the fundamental agents of public prosperity and where, as a result, we cannot pay too much attention to the establishment of what has so justly been called the repair shop for human equipment." [60] From 1899 to his death in 1930, except for a brief interlude after the war, he was a very powerful mayor of Tourcoing and an architect of the municipal socialism Waddington's newspaper admired.[61]

Yet it took more than two decades to remove the Sisters of Charity, who visited homes to identify and distribute relief to indigent families. Like other doctors engaged in a struggle with the traditional health and welfare agents, Dron denounced the sisters for pressuring patients to attend Mass and orphans to attend parochial schools, as well as for poor hygiene. When the Catholic majority on the Hospices Commission resisted, Dron arranged to replace intransigent Catholics with republicans. In the 1890s he and other anticlerical councillors berated the sisters for distributing relief packages displaying the name of a Catholic benefactor (one of Dron's political opponents). City council replaced three nuns with civic inspectors. In 1908 anticlerical councilmen accused the sisters of refusing home visits unless the children were in parochial schools. Over the next four years, the council released all the sisters and, in a highly symbolic gesture, transferred their convent to Dron's favorite lay service, the "Infant Protector." [62]

Dron's actions on the Hospices Commission reveal demographic concerns and social paternalistic solutions. In response to a local Catholic employer who complained that maternal assistance was limited to unwed mothers, he bluntly responded that the point was to prevent single mothers from committing infanticide.[63] If he accepted the reality of single motherhood, he insisted on state supervision of nonpatriarchal (mother-child) families. Generally, Dron tried to foster state supervision *and* family responsibility. While he approved the Roussel law providing wet nurses for abandoned babies, he thought that grandparents should be involved, since they owed "guidance" to their grandchildren. "By what right would the State interpose as tutor?" Similarly, he arranged for home rather than institutional meals for the able-bodied elderly and for family housing, not single-sex dormitories, for the elderly on medical assistance.[64] However, his preference for outdoor relief and family residences presumed state surveillance—and standards—in the home.

Although Dron championed labor regulations in the general council of the Nord, he emphasized health and welfare. He supported subsidies to tuberculosis dispensaries and sanatoriums for crippled children, justifying them with an economic analogy and a labor market metaphor: "What is this expense compared to the savings to be realized in human capital?" Like Waddington and Strauss, he advocated lifesaving assistance, not morally conditioned relief, to infants. Opposing the withdrawal of assistance on the birth of a second illegitimate child, he said: "A single mother has a second baby; I neither criticize nor excuse her; as individuals, we can think what we wish from a moral point of view, but the issue here is to give assistance to poverty and to stop infanticides."[65]

Aid to children preoccupied him, possibly because, like the Strausses, the Drons had no children.[66] In his will, he wrote that his life purpose had been "to encourage the growth of working-class children and to fight above all for the prevention and treatment of . . . social ills." He felt he had spent "the most continuous and productive part of [his] life in philanthropy."[67]

Influenced by Pierre Budin, the founder of the first free baby clinic, and Paul Strauss, champion of infant welfare, Dron launched the "Infant Protector" to distribute pasteurized milk to indigent mothers as well as to subsidize breast-feeding mothers in their homes. Most of the funding came from the city, but private donations, including a generous one from Pierre Wibaux, the son of a local industrialist who had settled in Montana, were welcomed. In order to qualify, new mothers had to allow investigators in their homes and answer questions about feeding and child-care practices.

Although lay women continued the sisters' practice of home visits, they were interested in instilling new standards of physical care, not in encouraging religious observance: they were carriers of a hygienic rather than a spiritual message.[68]

By combining private donations and public subsidies, like Strauss, Dron offered more comprehensive child care than Waddington did.[69] Home visitors' reports on health and living conditions led to school medical inspections, school canteens, a dispensary, free vacation schemes, and a clinic for children with orthopedic problems. Passionately concerned with education, especially vocational education, Dron pursued school secularization. Since the primary and boys' secondary systems had been secularized before he became mayor, he established girls' senior primary and technical schools. These schools attempted to broaden the range of occupational options for working-class girls.[70]

Like the Waddington women, Dron's mother-in-law and wife were involved in charitable activities. With other republican ladies, they founded and gave most of their personal fortunes to the Dames charitables. The members made and dispensed clothing to poor children in the public schools, a secular parallel to the sisters' activities in the private schools. Over the years, the Dames charitables also visited homes, where they advised on cooking, cleaning, and child care. Sixty years later, one recipient of their charity still resented their meddling and their anticlericalism.[71] Educated by Jean Macé, a popularizer of lay female education, Marie Dron raised money for a "Practical Housekeeping School" to teach poor girls basic household management. She had "her own conception of women's mission in society," one that did not involve "dragging them beyond the permitted limits." Although her endeavors were more overtly class and gender bound than her husband's programs, he continued subsidizing them after her death.[72]

More directly than Waddington's position as a secure industrialist, Dron's profession drew his attention to infant care. Reproductive concerns brought him into contact with charitable institutions. Scientific training imbued him with a utilitarian conception of philanthropy that emphasized saving lives. Dron took this public health approach into his legislative campaigns for regulation of productive work. His modest background and political allies made him more dedicated to universal labor standards, but he too was adaptable. Entering the Chamber after it approved feminine hours standards, he concentrated on banning women's night work and enacting maternity leaves. Presenting measures no one proposed to apply to men, he tried to slip through the barriers between private and public realms.

After aggressive lobbying from industrialists, the Chamber had adopted an amendment to remove women from the night-work article. Now Radicals developed the idea that women's nocturnal labor disorganized the family, reduced the number of births, and increased infant mortality. Without dropping humane concern about women's fatigue due to the poor quality of day sleep and "their second burden, housework," they pleaded the "superior interests" of children, country, and social cohesion. Tired mothers meant "physical degeneration" in succeeding generations; poor maternal guidance meant "moral decay" among their progeny. The absence of the housewife at night, when other family members could assemble, meant the dissolution of the family. "Abandoned" husbands went to the bar; "deserted" children fled into the streets. At home, the housewife could "inculcate the habits of order and economy," which were the "strength and security of the French worker." [73]

Dron's critique of nocturnal labor combined "common sense" and clinical and "scientific" medical arguments. After brief reference to the usual social consequences of separating families at night, he insisted that night work was "above all, injurious to health." "In the natural order, night and sleep are made for one another." Everyone agreed that daytime sleep was less restorative, and Dron added that this was particularly true for women, who could only hope for intermittent sleep, since they had to wake up to prepare meals. Drawing on his own medical practice, he sketched horrifying vignettes of women toiling twelve or thirteen hours in hundred-degree heat and claimed that more accidents happened in artificial lighting. To add substance to these anecdotal and emotive appeals, he cited a resolution of the Academy of Medicine and a survey by a prominent hygienist on the pernicious effects of night work. [74]

At the request of one of the other doctors on the labor committee, the Chamber had solicited the advice of the Academy of Medicine. [75] A commission of two hygienists and two eminent obstetricians appointed by the academy promptly reported that night work was "prejudicial" to women's and infants' health, as well as to their morality and family interests. Because close work in gas light caused loss of eyesight and because night shifts contributed to women's predisposition to anemia and (alleged) susceptibility to nervous disorders, the commission pronounced nocturnal labor "especially fatal" for females. Although studies had indicated a high incidence of anemia and poor eyesight in workshops employing women at night, neither medical condition was normally fatal. But the report did mention France's high rate of infant mortality, after referring to babies languishing from lack of nourishment and nurturance because of maternal absence. Since the report provided no statistics on mortality among infants of mothers employed at night, it simply inferred a causal connection. The report concluded that banning women's night work would complement the recent Roussel law to protect newborns by supervising wet nurses. With very little discussion, the academy resolved that women's nocturnal work had "the most disastrous consequences."[76] Dron quoted this hasty, undocumented, and overstated resolution as definitive proof of the health (and moral) hazards of women's night labor.

The medical profession had acquired new authority with the Pasteurian revolution. Since physicians had done little research on the impact of nocturnal labor, the first major survey responded to the political controversy. Presuming that night work implied exhaustion and that women's physiology endowed them with "a special fragility and delicacy," Professor Proust concluded that night shifts destroyed women's "already unstable equilibrium"—a typically discreet reference to women's menstrual cycle and reproductive functions. Proust's only data on women's greater vulnerability showed that they took more sick days than men, with no correlation to night shifts, and higher rates of tuberculosis among women in sweated trades, with no control for other causes of consumption. Despite rhetoric about the dual role in the political debates, Proust did not consider the physiological effects of exhaustion from the double burden; ignoring contemporary theories about the influence of poverty on the incidence of tuberculosis, he did not consider the implications of malnutrition from low wages.[77] Since Proust prescribed a legal prophylaxis, Dron cited his study. He must have assumed that deputies shared Proust's opinions about women's physical fragility; certainly no deputy challenged them.

Dron also took up maternity leaves, a Social Catholic concept incorporated in the bills of the late 1880s but returned to committee, for further consideration, in 1890. He tried to salvage the measure as a separate bill.[78] Once again he utilized medical evidence and utilitarian but now primarily demographic reasoning. His 1892 report asserted that mandatory leaves and benefits would improve maternal and infant health, halt the natural decrease in population, and, in a new note, ensure "the very existence of the race." He based his conclusions on "medical treatises, the authorities in this matter," cited two medical monographs, and appended a third. Another sign of a new scientific mode of documentation was his detailed reporting of infant mortality statistics compiled by the physician-statistician Jacques Bertillon. Although he limited leaves and benefits to industrial workers, he offered daily assistance to all poor women. Questions about this extension of coverage degenerated into ideological exchanges about state socialism. The committee abandoned the bill, ending parliamentary debate on maternity leave for more than a decade.[79] The fragile coalition that had just passed gendered labor standards had disintegrated. After 1892, Dron continued to express concern about infant mortality, but Strauss led the legislative crusade for the maternity leave law of 1913.[80]

Instead, Dron conducted an unsuccessful campaign for universal hours standards. The contrast to the motivations and rationales for feminine standards was immediately apparent.

Neither unions nor unorganized workers had much influence on Waddington's and Dron's position on gender-specific restrictions. Although five labor federations demanded the suppression of women's work during the legislative debates, the largely male unions were not unanimous or vociferous about suppressing women's work.[81] Indeed, discord in the 1880s and disavowal of electoral politics in the early 1890s ensured that the labor movement had little impact on the debates on feminine restrictions.[82]

Experience with mixed-sex manufacturing and infant charities discouraged Waddington and Dron from consulting the women they proposed to protect, except in personal conversations with local operatives. Working women were not systematically consulted until industrialists from the Vosges organized petitions against the article prohibiting female night employment. In 1888 a deputy from the Vosges, Albert Ferry of the influential Ferry clan, presented a petition signed by eight thousand workers organized by the Eastern Cotton Syndicate. Members of the labor committee representing regions with women on night shifts suggested interviewing workers from their districts. Waddington demurred on the grounds that receiving delegations would slow reform. When the majority agreed to interviews, he exploited them to ask difficult questions of the mainly male workers.[83]

After Senator Charles Ferry of the Vosges used the petition to get a Senate veto of the night-work article, reformers were more open to consultation. Waddington advised sending questionnaires to large workshops; Dron recommended interviewing union representatives. Both methods would have elicited the opinions of working men, not women. Other Radicals and a conservative, Baron Pierard, insisted upon hearing the testimony of cotton and woollen operatives in the Vosges and the Nord and several hundred seamstresses in the capital. Waddington and Dron then showed excessive interest in the location and conduct of the hearings, disclosing an intention to manage testimony. If their interest reflected real concern about employer coercion of vulnerable witnesses, it also belied a paternalistic or tutelary complex.[84]

Although the Parisian witnesses unanimously opposed late-night over-time (*veillées*), a third of the 944 seamstresses who petitioned against *veillées* added that they were willing to stay late if paid overtime. Many cotton spinners explained that they preferred night shifts because they could leave their children with their husbands. One hundred and eighty-six wool carders protested the prohibition of graveyard shifts because they feared the loss of their jobs. The committee report to the Chamber of Deputies dismissed these women's anxieties about wages, jobs, and child care as expressions of employer "manipulation." Neither the revised bill nor the final act provided pay, employment, or child-care assurances. Before the hearings, the committee rejected wage and job guarantees because opposition to them would kill the whole bill. Instead of contemplating provisions for child care such as was already provided by enlightened employers, the committee blamed mothers who "left" their children at night. The report approved male cotton workers' criticisms of women's nocturnal work as "unnatural, debilitating and deathly," no doubt because it regurgitated the committee's own propaganda.[85]

Conversely, organized working men's agitation for the eight-hour day in the late 1880s and early 1890s bolstered Dron's commitment to universal standards of ten hours. His first (1893) report on universal hours standards featured the high percentage of working men's petitions favoring legal limits on their labor. However, a public opinion survey found mixed reactions. If nearly half of the 422 unions wanted an eight-hour day, overwhelming majorities of 235 employer syndicates and 191 other economic organizations were hostile to any regulation of men's labor. Even without the division of opinion, Dron's bill had little chance, because it was tabled shortly before prorogation.[86]

In 1895 Dron retrenched and adopted an incremental approach with a familiar pitch: he suggested correcting the flaws in the 1892 regulations, for the sake of the family. He contended that the three-year-old act had not fulfilled expectations because of employers' ruses. Drawing upon inspection reports about the new system of relay shifts, he described women spending less time at home and leaving their children without supervision. Since the Senate preferred "unification" at eleven hours, he obliged with a transitional eleven-hour day. Another concession was to cover men only in workshops employing women and children.[87] When the Chamber debated his bill in 1896, the very notion of intervention in men's labor provoked potential allies on the left and right into unprecedented polemics, which now included exposition of Marxist as well as liberal doctrines. To distance himself from socialist assertions that labor reform would open the door to socialism, Dron warned that employers who did not show solidarity with workers pushed workers into socialism. Although similar to earlier exhortations to employers to "settle accounts" to halt the advance of socialism (in *Le Petit Rouennais*), Dron's warning pleased neither Right nor Left. The loose coalition that had passed the gender-specific law had dispersed.[88]

In 1899 the reform socialist minister of commerce, Millerand, wore down opposition by threatening to enforce the shelved ten-hour rule for adolescents. The 1900 act duplicated Dron's 1895 bill. After intense lobbying by industrialists and compromises by both parties, standards were applied to men working "in the same places as the protected population." The legal workday fell in two stages to ten hours. Moderate republicans accepted the bill to eliminate "the intolerable abuse" of relay shifts of young people.[89] Two years later, Dron returned to his tactic of criticizing the law, in this case for provoking mass dismissals of apprentices so men could continue to put in twelve-hour days. This bill languished in committee.[90]

Eventually, solidarists such as Justin Godart realized that reformers had to offer something more than a negative case against the existing law. As early as 1906, Godart revived Waddington's argument that ten hours would not reduce output because of more rational deployment of technology and better disciplined labor. His 1910 report offered statistics about a higher incidence of industrial accidents after nine hours work.[91] When reformers returned to universal standards, they stressed production and workers' health, not reproduction or family life.

Unable to enact universal standards, reformers such as Waddington and Dron switched to gender-specific regulations. Contending that limits on women's hours would mean healthier births and better child care allayed anxieties about depopulation, degeneration, and the disintegration of the working-class family. Their concentration on biological and social reproduction may have defied liberal myths about distinct public and private realms, often interpreted as synonymous with separate masculine and feminine spheres, but it reflected bourgeois gender assumptions and male workers' aspirations about full-time housewives and domestic life. Their case was socially conservative, for alarm about the collapse of the working-class family was linked to apprehension about social disorder. Their presentation was also politically expedient. Projecting lower infant mortality and better disciplined children appealed to patriots in the aftermath of the Franco-Prussian War, while promises to reinforce the family united working-class and bourgeois republicans in the age of republican defense.

Yet their position was not fabricated to build a voting block. Waddington, because of his vision of future labor and military requirements, and Dron, because of his public health orientation, were sincerely concerned about depopulation and degeneration. Their experience with workers in their constituencies and their engagement with local charities and welfare programs promoted a practical approach to reform. Their rationales were economically viable: Waddington recognized that entire industries depended on cheap female labor; both realized that working-class women had to work for wages. Far from being simple exponents of a bourgeois ideology about women as full-time housewives, they articulated a dual role for working-class women as short(er)-time paid laborers and part-time homemakers. Unfortunately, if understandably, these paternalists presumed that they knew what was best for working women without asking them. Their class and gender prejudices and their philanthropic credentials prevented a realistic assessment of working women's needs for flexible schedules to accommodate child care, for convenient and affordable child care, and for their current jobs and pay, not to mention better job and pay opportunities.

While appeals about child care and family life accelerated passage of special/feminine labor standards, they did not advance the cause of universal/masculine standards. Even criticizing gendered regulations did not convince opponents of universal standards. A new assault on the liberal ramparts had to be mounted, one that confronted concerns about production and individual rights. The campaign for labor reform remained gendered, in this case masculine, but the intellectual battleground was definitely in the public sphere. Of course, the tactic of manipulating gender and family anxieties, and thereby confounding distinctions between public and private, remained in the arsenal of social reformers.

Six

Bringing Feminine Qualities into the Public Sphere

The Third Republic's Appointment of Women Inspectors

LINDA L. CLARK

Politicians' statements designating women's appropriate social space as the private sphere of the home abound throughout the nineteenth century. Napoleon I, who scorned the "weakness of the brains of women, the changeableness of their ideas," insisted that the new schools for daughters of members of his Legion of Honor should prepare "useful women" able to run a household, a mission requiring the teaching of sewing and other practical subjects.[1] At the end of the century republican reformers, who founded the first full-fledged public secondary schools for girls and expanded girls' primary education, also considered the domestic role central for most French women: they specified that primary schools for daughters of *le peuple* should initiate girls in the "care of the household and *ouvrages de femmes*" and that the new secondary schools for middle-class girls should prepare "future mothers" for "a more complete and intimate community of ideas . . . with their husbands."[2] Frequently linked with the domestic role were characterizations of the feminine personality presumed to enhance women's fulfillment of that role but also to make them unsuited for activity in the public domain. Nineteenth-century opinion brokers thus repeatedly articulated the assumptions about appropriate divisions between masculine and feminine roles and personalities which Jean-Jacques Rousseau had defined in *Émile* (1762) and which French revolutionaries of the 1790s drew upon to justify excluding women from the new rights of citizenship provided to men.[3] Nonetheless, France's revolutionary upheavals from 1789 to 1848 also prompted both conservatives and reformers to emphasize women's role in the transmission of social values to children, thereby assuming that women should possess some knowledge about public issues and so blurring the separation of the public and private spheres for women.[4]

As industrialization increasingly separated the workplace from the home, moralists of various political leanings found new reasons to object to women's leaving the home to earn a living.[5] Yet some contemporaries, such as the prison reformer Charles Lucas, also did worry that the growing European tendency to tell women to remain at home—a message that still seemed new to inspector general Lucas during the 1830s—posed special and even unnecessary problems for poor women obliged to work for wages.[6] Indeed, Lucas's concerns foreshadowed the more recent judgment of historian Joan Scott that the nineteenth-century discourse on separate spheres was not simply a reflection of changing economic and social realities for women but was itself a cause of sharpening notions about divisions between male and female roles.[7] The many women who left home daily for the workplace led lives unlike those anticipated for them in the rhetoric of public officials and moralists. Because women constituted 34 percent of the workforce by 1886,[8] their wage labor could not be ignored by the early leaders of the Third Republic. As Mary Lynn Stewart demonstrated, legislators' preoccupation with the negative impact of women's work on both the family and the nation led in 1892 to the first comprehensive French law to protect women employed in factories and ateliers, child laborers having already received some protection from laws passed in 1841 and 1874.[9]

Within a society marked by ubiquitous rhetoric about women's place in the *foyer* and the eventual political consensus that protecting the family necessitated some restrictions on women's work outside the *foyer*, there also existed several relatively small groups of women inspectors whose very existence seemed to defy contemporary beliefs about womanhood and women's appropriate roles. Paid by the French state, these inspectresses worked in the public sphere and helped implement official policies affecting other women and children. Why did the French state create women officials whose jobs seemingly contradicted ideas about women's place shared by most politicians from not only the conservative Right and large republican Center but also the socialist Left?[10] That general question and several related questions are addressed in this essay. Although the Third Republic did not appoint the first inspectresses on the national payroll, it added new categories of inspectresses and altered other categories. Why did policy-makers decide that implementing certain plans required women officials? How did the government's definition of inspectresses' tasks relate to widely shared attitudes toward gender traits and gender roles? How were the in-spectresses greeted by male supervisors and colleagues, women affected by their official activities, and other interested onlookers, such as feminists? Finally, how did women inspectors themselves view their responsibilities to both the state and the people touched by their services, and how did their views compare with those of politicians who had created their jobs? Addressing these questions illuminates the importance of gender and atti-tudes toward gender in the pre-1914 Third Republic's development of new social and educational policies.

The national government's employment of women in investigative and supervisory positions began during the July Monarchy when the education minister, Baron Narcisse-Achille de Salvandy, appointed Mme Fortunée Eugénie Chevreau-Lemercier to the new post of inspectress general for nursery schools (*déléguée générale des salles d'asile*). This position was part of Salvandy's comprehensive ordinance of 22 December 1837 concern-ing the organization of the *salles d'asile*, nursery schools created since the late 1820s by philanthropic men and women eager to provide a haven for the very young children of working mothers.[11] Hoping to perpetuate the combination of "municipal authority and maternal authority" which had colored the nursery schools' beginnings, Salvandy considered that women's maternal and nurturing qualities could benefit the larger society as well as their own families. His interest in utilizing feminine attributes in the public sphere was consistent with postrevolutionary France's emphasis on women's role as "mother-educators" (*mères-éducatrices*), the counterpart, albeit in a very different political context, of the post-1776 American "re-publican mothers" discussed by historian Linda Kerber.[12] The July Monar-chy's vision of the nursery school, like that of the founders of some German kindergartens,[13] also represents an earlier-nineteenth-century instance of "maternalism"—a label recently applied by many historians to the con-victions of the late nineteenth- and early-twentieth-century reformers who justified a larger role for women in the arena of social action by contending that women's nurturing qualities could thereby benefit the larger society.[14] Salvandy persuaded Madame Adélaïde, King Louis-Philippe's sister, to become the "protectress" of nursery schools, and he also created a central supervisory commission (Commission supérieure des salles d'asile) with a predominantly female membership, including his aunt, Mme Jules Mallet, an early philanthropic sponsor of the schools.[15] The commission described the nursery school as a "work of faith, charity and maternal love," and the first inspectress general, in turn, saw her functions as less a job than "an apostolate."[16]

Although the department of the Seine had set a precedent for employing women to inspect its schools,[17] Chevreau-Lemercier, a former teacher, knew that her visitation of nursery schools throughout France "was the first time that a woman was officially charged with a task of this nature." She also realized that many people doubted a woman's ability either to travel widely or to deal successfully with local officials. After a decade on the job, she argued pointedly that inspecting nursery schools could be done "usefully and suitably only by women." Convinced that men typically disdained what was "not in the destination of their sex," Chevreau-Lemercier insisted that women inspectors, endowed by "nature" with a maternal "instinct," could better understand and serve children and also give more help to women teachers, whom they intimidated less and yet persuaded more effectively than did men.[18]

In later decades government officials continued to employ traditional notions about gender to justify inspectresses' assumption of untraditional roles, intended not to effect a revolution in mores but rather to enlist women's help with problems in a presumably feminine domain—that of contact with other women and children. Thus the July Monarchy's second national inspectress was to visit women's prisons. Concerns about propriety and morality had prompted the government's decision in 1839 to require that women prisoners be guarded by women.[19] Replacing male guards with nuns created an administrative problem because many nuns were uncomfortable dealing with men not in religious orders. Believing that nuns' "relationship with a person of their own sex" would provide "more expansion and more truth," officials of the interior ministry recommended the appointment of a woman inspector.[20] In 1843 the interior minister, Count Tanneguy Duchâtel, named Antoinette Lechevalier, an artillery officer's wife who had assisted Mme Alphonse de Lamartine with her new charity (*patronage*) for recently released women prisoners.[21]

Napoleon III's Second Empire noticeably increased the number of nursery school inspectresses and also added a second inspectress to the penitentiary administration, now responsible for a larger number of girls' reform schools. Because most departments would not pay for special inspectresses of nursery schools, the national government in 1855 appointed a "special delegate" (*déléguée spéciale*) for each of the sixteen regional "academies" into which education was administratively divided.[22] Additional "general delegates" were named in 1847 and 1862. The "delegates" typically held a certificate for directing nursery schools, awarded by departmental educational authorities and sometimes earned after several months of study in Paris at a *cours pratique* headed from 1847 to 1874 by Marie Pape-Carpantier, herself a *déléguée générale* as of 1868.[23] Political connections often influenced appointments, and many aspirants wrote directly to Empress Eugénie, the nursery schools' official "protectress."

How did the Third Republic define women's position within national inspection corps? During and just after the Franco-Prussian War an immediate concern with restoring social order, exacerbated by the Paris Commune of 1871, prompted the Ministry of the Interior to add three adjunct inspectresses for women's prisons and girls' reform schools. For the next three decades, following the involuntary retirement of the two previous senior inspectresses in 1872, one inspectress general and two adjuncts typically served the prison administration.[24] After republicans replaced the postwar monarchist governments of "moral order" by winning control of the Chamber of Deputies in 1876–77 and the Senate in 1879, education minister Jules Ferry reorganized and also appreciably reduced the ranks of nursery school inspectresses. In 1879 he announced that the post of special delegate would be eliminated as incumbents retired, explaining that it duplicated many of the general delegate's functions. His reorganization effectively removed women whose political or religious allegiances clashed with the new leaders' democratic and secular goals. Although Ferry did raise the number of general delegates—renamed *inspectrices générales* of *écoles maternelles* in 1881—from five to eight, their number shrank to four in 1885 because of legislative cost cutting. Furthermore, few departments replaced the "special delegate" with their own inspectresses, as Ferry had recommended, because the state required departments to pay half of their salaries.[25]

As the corps of nursery school inspectresses shrank during the 1880s, some inspectresses general tried to reverse the trend by inserting requests for more women inspectors in their annual reports and in *L'Ami de l'enfance*, the major pedagogical journal for nursery school teachers.[26] These inspectresses' central argument that women's maternal qualities had a natural application to educational leadership was not novel, but it had special utility during the famed decade of the Ferry laws, which in 1881–82 made primary education compulsory and public primary schools free and secular. Republicans retained the Catholic tradition of separate schools for girls and boys, but their goal of secularizing public schools required that lay women teachers replace the nuns who had taught the majority of girls in public as well as private primary schools as late as 1877.[27] Thus the Paul Bert law of 1879 required each department to provide a normal school for training female teachers—a responsibility previously left primarily to Catholic institutions. The Goblet law of 1886 required the eventual removal of religious congregations from public school teaching. To counter Catholic objections that secularization threatened public morality, republicans introduced a nontheological moral instruction and stressed that lay women offered girls and very young boys a maternal direction that celibate nuns could not provide. Previously the Second Empire's pro-Catholic policy had encouraged communes to make nuns a larger majority of the teachers of public girls' and nursery schools, and its education ministries understandably deemphasized the importance of maternal qualities for women teachers.[28] Although one inspector general from a clerical background had complained in 1857 that the lay inspectresses of nursery schools shared Parisian society's prejudice that mothers could teach small children more effectively than could nuns, the Second Empire did not provide enough funding to train or employ large numbers of new lay women teachers.[29] The republic's renaming of nursery schools from *salles d'asile* to *écoles maternelles* in 1881 signified not only that their central function was educational rather than charitable but also that their teachers offered a kind of maternal care to children aged 2 to 6 whose mothers worked outside the home.

Official curricula and textbooks for girls' schools spelled out the dimensions of republican motherhood. Republican mothers were dutiful and self-sacrificing. They also knew that they must yield to their husbands in family arguments because Article 213 of the Civil Code, framed under Napoleon I, required women to obey spouses. Nonetheless, female role models in textbooks also understood that they wielded influence within the family circle and that the family's well-being depended on the existence of a stable society. Thus textbook authors depicted women counseling sons and husbands to support the new republic and refrain from going on strike. The explicit emphasis on mothers' role in shaping the political and social values of future male voters resembled the delineation of republican motherhood in the newly independent United States of the late eighteenth century.[30]

Pauline Kergomard, a Protestant inspectress general of nursery schools appointed by Ferry in 1879, well exemplified a determined woman's ability to use familiar discourse about feminine maternal qualities to further women's access to the untraditional role of school inspection, which, unlike classroom teaching, put women primarily into contact with an adult public of women teachers and male officials. In an important article in the quasi-official *Revue pédagogique* of May 1889, she contended that women's inspection of schools was a natural "extension" of the maternal role and, furthermore, that inspectresses could handle "the most intimate educational questions" affecting female pupils and teachers, questions that men could not and should not address.[31] As the first woman elected by fellow educators to the Higher Council of Public Instruction (Conseil supérieur de l'instruction publique), the chief advisory body of the Ministry of Public Instruction, Kergomard hoped that her article would stimulate discussion at an international congress on primary education scheduled for August.

Kergomard's plea was timely, for women's role in education was one of three general topics on that congress's announced agenda. Moreover, in June 1889 Senator Agénor Bardoux, a conservative republican and former education minister, proposed that women join the ranks of departmental inspectors of primary schools, a corps created by education minister François Guizot in 1835 and now numbering about 450. Stating that some "aptitudes" were related to gender—an assertion quickly supported by other senators—Bardoux argued that "for certain questions of hygiene" and "quasi-maternal concerns," there were "gaps" in the service of male inspectors, "regardless of their respectability or development."[32] Thus he recommended appointing a woman inspector for the girls' primary schools in each department. Subsequently the Senate and Chamber of Deputies, with relatively little discussion, included a significantly revised version of his proposal in the law of 19 July 1889 on educators' salaries. Article 22 of the law did not require that an inspectress be named for each department; it simply stated that inspectresses "can be named."[33]

The emphasis on maternal qualities in rationales for appointing school inspectresses resembled the Ministry of the Interior's justification for introducing a few women in another of its inspectorates. While the government expected primary schools to turn the children of "the people" into loyal republicans and industrious workers, it charged the Ministry of the Interior's services for orphaned, abandoned, or needy children with the dual mission of ensuring that these disadvantaged youngsters respected the social order and also helping to curtail the menace of depopulation by protecting their charges' health. Thus the Republic improved public assistance for needy children (*enfants assistés*) and their mothers, as Rachel Fuchs and

Catherine Rollet-Echalier demonstrated.[34] To help assess its services for children, the Ministry of the Interior of the 1880s also sent a few women on special fact-finding missions. In late 1886 the ministry acquired a new division for public assistance, directed from 1887 to 1905 by a Protestant, Henri Monod, who soon urged the formal appointment of inspectresses.[35] The department of the Seine, which had its own director of public assistance since midcentury and a unique organization of services, already had set the precedent of employing women in two positions comparable to but less prestigious than those of its male inspectors: *dames visiteuses*, for infants placed with wet nurses, and *dames déléguées*, who checked on nursing mothers receiving aid.[36]

Premier and interior minister René Goblet, Monod's sponsor, decreed in March 1887 that women could become both assistant inspectresses and inspectresses in the departmental service for *enfants assistés*. An anticlerical republican whose name was attached to the recent law secularizing public school teaching, Goblet may have envisioned inspectresses as a new type of official lay caregiver at a moment when a lack of both money and trained lay female personnel made it impossible to remove most nuns from the ranks of nursing in public hospitals and other charitable institutions.[37] Armand Faillières, the next interior minister, named the first assistant inspectress (*sous-inspectrice*) to the department of the Eure in November 1887; and Charles Floquet, premier as well as interior minister after April 1888, sent a second assistant inspectress to the Nord and also appointed four inspectresses general for children's services. Although fiscal constraints had prompted abolishing the jobs of five inspectors general in February 1887, the Chamber of Deputies' budget commission later added fifteen thousand francs to the ministry's appropriation for the inspectorate concerned with children. The commission's *rapporteur*, Stephen Pichon, a Radical republican ally of Georges Clemenceau, explained in November 1887 that the extra funds were earmarked for the *dames déléguées* recently sent to rural areas to verify that children receiving public aid actually obtained proper care and schooling. "Women are especially qualified to understand the services for children and to devote themselves thereto; to note their gaps, to discern with a practical sense reforms that they require," Pichon noted. Enhancing inspectresses' "official situation" would produce a "very useful increase in [their] authority," the budget commission believed, but it minimized costs by not designating the future "*inspectrices générales des services de l'enfance*" as regular functionaries (*fonctionnaires*) with the right to a pension.[38]

Whereas the education and interior ministries acquired inspectresses general before adding lower-ranking departmental inspectresses, the reverse was true for the third ministry to appoint women inspectors. Women's inclusion in the Ministry of Commerce's new national corps of departmental labor inspectresses was part of the law of 2 November 1892, the first comprehensive protective legislation limiting the hours worked by women. Previously the state had provided fifteen (later twenty-one) "divisional" inspectors to enforce the child labor law of 1874, but it would not pay for the departmental inspectors who functioned, as of 1891, in only twenty out of eighty-seven departments and were often school inspectors taking on extra work.[39] Although opening the primary school and public assistance inspectorates to women had generated much controversy (as is noted below), the precedents set by earlier departmental inspectresses of child labor in the Seine evidently helped ward off prolonged legislative debate about their value in industrial cities with many women workers.[40] Indeed, the existing Seine inspectresses had such strong defenders that after commerce minister Jules Siegfried decreed on 12 December 1892 that there would be ten women's posts for the Seine and five for other urban administrative *circonscriptions*, the general council of the Seine protested successfully against the planned dismissal of some of its appointees. A new decree two weeks later retained the Seine's fifteen inspectresses and several adjuncts for a transition period, their number eventually scheduled to fall through retirements.[41]

We have seen that by the 1890s three ministries assigned inspectresses to serve a clientele of women and children. In each instance, officials justified their hiring by utilizing traditional ideas about feminine traits, just as contemporary maternalist reformers also did in other Western countries.[42] Thus women's maternal inclinations would presumably benefit French schoolchildren, infants and children receiving public aid, and girls in reform institutions; women inspectors' special understanding of other women was also expected to enable them to empathize with and help women teachers, workers, prisoners, and mothers receiving public assistance better than male colleagues could. If the nation was an extended family, then inspectresses were, in a sense, state-supplied mothers or sisters. Emphasis on women's maternal role also blended nicely with the political philosophy of "solidarity" (*solidarité*), in embryo during the 1880s and further developed during the 1890s by progressive republicans who eventually formed the Radical and Radical Socialist party. Solidarism's goal was harmonious relations between social classes, to be achieved by new reform legislation. Responding to the growth of socialism among the working classes, solidarists such as Léon Bourgeois—briefly prime minister in 1895–96—portrayed the nation as an organic entity whose health depended on the functioning of each part.[43] Women's activities thus contributed to the social organism's health, although there was tension between solidarists who believed that women's natural place was at home and other solidarists eager to apply women's natural talents outside the home to "social" housekeeping.[44]

The careful definition of inspectresses' functions as essentially feminine did not prevent opposition to their appointment. Male inspectors made frequent protests and, regardless of their ministerial base, displayed remarkably similar objections to female colleagues. Yet these opponents of inspectresses resembled their defenders in drawing heavily on prevailing assumptions about distinctive feminine qualities. Generalizations about women's innate personality traits, physical fitness, and appropriate social roles thus undergirded criticisms of inspectresses' abilities. Within a month after the opening of primary school inspection to women in 1889, male educators vented opposition at an international congress in Paris. Inspector Pierre Plazy of Angoulême pronounced that women were "naturally weak and impressionable" and so could not "discover the truth as easily as the male inspector." A normal school directress from the Hautes-Pyrénées also doubted women's psychological fitness for inspection and asserted that only men should inspect schools because "man is usually directed by reason; . . . woman, by the heart."[45] Administrator Louis Bouquet of the Ministry of Commerce summarized similar criticisms of labor inspectresses at an international congress in 1894 on accidents in the workplace. Opponents claimed that women inspectors lacked the necessary "patience, composure, [and] fairness" and were too "nervous, easily irritable [and] often biased." Inspectresses' supporters believed, however, that feminine "defects" could be attenuated by the "adaptability, tact, [and] cleverness" that woman "often possesses to a greater degree than man."[46] Such advocacy did not persuade divisional inspector François Gouttes, one of eleven regional supervisors of departmental labor inspectors, for in 1900 he asked the ministry to replace Bordeaux's departing inspectress with a man. "Experience has shown that the role of labor inspectress does not suit women; women have less authority than men," he insisted.[47] Whereas Gouttes believed that women could not persuade employers to rectify violations of laws concerning the workplace, Loys Brueyre doubted that women's psychological traits matched the job of inspector of public assistance. At a meeting of the Higher Council of Public Assistance (Conseil supérieur de l'assistance publique) in 1905, Brueyre, a philanthropist and former public assistance administrator in Paris, argued, in particular, that women could not manage adolescent males under the inspectorate's jurisdiction.[48]

Brueyre's opposition to inspectresses also demonstrated how assumptions about women's physical deficiencies could reinforce suppositions about psychological disabilities. Visits to assisted children might require hiking across fields to remote houses, and, asserted Brueyre, such travel "surpasses the forces of a woman," who also—for moral as well as physical reasons—could not endure the primitive travelers' accommodations in rural areas. A colleague on the council, Dr. Gustave Drouineau, an inspector general of the Ministry of the Interior, concluded not only that women's "physical imperfections" made them unsatisfactory inspectresses but also that the compensatory practice of assigning them shorter trips unfairly burdened male inspectors with extra tasks. Similarly, in 1889 education minister Faillières and others had doubted school inspectresses' ability to travel outside cities. In 1906 the permanent commission of the Higher Council of Labor (Conseil supérieur du travail) received a resolution calling for the abolition of labor inspectresses because the "weaknesses and maladies inherent in . . . [their] sex" hampered their climbing five or six flights of stairs to visit ateliers. Although the commission rejected the resolution, several male workers on the council argued that inspectresses had serious deficiencies.[49]

Both the alleged incompatibility of a public function with women's appropriate domestic role and the presumed impropriety of such functions for women were other common objections to inspectresses. Thus school inspectresses' critics judged it inappropriate for them to deal with male local government officials or higher-ranking educational administrators—although they never objected to male inspectors observing women schoolteachers. Labor inspectors' task of stopping violations of the ban on most women's work at night prompted Gouttes to object also to the unsuitability of inspectresses being on the streets long after dark. Brueyre further pronounced that men would be unacceptably humiliated if a departmental inspectress of assistance supervised a male assistant inspector. Opponents of school inspectresses also alleged that the nation's families would be harmed by the bad example of a married inspectress whose work took her away from her own children.[50]

Behind arguments that inspectors' tasks were not suited to feminine traits or appropriate social roles there often lay, as Brueyre revealed, male

resentment of additional competitors for a limited number of jobs offering
the lower middle classes a step upward on the ladder of social mobility.
Male teachers, for example, aspired to become not only primary school
inspectors but also inspectors of labor or public assistance. Whereas the
base pay for a male teacher (*instituteur*), before the addition of variable
departmental supplements and the provision of housing, was set in July
1889 at 900 to 2,000 francs, primary inspectors outside the Seine earned
3,000 to 5,000 francs and a departmental indemnity of at least 200 francs.
Departmental labor inspectors' pay range was also 3,000 to 5,000 francs,
with untenured beginners starting at 2,400 francs. Departmental inspectors of public assistance earned 3,500 to 5,000 francs prior to a pay hike
in 1906 and assistant inspectors 2,400 to 3,000 francs.[51] Unlike the pay
differentials established between male and female inspectors general, primary school teachers, or normal school and secondary school professors
and directors, the same scale prevailed for male and female inspectors of
primary schools, labor, and public assistance.

Faced with multiple objections to inspectresses, politicians and high-
ranking administrators often tried to reduce controversy by moving slowly
to appoint women, keeping the female inspectorate limited in size and
giving women fewer responsibilities than male colleagues. Even before the
legislature voted for appointing primary school inspectresses, education
minister Faillières warned that the lack of funds to enlarge the inspectorate would dictate the selection of a woman only if a male inspector's
post could be suppressed. Bourgeois's decree of 17 January 1891, which
defined primary inspectresses' duties, restricted women to inspecting girls'
schools, small coeducational schools (*écoles mixtes*), and nursery schools.
Although inspectresses, like inspectors, made recommendations concerning teachers' appointments and promotions and also disciplinary actions,
only male inspectors could work directly with municipalities or the upper
echelons of the educational bureaucracy to create new public schools or
handle the often controversial procedures for opening private (and typically
Catholic) schools. Inspectresses' special responsibility was ensuring that
women teachers gave daughters of *le peuple* a distinctly feminine moral
instruction and homemaking lessons.[52] The important differences between
male and female assignments limited inspectresses' utility outside big cities
with many girls' schools. Before 1914 only the departments of the Seine
and adjacent Seine-et-Oise acquired primary inspectresses. The first began
in the Seine-et-Oise in 1891; the second served in Paris as of 1895 and was
joined by additional inspectresses in 1896, 1904, and 1912.

The appointment of primary school inspectresses, limited though it was, owed much to the support of two influential administrators: Octave Gréard, vice rector of the Academy of Paris from 1879 to 1902, and Ferdinand Buisson, a liberal Protestant who was the Ministry of Public Instruction's director of primary instruction from 1879 to 1896 and later, as a Radical deputy, a leader of the Chamber's suffragist bloc.[53] The education ministers who added posts for inspectresses came from both Radical and moderate republican groups: Bourgeois (1891), Raymond Poincaré (1895), Alfred Rambaud (1896), Joseph Chaumié (1904), and Gabriel Guist'hau (1912). Bourgeois, a creator of the Radicals' solidarism, and Poincaré, a moderate, also worked for the passage of a special law of 1900 to admit women with university law degrees to the bar; and Bourgeois later backed retaining the Ministry of the Interior's inspectresses general. Rambaud, once Ferry's private secretary, was responsive to the urgings of Buisson, also Ferry's appointee. During the post-1899 era of Radical predominance ushered in by the resolution of the Dreyfus Affair, Chaumié, a moderate in Émile Combes's cabinet, designated as an inspectress a normal school directress who had once served in Agen, his political base, and become his wife's friend; Guist'hau, a Radical in Poincaré's prewar cabinet, elevated still another normal school directress. Although only five women were in the corps of 450 primary inspectors by 1914, their restriction to the Paris area had generated male colleagues' additional complaint that they unfairly hampered men's ability to obtain the most desirable and highly paid inspection posts (6,000 to 8,000 francs for the Seine) after serving many years in provincial backwaters.[54]

Men could not become departmental inspectors of nursery schools, but because primary inspectors long visited these schools and the government refused to pay the full salary of departmental inspectresses, this woman-only category showed little increase before 1912. Indeed, requiring departments to pay half of their salary actually caused a drop in their numbers from twelve in 1885 to eight in 1910. Furthermore, five of these inspectresses served in the urbanized Seine, which typically spent more on public services and set precedents for hiring women administrators. Mounting concerns about depopulation which affected other areas of policy also eventually helped to revive politicians' interest in this post for women. In 1910 education minister Gaston Doumergue, echoing the sentiments of a predecessor, Jean Bienvenu-Martin, strongly urged departments to support nursery school inspectresses because women's "sex, credentials and experience" uniquely suited them to deal with "the hygiene and education of early childhood," a major concern in view of France's "crisis . . . from the standpoint of natality." Doumergue also reminded prefects that two or three departments could share the cost of a nursery school inspectress, whose pay, in any case, was less than that of a primary inspector: 2,000 to 2,400 francs, raised to 2,400 to 3,400 francs in 1912. By 1913 there were fifteen departmental inspectresses of nursery schools, but only in 1923 did the state pay their entire salary.[55]

Just as school inspectresses went only to women teachers' classes, inspectresses of labor visited establishments employing only female workers. Furthermore, men inspected such workplaces if they used motors operated by steam or electricity.[56] The female contingent in the labor inspectorate began in 1892–93 with a larger number than was ever attained in the pre-1914 inspectorates for primary schools or public assistance, but the women's section increased less rapidly than that of men. Whereas the primary inspection corps did not grow after 1889, reflecting stagnation in school enrollments because of the low birthrate, the departmental labor inspectorate went from 92 authorized positions in 1893 to 133 by 1914. The passage of more protective laws dictated the increase, but inspectresses were initially excluded from many of the new tasks of enforcement. While the number of positions formally authorized for women rose from 15 in 1893 to 19 in 1914, the number of men's posts rose by nearly 50 percent, from 77 to 114. After the initial assignment of women to the Seine, Lille, Lyons, Nantes, Bordeaux, and Marseilles, inspectresses were added for Rouen and Toulouse, and not all of the pre-1893 Seine posts scheduled for abolition were dropped. The smaller number of women's slots also dictated fewer entrance competitions: the only prewar *concours* for women (aged 26 to 35) were held in 1893, 1901, 1907, and 1911; and the lack of openings delayed the appointment of one woman qualifying in 1907 until 1914. Furthermore, inspectresses obtained promotions less rapidly than men and could not attain the higher rank of divisional inspector.[57]

The modest increase in positions formally authorized for labor inspectresses owed much to two independent socialist ministers, Alexandre Millerand and René Viviani, and also to Arthur Fontaine, named by commerce minister Millerand to the new post of director of labor in 1899 and still its holder in the new Ministry of Labor created by Clemenceau in 1906. Millerand, the first socialist to enter a republican cabinet, decreed in 1902 that the Seine had fourteen inspectresses and other districts five. He opened the second *concours* for inspectresses and also hired the first female clerk-typists in the central offices of a ministry. Yet Millerand also sometimes lacked total confidence in the inspectresses. In October 1899 he had instructed divisional supervisors to send male inspectors to religious establishments that ran workshops employing young women because he doubted that inspectresses could exercise enough "authority." At the time, anticlerical republicans were in heated conflict with clerical anti-Dreyfusards, and recalcitrant local authorities did not always adequately support inspectresses' recommendations.[58] In 1909 labor minister Viviani, a feminist as well as independent socialist, increased women's representation in the provincial inspectorate from five to six, but the Seine's number of posts fell. Fontaine, in turn, lobbied persistently for increases in the inspectorate's budget.[59] He also won praise from the moderately feminist National Council for French Women (Conseil national des femmes françaises) because he advocated providing working women with additional job opportunities, including hiring more women above the rank of clerk-typist in the Ministry of Labor's central offices.[60]

Before 1914, however, Fontaine was more successful in defending existing inspectresses than in adding new ones. In 1906 he supported inspectresses when several male workers on the Higher Council of Labor questioned their competence. He also defended them after the Paris region's divisional inspector, Boulisset, complained in 1911 about their completion of an assignment to measure the cubic meters of air in workshops. Inspectresses, wrote Boulisset, feared taking action against employers violating the air standard set in 1904, and they were fatigued and annoyed by the extra labor and the "unfeminine task" of climbing ladders to measure rooms. Fontaine replied that inspectresses certainly did exercise their authority. By also reminding Boulisset of his duty to instruct inspectresses and by reiterating that the measurement of breathing space was a standard part of all inspectors' assignment, the director conveyed that some inspectresses' inefficient performance might stem from their immediate superior's poor leadership.[61]   •

Whereas school and labor inspectresses were securely established, albeit in limited numbers, before 1914, the departmental inspectresses of public assistance had a more dismal prewar fate. Goblet's decree of 1887 had envisioned the eventual appointment of departmental inspectresses as well as assistant inspectresses, but no departmental inspectress was ever named, and the number of assistant inspectresses did not increase beyond three after 1890. Indeed, both positions long seemed destined for extinction. Because there was no reference to departmental inspectresses in the important law of 27 June 1904 concerning services for assisted children, the

Higher Council of Public Assistance debated whether the law had truly excluded them. This discussion in 1905, during a review of a policy statement on personnel, produced a revealing interchange between proponents and opponents of women inspectors. In partial rebuttal of the opposition of members Brueyre and Drouineau, cited previously, former deputy Ferdinand Dreyfus insisted that feminine qualities could offer much to public assistance efforts, and he claimed to know of private charities where women's influence on adolescent boys was more beneficial than that of men. A self-styled "feminist" whose support for women's demands did not extend to awarding the vote, Dreyfus conceded to Brueyre that French society was not yet ready to accept a woman heading a departmental inspection service, but he favored assistant inspectresses, whose task seemed no more burdensome than that of women teachers in rural areas. Thus he urged the council to recommend that the Ministry of the Interior specify that the inspectorate was indeed open to women.[62]

Also entering the council's discussion were two advocates of inspectresses whose backing had become limited by political "realism." Monod, director of public assistance, affirmed his support for women's participation in some assistance services, and he reviewed his appointment of departmental assistant inspectresses during the late 1880s. At that juncture, he also had worked with two eminent Protestant women, Kergomard and Caroline de Barrau, to start a private charity for abandoned children. In 1905, however, Monod claimed that assistant inspectresses "could not carry out their functions," and the women themselves "were the first to state this." Asserting that the two remaining inspectresses simply did office work, contrary to the "hopes that [one] had conceived" for them,[63] Monod probably did not do justice to the active efforts of the assistant inspectress in the Bouches-du-Rhône.[64] Senator Paul Strauss, president of the Higher Council of Public Assistance and a major promoter of increasing women's role in public assistance, also judged the moment not propitious for demanding departmental inspectresses. During the Senate debate on the 1904 law, Strauss instead had helped insert the option of departments appointing (and paying for) *dames visiteuses*. In 1905 he was more interested in saving the position of the inspectresses general, destined by a decree of February 1901 for elimination as current appointees retired but included nonetheless in the law of 1904. Strauss had enlisted the support of Bourgeois for a better "organization of *l'inspection générale féminine*," and he read to the council Bourgeois's letter asserting, "The domain of assistance is incontestably the one where the intellectual and moral qualities of the woman should find their most natural and happy employment." Strauss in turn predicted that once *visiteuses* and inspectresses general had demonstrated more of their talents, women could acquire other roles in public assistance. Despite Monod's and Strauss's caution, Dreyfus persuaded the still all-male council to add to the proposed regulations the statement that women were "admissible" to the departmental inspectorate.[65]

Feminists interested in the inspectresses' fate hoped that the council's vote and the related action of another council member, Senator Adolphe Pédebidou, meant a victory for their cause. In April 1906 Pédebidou had persuaded interior minister Clemenceau to agree during Senate debate that qualified women deserved a role in inspection.[66] Nonetheless, Clemenceau's future actions affected only the inspectresses general. No more assistant inspectresses of public assistance were named until after World War I, by which time the post was under the jurisdiction of the new Ministry of Hygiene. Strauss, as hygiene minister in 1923, helped secure approval for a law explicitly opening the post to women; but even then no assistant inspectress could be promoted to departmental inspectress until another law so provided in 1938, fifty-one years after Goblet's decree had first envisioned the possibility. Considerably more women had the educational credentials expected of a professional administrator in 1923 than in 1887, but discussion in 1923 of women's qualifications still focused heavily on the value of their "maternal" qualities for this particular service.[67]

That postwar reference to distinctive feminine talents notwithstanding, prewar advocates of inspectresses also had sought to demonstrate women's competence by requiring certain educational or professional credentials. Before the 1880s, administrative appointments for men and women often owed much to familial connections with members of the government. After 1879 the expansion of women's education permitted greater emphasis on their professional qualifications and competitive examinations. Inspectresses of primary schools or the workplace always had to pass a written and oral examination that covered much, if not all, of the legal, administrative, and practical information that men likewise mastered. Primary inspectresses held not only teaching credentials but also the certificate created in 1880 for the professoriate in departmental normal schools and another certificate qualifying one to direct a normal school and inspect primary schools. Frequently labor inspectresses had teaching credentials, too, although initially no specific diploma was required.[68] There were no comparable standards, however, when the education and interior ministries created their *déléguées générales* or *inspectrices générales*. During the Second Empire and early Third Republic nursery school inspectresses needed only the certificate for directing nursery schools, and a few lacked even that. After 1879, republicans introduced the certificate of aptitude for the inspection of *écoles maternelles* as a requirement for both departmental inspectresses and inspectresses general of nursery schools, and as of 1908 the teaching experience required for an inspectress general was raised from five to ten years.[69] Nonetheless, the nursery schools' inspectresses general actually needed less academic training than normal school professors and directresses or primary school inspectresses, and their salaries reflected their inferior training. Unlike *inspecteurs généraux, inspectrices générales* long earned no more than departmental primary inspectors outside the Seine (3,000 to 5,000 francs), and after a pay increase in 1912 (5,000 to 6,000 francs) they still earned less than the Seine's primary inspectors.[70]

Differences in the formal education of the Ministry of the Interior's male and female inspectors general also helped account for disparities in pay and duties. Indeed, after 1872 the inspectress general for prisons and reform schools earned less than the first appointee, Lechevalier.[71] In 1901 premier and interior minister Pierre-Marie René Waldeck-Rousseau turned the Ministry of the Interior's inspectors general, previously assigned to specific services, such as prisons or public assistance, into a single corps with broader responsibilities. At the same time, he planned to keep only one post for an inspectress general and to abolish the jobs of adjunct prison inspectress and inspectress general of *enfants assistés* as incumbents retired.[72] The reorganization followed a sharp drop since the 1870s in the number of adult and juvenile prisoners, the number of incarcerated females having declined even more than that of males.[73]

In response to the Ministry of the Interior's reorganization, supporters of inspectresses began a lobbying effort to save additional positions for inspectresses general and also women's access to the departmental inspectorate. Strauss and other members of the Higher Council of Public Assistance aided the cause, as did the new National Council of French Women (CNFF), which helped obtain backing from the League for the Rights of Man (Ligue des droits de l'homme), a republican pressure group especially influential since the Dreyfus Affair. Mme Olympe Gevin-Cassal, an inspectress general of children's services since 1896, kept the CNFF informed about administrative developments.[74] Others worked to overcome opposition based on earlier inspectresses' inadequate administrative knowledge by proposing a new *concours* for the position. A "remarkable campaign" for a competitive entry examination was waged, judged

Strauss, by Hélène Moniez, wife of the rector of the Academy of Grenoble and a disciple of Bourgeois.[75] This tactic eventually won over some reluctant inspectors general, and in December 1907, a year after the death of the longtime inspectress general, Marie-Anne Dupuy, premier and interior minister Clemenceau decreed that three *inspectrices générales* would be selected through a *concours*. Although the anticlerical Clemenceau vehemently opposed women's suffrage on the grounds that too many would vote as their priests dictated, he conceded that public assistance was an arena in which women's "intelligence and heart" had special application. Already in 1906 he had added women to the Higher Council of Public Assistance, as the CNFF urged.[76] Moniez, a temporary inspectress general since 1906, subsequently qualified as an *inspectrice générale* through the *concours* of May 1908. The pay scale accorded to her and two colleagues was 4,000 to 5,000 francs, whereas *inspecteurs généraux* earned 8,000 to 14,000 francs and *inspecteurs généraux adjoints* 5,000 to 7,000 francs.[77]

Who were the inspectresses of the pre-1914 Third Republic? Like the great majority of French working women (half of the female population aged 15 and over in 1906),[78] most inspectresses needed to earn a living. Unlike most working women, however, they had jobs conferring both professional status and an income adequate for a modest middle-class living standard. For male inspectors, official functions typically represented either maintenance of social status or a step upward on the ladder of social mobility. The same was true for some inspectresses, but in a society that expected elite and middle-class women to limit activities outside the home to charitable endeavors, it was also more likely for women than for men that government employment represented a kind of downward social mobility.[79]

Françoise Huguet's study of the family backgrounds of 356 male inspectors general of education, appointed between 1802 and 1914, and 66 pre-1914 inspectresses general or "special delegates" for nursery schools reveals that most of the women came from middle- or upper-middle-class families whose status equaled or surpassed that of the men. Inspectresses' entry into the workforce also frequently indicated, however, that their parents or husbands had suffered a reversal of fortunes. Of 53 female "general" or "special delegates" appointed before the Ferry reforms began in 1879, 43 percent were single, about one-quarter were impoverished widows, and many of the married had husbands who were ill or earning very little.[80] Their average age when first appointed was 41, as compared with 49 for male inspectors general. Huguet's analysis of the social origins of 49 women in the entire 1837–1914 group places 40 percent in the *haute bour-geoisie*, 30 percent in the *moyenne bourgeoisie*, and 30 percent in the *petite bourgeoisie*. The pre-1879 appointees included at least five from modest backgrounds: the daughters of an innkeeper, a printer, a watchmaker, and a boilermaker, and the illegitimate daughter of a linen maker.[81] The presence of some military officers' daughters in the pre-1879 contingent correlates well with Rebecca Rogers' discovery that mid-nineteenth-century officers—whose own social origins were increasingly modest—frequently wanted their daughters prepared for some type of work.[82]

The smaller group of nine inspectresses general of nursery schools named between 1879 and 1914, after the abolition of the special delegate's post, resembled predecessors in marital status and age: four were single when first designated, two were widows, and three were married; and their average age when first appointed was 43. The group's social origins suggest the tendency of the post-1878 Republic to provide more opportunities for the *nouvelles couches sociales*, Léon Gambetta's famous term for the middling and lower middle classes who loomed large in the ranks of republican voters. Three post-1878 appointees came from humble backgrounds—the daughters of a hosiery maker, an employee, and a *huissier*; four had middle-class origins; and one was an English baronet's daughter.[83] Whereas earlier inspectresses used Bonapartist or royalist family connections to advantage, later appointees emphasized republican loyalties. Ferry's nominations in 1879 included Kergomard, the anticlerical daughter of a Protestant school inspector persecuted by Catholic clergy, and Marie Davy, the widow of a republican member of the constitutional assembly of 1848. Although five inspectresses designated in 1879–80 had credentials no more impressive than those of many teachers, two named in 1894 and 1904 had normal school credentials and also the certificate qualifying them to inspect primary schools or direct normal schools.[84] Indeed, that advanced certificate was held by all eight prewar primary school inspectresses, at least half of whom had utilized their education to rise above modest origins.[85]

A comparable evolution in the professional credentials of the Ministry of the Interior's inspectresses was slower. At least two of seven pre-1879 appointees had a teaching diploma, but in the background of the first pre-1870 inspectresses general and two adjuncts named in 1871, experience with charities seemed the most evident preparation for the administrative post.[86] Political and military connections figured in all five appointments made between December 1870 and 1878; and only Dupuy came from a distinctly humble background.[87] At least six of the seven had married, as was also the case for seven of the ten women added after 1880. Legal and administrative knowledge was to be tested after 1907, but a formal degree was not required. Thus the three inspectresses general who emerged from the first *concours* of 1908 were Gevin-Cassal, born in 1859, a previous appointee and friend of Monod's, member of republican families of 1848, and author of children's books but without any formal educational credentials whatsoever; Moniez, born in 1865, a high-ranking education official's wife, sponsor of charities, and author of a girls' primary school textbook; and Mlle Josephine Fournier, born in 1848, the holder of a teaching diploma and evidently owing her first appointment in 1881 to her father's record as a senior clerk in the ministry. Fournier's replacement in 1909 was a former primary school teacher, Louise Thiry, who, like Gevin-Cassal, had married a painter without an adequate income.[88] Only in 1914 did an interior inspectress general have a professional credential comparable to those of male colleagues: Mlle Marie Galtier, born in 1887, held a university degree (*licence*) in law and had worked for Poincaré, now president of the Republic.[89] The three women who served for any length of time in the ill-fated post of departmental assistant inspectress of public assistance were all widows in their mid-30s when appointed and thus younger than most inspectresses general.[90]

Just as the primary school inspectresses named after 1889 had far better credentials than earlier nursery school inspectresses, so, too, among the more numerous labor inspectresses there was a difference between the professional qualifications of women selected after 1892 and the former appointees of the Seine department retained in the national service. Although the Seine had utilized a competitive examination to select labor inspectresses in 1878 and later, the republican departmental council also weighed individuals' neediness and recommendations from influential politicians, such as Clemenceau, Ferry, Buisson, and Floquet, when choosing appointees from among the highest scorers. Of eighteen former Seine inspectresses or adjuncts in the national service after 1892, eight were single, seven were widows, two were married, and one was separated. At least five had taught, and another was a teacher's daughter.[91] The next generation of twenty-one inspectresses, appointed between 1893 and 1916 after prewar *concours*, consisted of eight single, one widowed, and twelve married women, one of whom later divorced. Limited data on eight newer inspectresses' backgrounds reveal that five came from middle-class families (two of which had suffered financial reverses), and three had more humble origins. At least seven had once taught, four in public schools and three in private ones.[92] Entry into the inspectorate was highly competitive: the *concours* of 1911 for four positions attracted 150 women, including 38 teachers.[93] The post-1892 appointees included Marie-Jeanne Jourdan, a widow who remained on the job after marrying a bureau chief in the Ministry of Agriculture, and Marguerite Bourat, a single woman of humble origins who explicitly defined her job as a "vocation."[94]

In summation, the profile for seventy-one inspectresses hired between 1879 and 1914 by the education, interior, commerce, and labor ministries reveals that they were single more often (39%) than the typical working woman of 1906 (33%), less often married (43%, as compared with 54.7%), but more often widows (18.6%, as compared with 12.5%).[95] First appointed at an average age of 38, they brought a variety of personal and professional experiences to their administrative assignment.[96] The primary school inspectresses had the most formal education as a group, but several labor inspectresses had attended secondary schools, and one interior inspectress general and at least one labor inspectress had university law degrees. Data on family backgrounds, although incomplete, demonstrate that for women from lower-middle-class or more humble families, formal education and the inspectorate represented noticeable social advancement, while for others the job meant, at best, a maintenance of social status if families could not shelter them from the workplace. The psychological benefits provided by the job are not easily measured by familiar sociological markers but are suggested below.

Because of the intense controversies over women's fitness for inspection posts, the inspectresses' own assessments of women's abilities are of special interest. We have seen that officials advocating inspectresses' appointment often argued that women possessed special insights useful for inspecting schools, assistance services and disciplinary facilities for children and women, and women's workplaces. Not surprisingly, women appointees also cited traditional ideas about femininity to demonstrate their fitness. Furthermore, they echoed their sponsors' insistence that women functionaries could play a unique role in addressing important national issues, such as creating loyalty to the new Republic, maintaining social solidarity, or combating depopulation. They also knew that their jobs made them female pioneers. Thus Aldona Sochazewska Juillerat recalled that as Rouen's first labor inspectress during the 1890s she had been mocked by the attorney of an employer against whom she had drawn up a complaint.

The lawyer had stated that a woman with official functions ceased to be "feminine," a characterization denied by Juillerat, who eventually stopped working after marriage to a Paris administrator. Women were "more nervous . . . , more emotive and more sentimental" than men, she stated, but such qualities helped them excel in activities inspired by "the heart and sentiments." Interior inspectress Gevin-Cassal saw her work with assisted children as a "comforting moral bath," and in the feminist newspaper *La Fronde* she argued that women deserved more jobs at all levels of public assistance because they were better prepared than men for "that joy without parallel of loving and soothing those who suffer." At the same time, she believed that her official title, like her less lucrative literary works, made her "someone." Primary school inspectress Marguerite Ginier similarly emphasized that women inspectors could contribute more than men to the teaching of home economics and moral lessons appropriate for girls. Labeling these two curricular emphases particularly important for uplifting the working class, she also conveyed the typical middle-class official's view that working-class families often failed to give daughters an adequate upbringing.[97]

While citing special feminine qualifications for their jobs, inspectresses also underscored their ability to do the same rigorous work as men. Mme Sara Arnaud, the last prewar assistant departmental inspectress of public assistance to remain on the job, took pride in her travel to southeastern France's mountainous areas and carried out difficult assignments that adversaries hoped would discourage her. The highly visible Kergomard, a persistent advocate of inspectresses, also cited her own record of visits to provincial nursery schools when she dismissed objections that women could not travel extensively. Furthermore, she asked pointedly whether trips across France were really more difficult than running a nursery school classroom, which might have more than a hundred pupils.[98] Similar records of provincial travel by other inspectresses since the July Monarchy and Second Empire also made dubious the objection that an inspectress of public assistance could not do the required travel within a department.

The need to defend one's right to a job led some inspectresses to support contemporary feminist efforts to extend women's legal rights. Their reactions to feminism were varied, however. Some eventually concluded that winning the vote was the key to ending discrimination on the job, but others scorned part or all of organized feminism as ridiculous or radical, perhaps hoping thereby to dismiss charges that work had defeminized them. Juillerat advocated better pay for most women workers and also access to the supervisory rank of divisional inspector of labor, but she believed that female suffrage should be "strictly limited" to exceptional cases and not pursued if it caused antagonism between the sexes. Most women did not need the ballot, she judged, because their distinctive qualities, which complemented those of men, already gave them the "sufficient" role of inspiring and guiding men within the family. Moniez, who had campaigned effectively to preserve the Ministry of the Interior's inspectresses general, also rejected votes for women and belittled feminism as "this very disgraceful part of the social Revolution." Moreover, she complained that educators who encouraged young women to enter "male" liberal professions were diverting them from their appropriate role of child rearing. Because France's high infant mortality rate contributed to the much discussed "crisis" of depopulation, she recommended that both primary and secondary schools offer more lessons on child care (*puériculture*) and home economics.[99]

Unlike Juillerat and Moniez, many school inspectresses joined feminist ranks. Both Kergomard and Ginier argued that without the vote women were unlikely to gain their deserved place in the inspectorate. Ginier and colleague Eugénie Kieffer served on the central committee of the Union française pour le suffrage des femmes (UFSF); Lucie Saffroy supported the suffragist group of Maria Vérone; and Marie Rauber attended feminist meetings and recorded examples of male officials' mistreatment of women in her diary. As head of the École normale supérieure of Fontenay-aux-Roses, former inspectress Jeanne-Adèle Dejean de la Bâtie invited UFSF leader Cécile Brunschvicg to speak to her pupils, destined to become professors at departmental normal schools for women.[100] Recognizing that more schooling improved women's qualifications for jobs, Kergomard headed the education section of the National Council of French Women from 1905 to 1920 and was succeeded by a later inspectress general of nursery schools, Rose Evard. Interior inspectress Gevin-Cassal, whose work supported her four children, also embraced the feminist label, backed women's suffrage, and, like Kergomard, contributed to the feminist *La Fronde*. Her younger colleague Galtier had participated in a feminist congress before she was 30.[101] Among the labor inspectresses, Bourat, Alice de la Ruelle, and Gabrielle Letellier favored the vote, but Bourat explicitly rejected some English suffragettes' more radical methods. Bourat and her friend Letellier also supported the Congrès des oeuvres et institutions féminines in 1913, as did Kergomard, Ginier, Kieffer, Dejean de la Bâtie, and Gevin-Cassal.[102]

Those inspectresses who affiliated with feminists did not radically reject prevailing beliefs about women's domestic destiny, however. They often asserted that, ideally, women belonged at home, caring for husbands and children and thereby serving France. Their attitudes toward gender roles thus exemplified the "familial" or "relational" variety of feminism typical not only of many pre-1914 French feminists but also of some Anglo-American maternalist reformers and suffragists.[103] Feminist inspectresses recognized, nonetheless, that economic need forced many women into the workplace, and so they found it unfair to pay women workers less than men in comparable jobs. Indeed, that message was publicized not only by the feminists Kergomard, Ginier, Kieffer, and Gevin-Cassal but also by the antisuffragists Moniez, Juillerat, and Mlle Charrondière, another labor inspectress. If women had to work, then Kergomard, Ginier, Juillerat, and Moniez especially recommended work in an appropriate feminine sphere, such as teaching, nursing, or inspecting institutions for women and children.[104]

The job of inspectress existed, of course, not for the gratification of individual officeholders but to provide a state service to society. Inspectresses' relationships with an assigned clientele thus figured in judgments about their abilities. For school inspectresses, verdicts concerning their dealings with women teachers were mixed. During the initial secularizing of public schools in the 1880s, Kergomard and other inspectresses general of nursery schools probably encountered as much resistance from nuns as did male inspectors.[105] Later Kergomard and Ginier also conceded their adversaries' point that some lay women teachers remained hostile to inspectresses. Whereas Kergomard and Ginier thought that some women teachers (*institutrices*) preferred *inspecteurs* with whom they could flirt, another feminist suggested that *institutrices*' receipt of less pay than *instituteurs* caused them to resent especially successful women like the inspectresses.[106] Nonetheless, Kergomard asserted in 1906 that women teachers supervised by inspectresses were "agreeably surprised" and no longer felt "sacrificed." [107] Furthermore, the minority of women teachers who joined the Fédération féministe universitaire recognized inspectresses' value as role models and as administrative advocates for ending such injustices as *institutrices*' lower pay scale.[108]

Critics did not typically challenge school inspectresses' understanding of women teachers' situation, but labor inspectresses faced that charge from workers who saw them more as the agents of bourgeois society than as sisterly allies. Thus in 1906 Anna Blondelu, an artificial flower maker and the only woman among the more than sixty members of the Higher

Council of Labor, called for appointing women workers as inspectresses because "bourgeois" inspectresses were ignorant of "the realities of the life of work." Current inspectresses had the credentials required for "a very honorable and well paid job," but their boarding school education and comfortable families did not prepare them for its demands and fatigue, she alleged.[109] In reality, however, many labor inspectresses were lower-middle-class women who needed to work, not comfortable bourgeoises.[110] Some inspectresses tried to improve relationships with workers, particularly after Millerand called for frequent contacts between the inspectorate and labor unions. Ruelle, for example, spoke on protective legislation at a congress on women's work attended by both feminists and female workers. Bourat brought to her job the insights gained from studying workers' problems with the Fabian socialist Sydney Webb in London; and she and Letellier had regular contact with Jeanne Bouvier, a seamstress and the one woman on the Higher Council of Labor after 1909.[111] Nonetheless, a sympathetic study of the labor inspectresses concluded that the relationships of both male and female inspectors with workers were generally less satisfactory than those with employers.[112]

Inspectresses of public assistance, like those of schools and labor, also understood that the state expected them to help moralize and discipline the lower classes and thereby promote social stability and harmony. Apart from her official functions, Gevin-Cassal maintained connections with various charities and believed that bourgeois women's participation in *patronages* for working-class girls helped create a "harmonious fusion of classes." Her book *La Fraternité en action* provided examples of the contribution of both public assistance and private charity to social "solidarity." She also asked philanthropic women and feminists to circulate information about the importance of breast-feeding for lowering infant mortality rates and thus helping to check depopulation. Like Kergomard and Rauber, she readily embraced republican anticlericalism when called upon to help oversee the turn-of-the-century laicization of some personnel in public hospitals.[113] Moniez had tried to produce class harmony among schoolchildren by encouraging youngsters with extra centimes to contribute to summer camps (*colonies de vacances*) for poor schoolchildren. Later, as an inspectress general, she endeavored, with little success, to reconcile private charities to governmental plans for more state regulation, especially when charities received state subsidies.[114]

Ultimately inspectresses' efforts won commendations from some, if not all, male supervisors and politicians. Although certain *inspecteurs pri-*

maires tried to discredit *inspectrices primaires* for at least a generation, all prewar primary school inspectresses earned praise for helping to increase support for their position. Rauber, for example, experienced a cordial working relationship with her immediate superior, inspector of academy Emilien Cazes, and he and Gréard agreed that she, as France's second primary inspectress, had demonstrated the female inspectorate's value.[115] Similarly, Gevin-Cassal enjoyed the support of Monod; and Strauss and inspector general Georges Rondel commended Moniez for helping to overcome objections to the Ministry of the Interior's inspectresses general.[116] Indeed, in 1911 Moniez joined male colleagues to give testimony to the Chamber of Deputies' commission then evaluating proposals to extend state regulation of private charities.[117] Fontaine, the longtime director of labor, displayed his confidence in inspectress Letellier by selecting her to represent France at postwar conferences held under the auspices of the International Labor Office, which he served after 1920 as president of its administrative council.[118]

On the eve of World War I three ministries had women inspectors assigned to investigative and supervisory positions directly affecting women or children. These inspectresses held a unique place within French administration, for at the same time cabinets still refused to permit women with university training to start up the professional career ladder in the central offices of government ministries.[119] We have seen that women's entry into the "exterior" administrative services of the education and interior ministries began when officials of the July Monarchy decided that certain administrative functions required special feminine talents, including the ability to deal with nuns and very young children. The nursery schools and prisons visited by the first inspectresses were institutions designed to promote social order at a time when the postrevolutionary state had become more active in the "policing of families."[120] Nursery schools were to moralize the neglected offspring of poor working-class mothers, and the prison was to control and, if possible, reform social deviants. The goal of social regulation remained important during the conservative reactions after the Revolution of 1848 and the Commune of 1871. The Third Republic's inspectress general Kergomard later helped alter nursery schools by making their pedagogy more concerned with the physical and psychological development of individual children, but only after World War II did many middle-class families stop viewing them as institutions for the lower classes and begin enrolling their own youngsters. The late-nineteenth-century drop in the populations of female prisons and reform schools paralleled a decline in the number of incarcerated males and led to merging the prison inspectorate's responsibilities with those of other inspectors general of the Ministry of the Interior. Like earlier regimes, the Third Republic expected its new inspectresses general for nursery schools and public assistance and new departmental inspectresses for primary schools, public assistance, and the workplace to moralize the lower classes. When Radical republican politicians embraced solidarism as a goal, inspectresses, too, tried to promote harmony between social classes.

Other political reasons for naming women inspectors also warrant repeating. The secularizing goal of anticlerical republicans affected all categories of inspectresses. Ferry and his allies reformed girls' education in order to remove women from the influence of the church and its monarchical allies and to mold future generations of mothers supportive of republican ideology. The firing or retirement of politically unacceptable inspectresses appointed by earlier regimes and the nomination of replacements such as Kergomard was part of the process of republicanizing nursery schools, more often run by nuns than lay women before the 1880s.[121] Plans to appoint new departmental inspectresses for nursery schools and girls' primary schools were checked, however, by a combination of financial limitations, inadequate political support, and resistance from male inspectors. Nonetheless, the inspectresses of schools played an important role in introducing a secularized program and, in the process, endured attacks by clerical and conservative opponents. The Ministry of the Interior's inspectresses of female penal institutions and assistance services also became involved in the secularization of institutional personnel and policies, and labor inspectresses went to some ateliers run by religious congregations.

The turn-of-the-century campaign of doctors and politicians to heighten awareness of the crisis of depopulation posed by the low French birthrate and high level of infant mortality was an additional concern for all ministries' inspectresses. There were legislative and private efforts to introduce maternity leaves for women workers and also numerous efforts to convince parents that hiring wet nurses and using unclean bottles and unpasteurized milk contributed to many infants' deaths. A related campaign called for adding lessons on child care to girls' primary schools, something not done officially until 1923 but already encouraged after 1900 by some male administrators and women educators influenced by Dr. Adolphe Pinard's efforts.[122]

Like male colleagues, republican inspectresses also experienced the process of professionalization. They had to meet more substantial formal educational requirements and compete successfully on national *concours* designed to reduce the importance of political recommendations for obtaining government jobs. The questions on the pre-1914 *concours* for inspectresses were partly tailored, however, to meet the distinctly feminine aspects of their positions and so helped serve the dual purpose of giving women a place in public service but also not enabling them to leave that gender-segregated place.[123]

Named initially to carry out policies directly affecting women or children, the pre-1914 inspectresses established, for the most part, a record of successful performance of their duties and so helped pave the way for post–World War I additions to the female contingent in the corps of departmental primary school and nursery school inspectresses, labor inspectresses, and inspectresses of public assistance. Women's temporary replacement of male officials during World War I and a postwar shortage of qualified men interested in government jobs contributed also to the expansion of permanent opportunities for professional women not only in departmental inspectorates but also, for the first time, at levels above clerical ranks in central government offices. Nonetheless, the interwar period did not produce more women's appointments as inspectors general. There were no interwar inspectresses general of primary or secondary schools appointed as colleagues of those for nursery schools, and no women divisional inspectors of labor. In 1939 only one inspectress general still served the Ministry of the Interior. Although some politicians continued to cite the importance of uniquely feminine and maternal traits for such jobs as inspecting public assistance services, this argumentation did not help women gain more access to the highest level of inspectorates. In comparison with the pre-1914 decades, proponents of increasing women's representation in administrative posts after World War I and, even more so, after World War II more often cited women's completion of the same educational program as men. Recent studies well demonstrate, however, that appointments to the highest administrative echelons often have not been gender blind during the last half of the twentieth century, for after 1939 the Ministry of the Interior did not again acquire a female inspector general until 1984.[124]

Seven

France in a Comparative Perspective

RACHEL G. FUCHS

SOCIAL WELFARE REFORMS that set the foundations for a welfare state emerged in many countries of the Western industrializing world between 1870 and 1914. Why did France, other European countries, and the United States institute similar reforms in the same era? In which ways was France unique and in which measures did it resemble the other countries? Understandably, differences in timing and in the nature of specific social reforms varied according to the political, economic, and cultural climates of each country. Nonetheless, an international comparison of specific social reforms and speculation about the reasons for the development of the welfare state toward the end of the nineteenth century are warranted as a result of new research brought to light in this collection of essays and other recent publications.[1]

Just what happened, and why, become clearer when women and the family are brought into focus. Nineteenth-century European and North American culture emphasized the importance of the family and the mother's pivotal role within it and promoted values about the roles of women as mothers which shaped the political trajectory. In France, as in other countries, the politics of social reform focused on the desire of reformers to protect mothers, children, and the family in the context of related national concerns. Legislators in each country responded to the perceived needs of their national economy, to fears of social disorder, to intellectual currents, and to deep concerns about their nation's population. Reform legislation pertaining to gender and the family became the linchpin in the state's construction of programs to address issues in the national interest. Social reform movements and the origins of the modern welfare state are about prescribing gender roles, defining the family, and protecting childhood and motherhood. Only by examining social reform through the lens of gender can scholars adequately discern the origins of the welfare state and the nature of politics at the turn of the nineteenth century.

France was exceptional in that French reformers, more obsessed with national depopulation than their counterparts in other countries, made maternity a state preoccupation. Everywhere in western Europe birthrates were declining, much to the dismay of many politicians, but only in France did the threat of depopulation loom so central in reform debates. To remedy depopulation, which many intellectuals and politicians associated with degeneration, reformers placed reproduction at the center of the cultural crisis and positioned women as mothers, regenerators of a degenerating race.[2] The valorization of maternity translated into legislation, as French bureaucrats and social reformers enacted family reforms before they developed welfare regulations directly affecting men.

Little attention had been paid to the French welfare state until the 1980s, when France, like much of the developed world, confronted the financial limits, or crisis, of the welfare state. Great Britain under Margaret Thatcher and the United States during the twelve years of Ronald Reagan and George Bush began the devolution of the welfare state, while in France the system was relatively strengthened under the socialists and only began retrenchment in the 1990s. One possible reason for scholars' neglect of the French welfare state has been the misunderstanding of the French system as either underdeveloped or overly complex, because social security accommodates voluntary insurance, conceptualizes social insurance in relation to social risk, and operates with the help of advisory bodies composed of contributors to the system. The combination of social solidarity, mutual support, risk sharing, and interlocking social institutions in France is highly evolved, flexible, and competent.[3] In this volume, we have shown that this evolution took more than a century.

A consequence of this inattention to the French welfare system, especially in terms of gender, is an assumption that it developed later than in other Western countries. Political scientists usually date the French welfare state from the creation of the Ministry of Hygiene, Aid, and Social Welfare in the 1920s.[4] François Ewald's major study of the emergence of France's *état providence* (the welfare state) focuses on the long battle to achieve compensation for victims of industrial accidents and the elaboration of the concept of risk, which was accomplished by 1898.[5] Other historians add to the list of precursors of the welfare state disability and old-age insurance for miners, sailors, and railroad workers in the 1890s and a more general pension plan enacted in 1910. Some even date the French welfare state later, during the 1930s and the Popular Front, with the adoption of a government program of social insurance encompassing health, maternity, disability, death, and old-age insurance for all workers below a certain income level. They asked why France lagged twenty or more years behind Great Britain and Germany. Explanations offered included late industrialization, the prominence of small entrepreneurs and farmers who resisted mandatory social insurance, and political divisions over social insurance, notably on the left.[6] The answer, as the essays in this volume have shown, is that France did not lag behind. Rather, it was in the forefront of many social reforms.

This volume stakes a claim for an early, if uncoordinated, introduction of welfare measures in the form of family policy acts. The essays place the origin of family policies after the Franco-Prussian War of 1870–71. They focus on disparate, piecemeal, but nevertheless related acts that began to interpret social rights and responsibilities, specifically those that redefined the family.

Previous historians emphasized the role of the Left in introducing social reforms. Supporters of social security programs undertook most initial studies of the origins of the welfare state in France, as elsewhere. Accordingly, these historians did not seriously scrutinize claims that welfare programs protected client populations, which they treated either as undifferentiated citizens or as disadvantaged people.[7] Few of them expressed the social-control aspects of welfare articulated by other scholars of the 1970s and 1980s.[8] Some recognized the priority given to children as deserving of protection; fewer noted any priority given to women. More recently, historians acknowledge the responsibility of the bourgeois political discourse or of the middle-class political parties that dominated the legislature during most of the key period of 1890 to 1914.[9]

Recent philosophers, most notably Jürgen Habermas, have argued that welfare state capitalism rises in response to crises in classical capitalism. Furthermore, Habermas argues that the welfare state contributes to the disintegration of the bourgeois public sphere; it becomes repoliticized.[10] Incorporating some of Habermas's notions, the essays in this volume illustrate that the social reforms leading to the development of the welfare state embodied a blurring of the lines between the public and private spheres. The politicians of the social welfare state have made *la vie intime* of the family and reproduction public. The public and private have become indistinguishable. Private persons deliberated about public matters, and public persons, mostly men, made decisions on the most private matters of reproduction and motherhood.[11]

Contemporary feminist scholars have developed the importance of gender in the relationship between the public and private spheres. In her analysis of Habermas's theories, Nancy Fraser argues that welfare state capitalism "partially overcomes the separation of public and private at the level of systems." Since spheres are gendered—the public is male and the private is female—problematizing the boundary between public and private imparts new meaning to social welfare reform. The public sphere becomes an arena of discourse in which opinion is formed and reformed. It is the site for the construction of consent necessary for hegemonic domination. Participants are continually negotiating and renegotiating positions of power in everyday life.[12] With an understanding of the gendered nature of welfare reform, it becomes arguable that power relations are not a one-way street but an area of contestation. This collection acknowledges the lack of distinction between public and private in a system that could conceive of state fathers for single-mother families and more generally working-class families, as well as state mothers producing healthy children for the nation.

Other scholars have raised serious objections to both the welfare state and much of the scholarship about it. They probe beneath facile claims about protecting the poor to reveal hidden assumptions about both gender and the family. Gillian Pascall examined state support and control of women in the British welfare system. Looking for what Nancy Fraser called the ideological underpinnings, "the tacit norms and implicit assumptions" in social policy and welfare practices, Pascall found that support for family almost always meant for a rigidly demarcated male breadwinner/dependent female model of family. She suggested that family policy sustained women's dependency. Feminists also critique scholarly fixation on the public realm, in general, and on the system of social insurance predicated on productive labor or paid employment, in studies of the welfare state. They draw attention to the aspects of the welfare state designed to regulate private life, or more precisely, reproductive labor, to wit maternity and later family policy.[13]

When issues of gender become central, as indeed they must in a discussion of welfare, the picture brings into clearer focus the myriad of regulations and social welfare legislation that was so important to state development at the end of the nineteenth century. It also indicates that France was a European leader in designing family policies and family allowances.[14] To exclude a gendered analysis of social reform is bound to falsify the picture because women have always constituted a preponderance of clients, some of the advocates of welfare, and many of the implementers.

Social reform involved a set of attitudes toward women as mothers and toward children as potential citizens in which they become part of a state-building project. From the viewpoint of the state, fetuses, infants, and children were future soldiers and workers. Mothers thus needed protection in order to produce good future citizens. Mothers, in turn, performed their service to the state by rearing these citizen-workers and citizen-soldiers in a manner approved by doctors, educators, and politicians. Before the twentieth century began, France, Germany, Great Britain, and the American states developed social policies based on this set of attitudes; motherhood was the center of many competing discourses and the resultant legislation. The "protection" afforded to mothers and children (in the interests of the state) encompassed a view of women as needing men's protection. The notion of the (male) citizen as the defender of the polity and protector of those who allegedly cannot protect themselves is paternal. Interpreting people's needs is itself a political act, with political stakes.

The male reformers in these essays are illustrations of political men interpreting the needs of the state, of its citizens, and of women and children. Gustave Dron, Alfred Naquet, Paul Strauss, Richard Waddington, the Radical politicians, and many others had a distinctly paternalistic approach to protecting women, one that treated working women and mothers as children and presumed that they knew more about these women's needs than the women themselves. The male power component of the category of citizen predates the elaboration of reform and in effect is essential in that category from its first development. Social reform and the welfare state provided men with a male power role of citizen over noncitizen; the systems brought women into the public sphere through legislation and regulations of private, intimate life but also under the aegis of masculine power.

As Theda Skocpol recently argued, European nations took the road toward a "paternalist welfare state, in which male bureaucrats would administer regulations and social insurance 'for the good' of breadwinning industrial workers." The United States, however, "came close to forging a maternalist welfare state, with female-dominated public agencies implementing regulations and benefits for the good of women and their children" from 1900 through the 1920s.[15] This collection has shown, however, that France was a modified "paternalist welfare state" because French bureaucrats designed legislation *not* exclusively for male breadwinning workers but, significantly, for women and children.

Maternalism is a curious paradigm. Maternalism extolled the virtues of motherhood but also empowered women in the community and in politics by bringing "feminine values" into the public sphere and by giving women a public and political arena. According to the carefully nuanced definition of Seth Koven and Sonya Michel, maternalism involved women's initiative and participation in designing a set of "political discourses and strategies" focusing on maternal and child welfare. It "exalted women's capacity to mother and applied to society as a whole the values they attached to that role: care, nurturance, and morality." Policies were maternalist when women "transformed motherhood from women's primary *private* responsibility into *public* policy." [16] Generally, middle-class women, often encouraged by male politicians, designed and implemented reforms for working-class mothers and children. Maternalism is a useful construct insofar as women design and implement a system for other women. When middle-class women seek to protect disadvantaged women and children, the bias becomes one of class and race as well as of gender.

The French social welfare state contained maternalist elements. If male bureaucrats designed legislation and regulations for mothers and children, female philanthropists and women's associations exerted political pressure on the legislators. The populationist discourse may have been male dominated, but it had many female voices. Furthermore, France had a long history of autonomous women's charitable organizations. Toward the end of the nineteenth century charitable and philanthropic organizations, frequently organized by women, became more secular in order to receive subsidies from the anticlerical Third Republic. Women in these societies, and as individuals, campaigned for social welfare for women and children. They used their own women's networks and their contacts through their husbands and fathers; and they published in journals such as *La Revue philanthropique* and *Le Journal des femmes*.[17] Moreover, since women implemented many of the welfare measures, they also helped formulate policy in a give-and-take relationship. Nevertheless, despite the sometimes strong voices of women, men's voices dominated Third Republic France.

Comparative Reform Movements

In most of the Western industrializing nations, legislators enacted piecemeal social reform measures such as gender-specific labor legislation and divorce laws in the last third of the century, but the earliest and most prominent reforms were to protect mothers and babies.

French social programs for mothers and babies started in the early 1870s. Other European nations had similar agendas and time frames for the development of maternal and infant welfare reform. In many Western countries, national legislators followed two ideological paths: on the one hand, politicians became increasingly willing to position the state between the family and the child and to intervene to protect children. On the other hand, politicians and reformers glorified, dignified, and sought to protect motherhood.[18]

Children's well-being became essential to the national interest. The desire to protect children was so great that child protection took similar forms and materialized at roughly the same time in France, England, Germany, and Russia. Public and philanthropic agencies developed infant day-care facilities and kindergartens whose goals were to protect and educate young future citizens. To protect children from abusive, alcoholic, or criminal parents, the French, British, and German governments enacted almost identical legislation enabling state welfare authorities to decide who were unsatisfactory parents and then deprive them of paternal authority by authorizing the removal of children from their families and homes. The French government enacted the Roussel law protecting these "morally abandoned" children in 1889, the same year that the British Parliament enacted the Law for the Prevention of Cruelty and Protection of Children, which "allowed children in certain circumstances to be removed from their families." Comparable German legislation came about a decade later.[19] Then in 1908, the Children's Act of Britain gave the state further responsibility to protect children by preventing their "deprivation in early life." In this measure, the state seemed less concerned with mothers than with the possibility that deprived children might become depraved or even die. To calm those who feared that "state action would contribute to the destruction of family responsibilities," the advocates of the law argued that it would "reinforce 'responsible parenthood.'"[20]

Public and private agencies in several countries established well-baby centers and free milk dispensaries to safeguard infants' health around the turn of the century. In England, voluntary societies organized and staffed well-baby clinics where infants could be weighed and where volunteers could give child-care advice to mothers. They also ran free milk distribution centers, similar to the French *goutte de lait*. With encouragement from political reformers, physicians, and legislators, British volunteer organizations developed programs to educate mothers in methods of efficient, "scientific," hygienic infant care; they especially encouraged breast-feeding to prevent infant mortality from diarrhea. Much of this resembled the situation in Paris, Tourcoing, and other French cities where private organizations worked with the government in providing milk and medical care to mothers and babies. The United States came late to the idea of governmental protection of children, although female philanthropies instituted day nurseries in the late nineteenth century; nevertheless, by 1914 the United States also had well-baby clinics and infant milk depots.[21]

In Russia, day nurseries and boarding institutions for infants of widowed, deserted, or working mothers developed as part of an effort to reduce infant mortality. There may have been more "public upbringing" of children in Russia than in the countries of western Europe, and such Russian efforts were in keeping with their philosophy that the state could raise children better than poor, uneducated working mothers. The Russian Society for the Protection of Infants' Lives and Childrearing, incorporating some new ideas about infant feeding and education in child care, constructed various welfare institutions for mothers and children. In 1904, the Union to Combat Child Mortality distributed free "cow's milk to infants and children at walk-in clinics," while some members provided advice to mothers on breast-feeding and child care. It also established day nurseries for children of working mothers. An organization called the Drop of Milk (an identical title to the French *goutte de lait*) "distributed free milk to infants while emphasizing the superiority and importance of breastfeeding." The major difference between child protection reforms in Russia and countries of western Europe and the United States revolved around concepts of women's roles as workers. Russians viewed women's major role as a worker—a role that interfered with her role of mother. In effect, Russian institutions became surrogate mothers, thereby enabling poor women to continue to work; but the major goal was protection of the children.[22]

Child protection is inseparable from the protection of motherhood, in part because children depended on their mothers for survival. Furthermore, in Western countries, unlike in Russia, motherhood became a social function, and authorities often believed that the child's own mother was the best person to take care of the baby. They consequently enacted aid programs to support maternity and tried to establish an "endowment of motherhood" as in England or a "*caisse de la maternité*" as in France. In Germany "the League for Protection of Mothers called upon the state . . . to provide financial support for motherhood in the form of maternity insurance, to free the mother from work obligation through maternity leaves, and to preserve the child's and the mother's health through state-supported maternity care and subsidies for nursing."[23]

Legislation in Britain, Germany, and France treating childbirth as an illness, entitled to medical assistance, shows the extent to which motherhood had become important. The French law of 1893 on free medical assistance assimilated childbirth with other illnesses and allowed women in childbirth free admission to the public hospitals. Britain's National Health Insurance Act of 1911 allotted a pittance to women who had enrolled in the program, either on their own or through their husbands.[24] The money, however, went to the husband. Women's groups protested and in 1913 succeeded in getting a provision that mothers receive the money directly.[25] The 1883 German law on health insurance entitled insured women factory workers to minimal benefits for three weeks of maternity leave after childbirth, but coverage was optional and rarely paid. Only in 1924 could "non-employed wives of insured husbands" receive benefits."[26] Even Russia had a workers' insurance law in 1912 that provided for maternity benefits.[27]

The creation of mothers' pensions provided another building block to the welfare state spurred on by concerns about children and motherhood. These began first in France in the 1870s with programs of aid to mothers to encourage breast-feeding and prevent child abandonment. During the First World War, British politicians endorsed mothers' pensions in principle, but it was not until 1918 that the Labour party made them part of its program. In that year, the British government enacted a major piece of legislation, the Maternity and Child Welfare Act, whose goal was to provide for the health of women before, during, and after childbirth.[28] Because of the war's devastation and the large number of fathers killed, measures to protect mothers and children, and thereby increase and improve the population, multiplied in England as well as in France. By 1939, in both England and France, a combination of social reforms provided mothers with pre- and postnatal care, medical care for childbirth, well-baby clinics, and health visitors for infants and parturient women.[29]

The United States enacted mothers' benefits later than the countries of western Europe, and the states took action before the national government. The earliest laws authorizing public expenditure for widowed mothers occurred between 1911 and 1920 when forty states passed laws to enable local governments to provide payments to needy widowed mothers (and occasionally others) in order to let them raise their children "properly" by staying at home and maintaining a suitable, stable home.[30] Yet it was not until the Federal Act for the Promotion of the Welfare and Hygiene of Maternity and Infancy, known as the Sheppard-Towner Act of 1921, that the U.S. government provided any effective national welfare. This welfare was in the form of subsidized infant "pre- and post-natal clinics to disseminate health-care advice to mothers, in the hope of reducing the high infant mortality rates."[31]

Although much of the British, American, German, and Russian legislation for the protection of children and mothers resembled French programs, the differences between France and the other countries are twofold. One is a question of timing. France's various programs for the protection of motherhood began in Paris and other cities in the 1870s, developed through the 1880s, and became nationally legislated in 1893, 1904, and 1913. Second, France was unique in offering programs of aid to nonmarried mothers to prevent infant mortality on a national scale in 1904. This legislation came after the institution and implementation of aid programs to single mothers on a local level which had existed since the 1870s. Other nations' laws restricted mothers' pensions to widows or married mothers. France's fear of depopulation resulting from high infant mortality, proven higher among babies born to single mothers, prompted this difference between France and other nations.

In western Europe and the American states, legislation favored women's reproductive role over their productive role in the workplace.[32] Protection of childhood and motherhood lay behind protective labor legislation for women as the Western debate over women's work considered working women as actual and potential mothers. Reformers and politicians maintained that when a woman worked outside the home in the weeks surrounding her baby's birth, her infant's health and survival could suffer. They further argued that a working mother could not properly care for her infant. In attempts to reconcile women's roles as workers and as mothers, the European countries instituted a series of maternity leave policies; several of these tied into general national medical assistance programs.

Since maternity leaves in different countries varied in their comprehensiveness and remuneration to mothers, a precise international comparison presents difficulties. It is not clear if France was significantly behind other nations when French legislators enacted maternity leaves and benefits in 1913. The Swiss were the pioneers in this area; their 1877 law provided for eight weeks of leave, before and after delivery, and prohibited women from returning to factory work until six weeks after childbirth. One year later, in 1878, Germany enacted a three-week leave after childbirth, but neither the Swiss nor the German leaves included benefits or pay. By 1883 both Germany and Austria-Hungary had paid maternity leaves of three weeks after delivery for insured women, but the amount varied with the discretion of the insurance program. By 1900, Great Britain, Portugal, Norway, Holland, and Belgium provided unpaid maternity leaves after delivery. France, along with Spain, Italy, Denmark, Russia, and the United States, lagged behind these other countries in instituting any kind of maternity leave, even without pay. But in 1899, when Paul Strauss proposed paid maternity leaves of two weeks before and four weeks after delivery, and when France enacted such legislation in 1913, only Switzerland had a maternity leave *before* delivery, and only Luxembourg, Germany, Switzerland, and Austria-Hungary had paid leaves.[33] Maternity leaves were just one example of legislation and programs that helped construct the welfare state in the nineteenth century.

Gender-specific labor legislation designed to provide better child care and household management provided another step in the development of social reform. It addressed widespread anxieties about the disintegration of the working-class family and apprehensions about social disorder. Working mothers, reformers argued, could not properly care for and supervise their children without shorter hours.

France's timing in enacting child and gender-specific labor legislation coincided with the adoption of partial labor protection in several European nations. The most industrialized nation, Britain, passed its first child labor law in 1803 and its first adult female labor law in 1844. France passed legislation limiting children's work and regulating women's working hours decades after Britain, in 1844 and 1892. Between 1878 and 1892 France, Austria, Germany, and Holland restricted industrial women's working day. In these countries, as in France, the laws specified a shorter workday for children than for women and allowed more exceptions to the bans on women's night work.[34]

The American states implemented labor laws designed for women later than France, Britain, Germany, Holland, and Austria. American protective labor laws sought to regulate women's working conditions by concentrating on the negative impact of nonregulation on women's reproductive capabilities. Like the British and French, they emphasized women's primary role as mothers at home with their babies. The National Consumers' League and the General Federation of Women's Clubs worked for improvement in women's hours laws and minimum wage statutes, arguing that "'employed womanhood [needed to] be protected in order to foster the motherhood of the race.'" Although a few American states enacted female hours laws in the 1890s, the lower courts were overturning these laws until the Supreme Court affirmed its commitment to female protective legislation between 1905 and 1920. The arguments for passage of laws limiting women's working hours which the courts upheld underscored women's role as mothers and potential mothers.[35]

Historians of labor standards account for the American delay by reference to the opposition of the dominant segment of organized labor (and, as elsewhere, of employers' associations). Not until 1911 was the American Federation of Labor prepared to support gendered hours limitations, and as late as 1914 it explicitly rejected limits on adult men's labor. Few unions promoted labor standards for women.[36] The socialists, who did support labor standards, were less threatening than in European societies, thereby obviating the political interests of conservative and republican politicians in competing with the socialists for the vote by enacting working-class labor protection laws, as in Europe—most notably France and Germany.

An analysis of gendered labor legislation uncovers sincere concern about the social issue of protecting women's role as mothers. Reformers and progressive welfare capitalists, such as Waddington and Dron in France, associated feminine labor standards with the battle against depopulation and degeneration. Their firsthand experience with working-class families through local charitable activities informed their recognition that working-class women had to work for wages and at the same time needed some relief to accommodate their dual roles as paid laborer and unpaid mother. They shared the contemporary stress on the importance of motherhood yet expressed more concern with infant mortality as a result of women working outside the home than did American and British reformers.

English reformers, unlike those in France, did not invariably link women's work outside the home with the high infant mortality rate, although they agreed that women's factory work had deleterious effects on their infants' health and that married women should devote their time to domesticity, dependent on the male breadwinner. Sociologist Sonya Rose observes that in the last quarter of the nineteenth century, discussion among doctors and the general public directly linked women's factory work to infant mortality. And Jane Lewis maintains that "the argument against women's employment outside the home stemmed more from the belief that women's place was in the home than from the evidence produced to connect it with infant mortality."[37] The 1901 Factory Act stipulated that women could not work at night in any industry, but the 1906 Conference on Infant Mortality wanted that act to go further. It resolved that women should be compelled to stay at home for three months after the birth of a child rather than the one month prescribed by the 1901 Factory Act.[38]

The tension in political and business circles between women's role as mothers and their role as workers varied from country to country. Most reformers wanted women to have dual roles but gave priority to women's role as mother. Only Russian ideologies "emphasized women's participation in the work force over their roles as mothers." Russian reformers did not disavow women's work in factories in favor of motherhood because Russia did not have a problem with a fertility decline or perceived depopulation and because Russia was so much less industrialized than the other nations. Maternal and child welfare movements there tended to treat the needs of mothers and children as separate and often in conflict.[39] Behind most Western movements, however, was the child's well-being and the preferred role for women as mothers.

The beginnings of the welfare state in labor and maternity legislation had their counterpart in increasing state concern with private lives. While desiring to protect the family from disintegration, reformers also had a changing conception of family life. They recognized that more freedom of choice in marriage partners would make for better and more prolific families. Similarly, they linked divorce to a prescribed role for women, definitions of the proper family, and the role of gender and the family in the state.

Divorce relates to ideas of women's rights, social purity, femininity, temperance, illicit sexuality, and the doctrines of domesticity, liberalism, conservatism, and nationalism. Liberals, believing in individual happiness and in the sanctity of private life, supported marriage and divorce policies that maximized individual personal freedom. Socialists also sought a loosening of marriage ties. Conservatives disagreed. Pope Pius IX's 1864 Syllabus of Errors decreed, "By natural law marriage is not dissoluble and it is an error to assert that . . . divorce may be permitted by the secular power." Pope Leo XIII later argued, "Divorces are in the highest degree hostile to the prosperity of families and states, springing as they do from the depraved morals of the people."[40]

Passage of legislation enabling divorce indicates governments' relationships with the church and the relative strength of anticlerical movements. In England, divorce had always been available to the rich and prominent through a private act of Parliament. The passage of the divorce bill in 1857 denotes the decline of the church's influence; it removed divorce from parliamentary jurisdiction, the Anglican Church, and ecclesiastical courts and put it in civil courts. As in England and France, divorce in unified Germany was an anticlerical issue. The imperial divorce law of 1875, enacted at the height of Bismarck's campaign against the influence of the Roman Catholic

Church in Germany, can be interpreted as a slap in the face of Catholics and Pope Pius IX. In Italy the power of the Catholic Church persisted, and divorce remained illegal in the nineteenth century, despite five divorce bills brought before the legislative commission of parliament and the strong anticlericalism of the political elite.

Divorce in individual countries also related to issues of adultery and the desire to protect the family. In England, adultery was the only grounds for divorce until 1937. The objection to the passage of the 1857 divorce bill rested on the belief that it would promote adultery and the breakdown of the family; the 1857 legislation prohibited a woman from marrying "her accomplice in adultery." Yet supporters of divorce in both England and France wanted divorce and possible remarriage as a solution to matrimonial problems, enabling people to forge new families, with children, when an old marriage had irretrievably broken down.

According to its proponents, divorce promoted morality and protected women. Advocates of divorce in England argued that in France and Italy, where divorce was prohibited, the "faithlessness of married persons [was] proverbial." The reformers also wanted women to have equal access to divorce. Yet to obtain a divorce, women had to prove aggravated adultery (adultery plus bigamy, incest, sodomy, desertion, cruelty, rape, or bestiality). Women also risked losing their children, since the courts operated under the principle that children belonged to their father. Nevertheless, after enactment of the English law, half the petitioners for divorce were women, and their petitions had a better success rate than did men's. In the belief that marital breakup led to children's deprivation, the Matrimonial Causes Act of 1907 tried to regularize child support payments to divorced and separated women but did not resolve their long-standing difficulties in obtaining these payments from recalcitrant or poor husbands. Payment could be enforced only by the courts and would achieve little when poor husbands could not afford to pay.

Nineteenth-century Prussian law recognized divorce for adultery, "unnatural vices," desertion, refusal of sexual intercourse, impotence, "raging madness," violence, attempted murder, repeated and unfounded defamatory accusations, felony, disorderly life, continued refusal of a husband to maintain his wife, giving up the Christian religion, or "insurmountable aversion" in cases in which there were no children. Attempts to reduce the grounds failed. Opponents of divorce stressed its implications for immorality and social instability; they also feared making divorce available for the poor. In 1871 unified Germany based divorce on the Prussian model.

German legislation between 1875 and 1900 ran counter to the trends of liberalization in England and in France and made the law more restrictive by removing "insurmountable aversions" as grounds.[41] By doing this, the German law compared with those in England and France, which were already more restrictive. Divorce in Germany was bound to the politics of national unification and the consolidation of the German empire.

In France, fears of national decline and the breakdown of the family fueled movements for and against divorce. Divorce was legal in France from 1792 to 1816 and then illegal until 1884. Advocates and opponents of divorce debated its effects on women. Supporters argued that women would benefit from the ability to free themselves and their children from oppressive marriages. Opponents insisted that if marriage was good for women, divorce must be bad for them. The religious issue was always crucial; Catholics strongly opposed divorce, but supporters of divorce said that Catholics could choose not to divorce. The divorce bill passed less because of direct fear of depopulation and more because of the specter of family breakdown. Moreover, divorce came to represent individual liberty and the reaffirmation of the secular nature of marriage, both concepts central to the anticlerical republican agenda.

Women's movements, spanning the spectrum from socialist feminists to conservative Catholic feminists, divided over the issue of divorce. A very small minority criticized marriage. Most agreed that women should have equal rights with men as well as property rights. They applauded the French 1884 divorce law, in part because it recognized abuse by enabling women to obtain a divorce in cases in which their husbands repeatedly beat them. Some women's groups, especially the Social Catholics, regarded the family as a guarantor of social stability and believed that making divorce available would weaken the family and society. Feminists on the left correctly envisioned the feminization of poverty resulting from divorce.

Feminists also divided on the issue of gender-specific (as opposed to universal) labor protection. Although some feminists and women's groups supported protective labor legislation for women, many feminists, especially in England and France, opposed restrictions on women's working hours. The French Congress of the Rights of Women in 1889 and the 1900 Women's Congress implicitly rejected exceptional laws for women. British feminists opposed the 1901 Factory Act forbidding night work to women. What they wanted was not "protection" but "'a real equality for women.'" American middle-class women, some of whom were feminists, generally supported such labor legislation, and in Germany some middle-class women sought more extensive protective legislation for work-ing women.[42]

Women's groups promoted welfare and family legislation by their vol-unteer political and philanthropic activity and by their paid and unpaid ser-vices as implementers of the reforms. In France this activity did not begin in the late nineteenth century. Bourgeois and middle-class women had served as nursery school inspectresses since the 1830s and took precedent-setting positions as advocates for reforms with increased roles for women in pri-mary education throughout the century.[43] In other countries as well as in France, toward the end of the nineteenth century middle-class women's roles generally changed from that of "charity providers" to "trained social workers" who helped formulate and implement public welfare programs and policy.[44] Women inspectors at the end of the century exemplified new careers for women, as well as the close interaction of women and the state. The German League for the Protection of Mothers argued that the open-ing of education and careers to women was vital to the biological and the social welfare of the state. Women's voluntary societies, what was really the sphere of civil society, took a prominent part in philanthropy and social work and formed cadres of policy implementers. Although not always in-spectresses in the sense of the women in France, women in countries lacking a formal state welfare system, even a nascent one such as in France, fulfilled an important public function.

Some Explanations for the Origins of Social Reform

Examining the development of social reform at the end of the century is comparable to the image of five blind people and an elephant. Each person seeking an explanation has focused on just one aspect of this enormous beast. The second part of this essay attempts to explore various explana-tions for the development of social reforms at the turn of the century.

Although the essays in this volume do not ignore humanitarian motives for social reform, they place the fear of depopulation and the related issues of nationalism and anxiety over perceived national degeneration as inspi-ration for the reforms in France. To a lesser extent depopulation and its related anxieties motivated reform in other countries as well.

The idea of depopulation took many forms in different countries, but the concentration on the family and women's role as mother, protector of the nation's children, remained constant. A powerful elite of doctors, businessmen, politicians, and reformers used the idea of depopulation to extend their influence within the family and the state. To some extent they constructed depopulation as a problem they could solve. They viewed the family as the foundation of the state; the state needed buttressing, and so therefore did the family and its children, who were future citizens, workers, and soldiers. Concern over the quality and quantity of population gave rise to social reform movements to increase the quantity and improve the quality. The fertility decline was a new phenomenon of the Western industrialized world and promoted national concern. France had the greatest decline in birthrate, followed by England and then Germany. Russia experienced no decrease in birthrate. Low birthrates, high infant mortality rates, and the concern with national depopulation are the keys to understanding the development of social policies regarding the family in France and in other European countries, save Russia.

The number of private societies for prevention of infant mortality increased from 1890 to 1914, although infant mortality actually declined slightly in most Western countries during these years. National legislators, medical and political leaders, and private volunteer societies established commissions, conferences, and organizations to study the nation's needs and propose reforms. The major debates of these groups centered on national depopulation, and on infant mortality as the major contributing factor. They sought methods to increase and improve the population. In France, Dr. Jacques Bertillon established the Alliance nationale pour l'accroissement de la population française in 1896. It was one of several volunteer societies to foster the protection of newborns by supporting maternal breast-feeding. The analogous German Society for the Prevention of Infant Mortality and the League for the Protection of Mothers arose around the turn of the century. The comparable British society, the National Conference on Infant Mortality, founded in 1906, became the National Association for the Prevention of Infant Mortality and the Promotion of the Welfare of Children under School Age in 1912. And the American Association for the Study and Prevention of Infant Mortality began in 1909. Even in Russia, so politically different from the nations of the West and not experiencing depopulation, child protection agencies appeared just after the turn of the century, beginning with the Union to Combat Child Mortality in 1904. Just a few years later, in 1909, eminent Russian male doctors founded the Society for the Protection of Infants' Lives and Childrearing.[45]

Preventing infant mortality became the motivating force for social reform. In Germany, according to Ann Taylor Allen, "among both health ministry officials and private citizens, a heightened concern for population growth was first expressed through concern with the infant death rate." At about 20 per 100 live births in 1903, the German infant mortality figure exceeded that of France (13.7) and England (13.2). German medical and governmental officials, like their French and English counterparts, fixed responsibility for these deaths on the mothers. They placed an almost exclusive emphasis on the importance of breast-feeding in preventing infant deaths, and they downplayed structural remedies such as better housing and hygiene. The Germans argued that humanity, the culture, and the race needed progeny.[46]

In England, as well, "child and maternal welfare began with the recognition that infant mortality was a problem of national importance. . . . It became part of the drive to improve the quality and quantity of population . . . and was included in the campaign to improve physical efficiency." The government and volunteer societies concerned with depopulation sponsored reports on infant mortality. In 1904 the British Committee on Physical Deterioration realized that infants and children were the future of the country; it therefore carefully considered the children's well-being. Politicians endorsed state intervention in maternal and infant welfare on the grounds that it was for the "national good and racial improvement."[47]

France took the initiative in forming parliamentary commissions to study the problem of depopulation and to propose remedies directed at mothers and babies. In 1902 the French prime minister, René Waldeck-Rousseau, convened the first extraparliamentary commission to study depopulation. Shortly thereafter, the British Parliament launched an investigation into the strength of the British population. Although societies for the protection of women and children formed in Germany around the turn of the century, not until 1916 did the German Reichstag appoint a committee on population policy which advised government measures, such as public day-care centers, protective legislation for women workers, and increased maternity insurance, as positive steps to improve the environmental circumstances of motherhood.[48] The earliest noteworthy governmental conference to address infants' needs in the United States was the 1909 White House Conference on Women and Children; this conference focused on pensions for "fit" mothers (generally widows), and infant mortality only indirectly.

A nation's perception of its population became particularly crucial after a war. In France, England, Germany, and the United States, many social policies were directly related to military concerns and occurred after wars or as part of the expansion of military service and international competition that preceded a major war. France's shocking war loss to Prussia in 1870 prompted vigorous concern with the relative number and strength of the population. French politicians denounced the comparative strength of Germany's population in relation to that of France. Likewise, the Boer War (1899–1902) affected British nationalism and population concerns. During the Boer War, newspapers reported that the army had to reject many volunteers because they were physically unfit. Furthermore, Britain had trouble defeating the Boer farmers, and some concluded that this resulted from the weakness and deterioration of the British population. Many feared that the poor performance during the Boer War would lead to military and economic defeat by Britain's chief rival, Germany.[49] Infants' and children's welfare became significant only after the war.

International economic competition and nationalism that marked the decades just before 1914 helped fuel fears of population debilitation and led to gendered social reform to enhance the citizenry. Britain and France were competing with the more rapidly expanding economies of Germany and the United States.[50] British businessmen and politicians toward the end of the nineteenth century foresaw industrial decline vis-à-vis Germany and the United States. In the interests of the nation, they emphasized the "need to improve the physical and productive efficiency of the mass of the population." They debated the issues of poverty, illness, and degeneration with renewed vigor and sought "methods of improving the numbers and environment of the masses rather than weeding out the unfit." Employers wanted healthy workers and applied pressure on the government to approve welfare measures to increase "national efficiency" and workers' health.[51]

Nationalistic German politicians also decried their nation's depopulation. This appears ironic, since France looked east to a larger and threatening German population. Germany's resurgent imperial ambitions coincided with a fall in German birthrates and the persistence of a high infant mortality rate. In Germany "politicians, military figures, and moralists pointed to the danger from Russia, where birthrates remained high, and to the [counter]example of France, where, they argued, low birthrates were linked to military weakness and cultural decadence."[52] They tied their views to their ideal roles for women—as nurturing mothers protecting their children from debility and death—and also to ideas of national competition and methods of improving the race. In this the Germans differed little from the British and French ideas of "racial improvement" through maternal and infant welfare reforms.

In all countries, the rhetoric of eugenics and racial degeneration linked the declining birthrates to other signifiers of cultural crisis, such as crime, insanity, tuberculosis, alcoholism, syphilis, and economic performance. The form eugenics took in each country related to specific cultural anxieties. The British eugenics movement, with the formation of the English Eugenics Education Society in 1907, was particularly strong before World War I, when reports gloomily assessed the falling birthrate and the "pauperism" of the working class. Its strength later increased with the activities of the Society for the Promotion of Race Regeneration. Members did not wish to increase the birthrate among all the British residents—just the "economically successful." Eugenicists objected that "saving infant lives would impair rather than improve the quality of the race." They maintained that infant deaths among the working classes " 'offered the strongest possible presumption of inherent worthlessness.' " Health officials and prominent politicians, however, took pains to refute these ideas because of "anxiety over the falling birth rate." They argued that "infant welfare work would improve rather than impede racial progress." In a broad sense, the British eugenics movement was to foster national efficiency by controlling crime, insanity, and illegal aliens through breeding.[53] In Germany, more than a decade before World War I, the eugenics movement flourished, leading to a new moral authority for the state and an expansion of the state's role in promoting public health. This included a campaign for the health of single mothers because of the high mortality of their children. Metaphors linking physical health to moral regeneration pervaded the rhetoric.[54]

A broadly based eugenics movement formed in France about 1912, later than in other countries. As Robert Nye cogently points out, eugenics related to anxiety over national degeneration in which depopulation was the "master pathology" in the biomedical analysis of France's ills.[55] The French eugenics movement "aimed at the biological regeneration of the population, such as natalism, neo-malthusianism, social hygiene, and racist immigration restrictions. . . . [It was] a biologically based movement for social reform" emerging from the earlier puericulture (maternal infant and child-care education) movement and from perceptions of French decline. It encompassed seemingly diverse groups such as the natalists, neo-malthusians, and outright racists by fostering ideas of biological regeneration; it also gained broad-based support by "stressing positive eugenics and the need to improve both the quality *and* the quantity of the population" through control over human reproduction.[56] Paul Strauss, Léon Bourgeois, and other leading solidarists became members of the French Eugenics Society; in 1912 Bourgeois was the first honorary president, and

Strauss was one of seven honorary presidents of the French Consultative Committee to the First Eugenics Congress in London.[57]

The rhetoric of the eugenicists combined with that of the population-ists fed the fears that inspired social reforms for women, children, and the family. These family and gender reforms marked the origins of the welfare state in the decades before World War I. Until recently, the issue of depopulation has received scant attention from historians and political scientists alike. Only those studying gendered social reforms, those acts that preceded measures for male workers, have considered that the fear of depopulation drove social reform.

Previously, historians and political scientists argued that the disloca-tion, depression, and unemployment resulting from industrialization and a changing socioeconomic structure advanced modern social policies. They linked social policies to social conditions, and social reform to the politi-cal and economic structure. For example, Jürgen Habermas argued that "the rise of industrial capitalism transformed poverty from a social into a political problem"; welfare state capitalism developed in response to crises in classical capitalism. Basically, economic transformation, the shift from agriculture, and advancing industrialization weakened important personal and community ties that had previously supported both the family and the poor. Politicians redefined poverty to justify the state's intervention in support of the patriarchal ideal and the *raison d'état*.[58] More specifically, historians point to the large-scale visible urban poverty between mid-1880 and mid-1900. The decline in agriculture and the migration of young to the cities in the late 1880s added to a large pool of urban labor (with many unemployed) and an elderly population remaining in the rural areas. His-torian Pat Thane sees a trend away from blaming the poor for their poverty to a recognition that the fault lay in the structure of the economy. Former means of charity and welfare were inadequate for conditions in 1900.[59]

Analogously, social reform emanated from a fear of civic disorder asso-ciated with economic dislocation and the depressions of the 1880s and 1890s. The poor and unemployed became more visible. The factory system combined with the fear of social revolution, especially in the wake of a de-pression, led to new types of solutions. Strike activity, much of it violent, arose all over Europe in the last third of the nineteenth century and pro-voked legislative action. Less than fifty years later, the horrific conditions occasioned by the world depression of the 1930s spurred massive welfare measures. Government leaders responded to crises in the economic struc-ture by social reform. Nevertheless, the programs first established were not those for the unemployed men nor the general welfare programs of the 1930s. The earliest welfare measures were intended to regulate the family, and as such, they targeted women and children.

In concentrating on economic rupture in the society, historians and political scientists focused on male unemployment and the potential threat and danger that unemployed men presented to the social order, which is why they have wrongly interpreted the timing and nature of the welfare state. These scholars differ, however, in assessing the motivations of the reformers—whether reformers were humanitarian in believing that the poor should be served or whether they had their own self-interests in mind in seeking to control the unemployed men.

Social reforms and welfare legislation are not necessarily progressive or humanitarian responses to economic and structural crises. Revisionist historians and political scientists have called into question the dominant model that had presented social reform as one of progress "from ignorance to expertly guided intervention, from cruelty and vindictiveness to scientific humanism" in attempts to alleviate the most serious social ills.[60] Revisionists are skeptical about the aims, beliefs, and intentions of reformers. They still locate reform efforts within the social, economic, and political structures of the period, but they see the reforms more as an effort to control a population than as an element of humanitarian progress.

In their pathbreaking 1971 book *Regulating the Poor*, Frances Fox Piven and Richard A. Cloward argued that the chief function of social reform and welfare arrangements was to regulate the poor, restore order, and control turmoil from the unemployed by enforcing work. Poor relief, social reform, and social welfare were the means by which society reasserted its authority when mass unemployment weakened the entire structure of society and social control. According to Piven and Cloward, social welfare was a political response to political disturbances. It pacified the "unemployed and turbulent populace" with public allowances to enforce work. The notion of the power of one class or race over another in state welfare policies is implicit in their work.[61]

Historians David Rothman and Andrew Scull present modified social-control interpretations of the origins of the welfare state. According to what Stanley Cohen and Andrew Scull depict as Rothman's "essentially functionalist and pluralist view, social control does not operate in the defence of any particular social interests, but rather originates as a broadly based corrective to *generally* perceived threats of social disequilibrium and disorder." The functionalists, such as Rothman, recognize the "limits of benevolence" and maintain that "conscience inevitably proves no match for convenience." Scull goes further and shows that reformers, operating in their own self-interest, would exaggerate the extent of the problem to achieve their ends. He is referring to the economic and social problems of industrialization, but he could just as well be referring to an exaggeration of the demographic imperative. Scull argues that an understanding of the development of social reform and institutions must be kept within the context of the society that led to those developments. Yet he rejects the notion of a structurally determined relationship between urbanization and industrialization and the development of social reforms.[62]

Structural analyses alone do not explain the social reforms of the turn of the century; economic change, poverty, and structural dislocation have been fairly constant throughout history. Theda Skocpol maintains that a structural economic approach to the origins of modern social reforms does not stand the test of research, at least for the United States. She concludes that it was not urbanization, industrialization, or depression that correlated with social reform, but rather it was literacy.

Linking social reform with literacy allows for an extension of Habermas's ideas of communication. Private people coming together in the public sphere to form public policy needed communication and pressure groups to mold public opinion to effect the reform. Literacy facilitated their efforts, as did a burgeoning number of international conferences and congresses disseminating information across Europe and the American states around the turn of the century. Government officials, feminists, women's clubs, doctors and social hygienists, demographers and other scholars, and international political parties met frequently to exchange ideas. This type of communication among private individuals in a public sphere spread information about one country to the next, fostering both international competition as well as ideas about social reform. Likewise, an extension of the electorate and the rise of competing political parties and ideologies encouraged more communication and new forms of political programs.

The European nations, and to a lesser extent the United States, faced threats to their political structure which came from both the political Right and Left. Socialist political parties and politically active trade unions increased in importance toward the end of the nineteenth century. Their programs offered welfare benefits and promised a plethora of social welfare reforms, such as universal labor standards. The governments of France, Britain, and Germany, fearing that workers' support for the socialists might topple their regimes, adopted welfare reforms as a means of undercutting the socialists or as a means of co-opting them. Politicians in power contended that welfare was a way to entice workers away from socialism and offered some of the benefits that the socialists promised.

The governments in power also considered the established church hierarchy a threat. Many of the measures adopted, especially divorce and compulsory public education, were distinctly anticlerical. In France, Alfred Naquet's anticlericalism drove him to prominence among social reformers involved in important family reform. The Vatican also played a role in spurring secular social reform. In 1891 the papal encyclical *Rerum Novarum* called Catholics to social action. Social Catholics argued that the family was the basis of society and solicited a restoration of Christian values. This could be done, they maintained, by strengthening the family through the intervention of the mother. The mother was the cement holding the family structure together, and the family was the basic block of the entire social edifice. The anticlerical governments borrowed some of the rhetoric and programs of the Catholic Church and endeavored to co-opt or undercut the established church.

Structural, social-control, and political arguments provide partial explanations for the development of the welfare state and the progression of social reform programs at the end of the nineteenth century. Social reform as a response to depopulation provides a more compelling reason for the reforms. Two social groups, the medical profession and women's organizations, were pivotal in elevating the broader issue of depopulation and the family onto the political agenda.

In the late nineteenth century, medicine was the handmaiden of the state. Doctors played a new, crucial role in politics and in setting standards of behavior. They extended their power to the realm of social problems by the creation of a new area of medical expertise that translated moral problems into technical ones.[63] Physicians became the widely noted, self-defined, and accepted "experts," using their professed knowledge of women's bodies to further their own position and programs in the political body.[64] They emphasized the "scientific" aspect of motherhood, and they desired to regulate women's sexual and reproductive lives.

In England, Germany, and Russia doctors played a particularly prominent position in recasting and developing social reform programs. In England, "because maternal and child welfare and particularly the problem of maternal mortality was treated primarily as a medical problem, the influence of the medical profession in formulating maternal and child welfare policy was particularly great."[65] In Russia physicians were instrumental in the "fight against infant mortality," and in Germany doctors and social hygienists recast moral reform as hygienic and medical reform, allowing for an expansion of the state's role in promoting public health.[66]

French physicians had enormous political power during the Third Republic, and they used the depopulation scare and ensuing debate to further their own political status.[67] The medical world formed a close alliance with the political world; doctors and many politicians were part of the same middle level of the bourgeoisie who sought expansion of social programs and of their own political and social power. Their interests in depopulation led to their legislative interests in gendered social reforms. Doctors served on parliamentary committees devoted to health, reproductive, and social issues out of proportion even to their high numbers in the National Assembly. Furthermore, they were outstandingly effective propagandists and legislators on gendered social and health reforms.[68] Their political power in France was linked to the strength of the anticlerical movement and the depopulation discussion. The medicalization of the depopulation debate enhanced physicians' power, forging a strong link between medicine, morality, justice, and notions of the French state.

In no other country was the national political power of physicians as strong. In 1902, a year in which the French assembly debated much legislation linked to depopulation, thirty-three doctors sat in the French National Assembly. At that time, there were only eleven doctors in the British House of Commons, six in the German Reichstag, and two in the United States Congress.[69] Physicians also achieved prominence on departmental and municipal councils and were replacing the clergy in authority. Georges Clemenceau, the most famous anticlerical doctor-politician, began his career on the local level as mayor of Montmartre and then rose to national prominence. Foucault's prescient analysis pointed out that doctors were the new confessors, replacing the church confessors.[70] Medical men held the health of future generations and the regulation of motherhood for the nation's health in top priority.

Doctors were only one segment of a new breed of men at the helm. The French government consisted of new politicians from a different social milieu—the *nouvelles couches sociales*. They were generally young professional men, doctors, and *arrivistes* who came to power with a new idea of the responsibilities and duties of the state. In France, the republican solidarist philosophy combined economic immobility with active policies toward women and children. Women were not full citizens, and therefore liberal republicans did not have to acknowledge a contradiction in their laissez-faire philosophy; laissez faire applied to citizens, and so there was nothing amiss in intervening in women's lives. By the same token, male children were future citizens whose rights the government sought to protect. Women, as noncitizens, did not have "rights" to protect, but their lives had to be regulated when the "rights" of future citizens came into question. The republicans used ideas of family values to support their conception of male citizenship. More important, they redefined citizenship for women as entailing the responsibility of maternity and breast-feeding (as forms of military service and suffrage) but without the rights inherent in men's citizenship. Women's bodies became part and parcel of the body politic.

In other countries as well as in France, a type of solidarist ideology arose based on the premise that the state was responsible for the health of its population. Thane posits a solidarist change from "individualism" to "collectivism" in Britain whereby state collectivism would supplement and reinforce self-help, philanthropy, and the duty to work. Furthermore, the British Fabians, intellectuals seeking reforms for the working class, represented a *nouvelle couche sociale* (newly important social group).[71] The German idea of the "great social household" was similar to the French notion of solidarism. And in the United States, the Progressives in power resembled to some extent the French solidarists. The American liberal tradition that eschewed government intervention in the lives of the poor and of women gave way to "republican civil virtue, as well as feminine ideals of 'social housekeeping' as alternative sources of legitimation for public social provision."[72] Yet the decline of liberalism, in the United States, England, or France, is not a sufficiently adequate explanation for modern social reform. As these essays on France have shown, liberalism itself could be reworked and become more nuanced to allow for government intervention if necessary.

These new politicians helped redefine the state and its relationship with women around the turn of the century. Under their leadership, the state was to institute social reforms to encourage their ideals of maternal behavior and model motherhood. In the Third Republic, motherhood was a woman's patriotic "natural" duty to the state which she must perform for "the grandeur of France."[73] Germany also had a concept of motherhood in the service of the state; women's duty was to prevent infant mortality as well as to bear and raise future workers and soldiers. The state stepped in to reinforce its norms; it sought ways to protect its patriarchal authority. The welfare state substituted the state patriarchy for the family patriarchy in families lacking a male head of household.[74]

Women themselves were not passive, either as welfare clients or advocates. To a large extent feminist and women's movements, even when women could not vote, became involved in public policy formulation and implementation. These women's groups helped instigate social programs for children and mothers by shaping public opinion and influencing legislators. As middle-class women increasingly entered the public arena in the last decades of the nineteenth century, motherhood became the center of their discourse. They championed the cause of motherhood as a "national duty" worthy of state support and a "mother's wage." Radical and moderate women alike in almost every country repeated the slogan that "motherhood is a social function." This concept meant not merely that women should become biological mothers, but it also implied that all women, whether or not they were biological mothers, should exhibit "spiritual motherhood" and be caring and nurturing people as philanthropists, in occupations such as teachers, health care workers, or inspectresses.[75]

Middle-class American women formed important gender-based associations that helped shape social welfare in the Progressive Era. Working toward moral and social goals, they launched the drive for social reform between 1890 and 1920. These women's groups formed alliances through local networks that spread across the nation; they also formed alliances with male reformist professionals to effect their programs for women workers, mothers, and children. The National Congress of Mothers and the General Federation of Women's Clubs petitioned for reforms in institutions for women, including factories, and pressed for legislation providing widows' pensions in the years before the First World War. In 1912 professional, reform-minded women addressed the needs of all American mothers and children (especially the poor), established and staffed the Children's Bureau, and successfully pioneered a drive for an explicit federal social welfare program for mothers and children. The 1921 Sheppard-Towner Act, promoted by associated women's organizations, incorporated a female vision of preventive health care; it "extended what was once domestic action into a new understanding of governmental action for societal welfare."[76] The legislation did not simply reflect a male state.

Maternalist legislation succeeded, according to Skocpol, because women had gender self-consciousness and a high degree of social organization and could mobilize to make demands for themselves and for other women. They projected "maternal values . . . from homes and local communities onto the agendas of state and national politics." Skocpol shows that "clubwomen made the transition from cultural to reform activities not by abandoning the Victorian conception of women's special domestic sphere but by extending it into what came to be called 'municipal housekeeping.' " The "cult of true womanhood" and the rhetoric of motherhood as a social function played in Peoria as well as in Washington and Paris. It appealed to the idea that women were selfless and concerned with family morality.[77] Yet maternalism had its limits, even in the United States beginning in the 1920s, especially between the termination of the Sheppard-Towner Act in 1929 and the inclusion of women under Title 5 of the 1935 Social Security Act. Many organizations became paralyzed; others splintered and became ineffective. Yet others lost their organization and authority to the domination of the male state and government bureaucracies.[78]

Women's activities help explain the rise of the welfare state in western Europe to a lesser extent than in the United States. In Europe, women became involved in issues of gendered social reform for many of the same reasons as the men: they wanted to strengthen the family and stem depopulation. They also saw their strength as women emanating from their duties in the home and as mothers. Their support of the male politicians' family-oriented agendas enhanced their own effectiveness. When they opposed the male political agenda, such as in the area of regulations of women in the labor force or in their advocacy of family limitation, women's words and actions often came to naught. The involvement of women as reform advocates and implementers does not make the European welfare state any less of a male state legislating in its own interest. The state's interests, however, were often the avowed interests of diverse women's groups. The interests of feminists and female philanthropists need not be mutually exclusive from those of male politicians.

Habermas's definition of the civil society as a sphere of interaction between social groups, economic institutions, and the state includes the "intimate sphere" of family life, forms of public communication, and voluntary associations.[79] A gendered civil society existed in most of the European countries and participated in the endeavors leading to gendered social reforms and the entry of women into public state positions. Women's illustrious roles in philanthropies and civil society empowered them and gave rise to women as inspectresses, as directors of institutions for women, and as prominent members of governing boards of charity and welfare societies. Women, active as paid inspectresses or in their voluntary organizations, bridged the gap between civil society and the more formal politics of the public sphere. They lobbied as pressure groups, or political action committees, spurring social reform in the intimate sphere of the family.

Middle-class women's organizations, instrumental in providing women with the means to enter the public sphere, also provided them with the practice and networks to reach poor and working-class women. French, British, German, and Russian women's groups supported many of the national policies for less fortunate mothers. As part of their "spiritual motherhood," or *devoirs*, they defended maternity leaves, divorce, protection for women and children, and especially child-care facilities.[80] In England as well as in France and Germany, women's groups, whether feminist, maternalist, or a combination, "found it impossible to separate the need for personal health services from the broader social and economic issues raised by maternal and child welfare." Groups such as the Women's Cooperative Guild took the lead in developing programs to educate mothers in methods of efficient, "scientific," hygienic infant care. They spearheaded the struggle to obtain maternity benefits as part of the 1911 National Health Insurance Scheme (albeit almost twenty years after France's male-sponsored 1893 legislation).[81] In Germany, feminists and maternalists made child rearing "an important public issue, vital to the well-being of the state. Therefore, the maternal role, whether conceived as biological or social, provided a basis for the entrance of women themselves into public life as speakers and actors." [82] Child care as a profession and instructing other women about motherhood became part of the feminist agenda for professional opportunities for women in all countries. Extolling the virtues and social importance of motherhood allowed female participation in the public world, muting the difference between public and private. Politically active women in France, however, had limited autonomy and roles in public policy formulation. What influence they did exert was on male republican politicians such as Strauss, Dron, Naquet, Waddington, and others.

Conclusion

These explanations amount to a shift in national values and political philosophies. The concept of national values, however, is necessarily vague. It is difficult to demonstrate "exactly how cultural values, intellectual traditions, and ideological outlooks have concretely influenced processes of political conflict and policy debate." [83] It is equally difficult to prove that a complex, integrated system of values held sway and that these cultural codes were primarily responsible for the development of social reform. The system of values in the arena of social reform involved a mixture of consternation over depopulation and national degeneration, nationalism, international competition, economic dislocation and depression, dread of worker unrest, new concepts of womanhood, and a host of other political, social, and economic anxieties surrounding the turn of the century. The mix depended on the particular country.

The cry of depopulation appears as the focal point for a myriad of national cultural values emerging in many Western countries at the turn of the century. The lament may have been most mournful in France because the French felt the population decline earliest and most acutely. Bemoaning national depopulation was also a political and nationalistic way to impose motherhood on women and thereby control them. The idea persisted that child rearing and breast-feeding served as moral restraints on women, keeping them from more public acts such as labor force participation or crime. If the cry of depopulation was a means to get women back into the home, it may have been louder in France because there was a much higher rate of married women's participation in the workforce there than elsewhere.

The concept of social control only partially works as a device to explain reform efforts. To succeed, reform efforts had to be accepted, at least in part by the objects of reform. Recent literature demonstrates the powerful part women and men played in generating reform and in using the reform measures in ways unintended by their authors. Groups may have had the means to resist control and limit the power of the reformers.[84] The dichotomy between the service state and the surveillance state is false; service has the potential for surveillance and vice versa. The essays in this volume point to a paucity of evidence that the reformers' primary goals were that of control.

Social and economic developments and structural crises (including the rhetoric about them) offer incomplete and inadequate explanations for why authorities chose the particular measures they did. In many respects industrial development established the need and context for welfare legislation by doing two things: it took work out of the home, and it created new spaces and roles for women. It ultimately created the leisure for maternalist activity as well as the need for "public motherhood." The social problems as well as the possibilities accompanying industrialization helped create the values underpinning welfare legislation. Yet industrialization is only a part of the picture.

Reforms would have been inconceivable without a definition or consensus on gender roles and a conception of the duties and responsibilities of the state and family. The consensus nature of social reform resulted from the need for economic and political stability and social cohesion mixed with a nationalistic fear of depopulation and a drive for survival, and with a clear role for women as mothers in the national welfare. Missing from this discussion of reasons for social reform is any serious consideration of a humanitarian impulse. Was the " 'humanitarianism' of the reformers . . . [just] 'so much incidental music,' " as Foucault says?[85] The men in this volume certainly demonstrated a humanitarian disposition, but it had mixed pragmatic national and personal goals.

This collection demonstrates the influence of demography on the change in perceptions and values that resulted in the welfare state. Obviously, it is not the only explanation. By looking at legislation for women, however, it becomes apparent that the welfare state emerged much earlier than the timing determined by previous historians, since they were focusing on men. Men are important here. Gendered political programs and power relations are part of a social system that not only includes men but in which men are some of the leading players. Although to some extent women were the catalysts setting into motion the decisions for social reform, women had to live with decisions they did not always make, decisions made for them by men.

Notes

One Gender, Social Policy, and the Formation of the Third Republic

I am deeply indebted to each of the contributors to this collection for their repeated readings of various versions of this essay and for the insights and suggestions they provided. I am especially grateful to Rachel Fuchs and Mary Lynn Stewart for the intellectual inspiration and friendship they have offered throughout this project. I also wish to thank Philippa Levine and John Merriman for their critiques and suggestions on previous drafts of this chapter.

1. See Landes 1988; Kerber 1980; Fauré 1991; Blum 1986; Sewell 1988, 105–23; Melzer and Rabine 1992; and Hunt 1992. For political theory undergirding the separation of spheres, see Elshtain 1981.

2. For example, according to Gordon Wright's assessment, the Opportunists "wasted most of their energies in what might be called France's last religious war" and failed to take any steps toward social reform and economic modernization. Radicals had little more commitment to any social and economic program. According to Alfred Cobban, only socialist pressure finally resulted in the "belated beginning of social reform" in the Waldeck-Rousseau government with the ten-hour law legislated in 1900 and implemented in 1904. See Wright 1987, 230–31, and Cobban 1981, 250. Theodore Zeldin's treatment of the Third Republic is one of the few that do note the extensive social legislation prior to World War I and points out that it is a common misconception that the Third Republic passed very little social legislation. See Zeldin, *France, 1848–1945: Politics and Anger* (1979), 301.

3. Stone 1985 and Elwitt 1986. For a more recent work on social reform and the development of the welfare state after 1870, see Mitchell 1991.

4. See, for example, Pateman 1988 and Fauré 1991. A number of excellent recent works have, however, begun to address directly the issue of gender in the Third Republic; see, for example, Berenson 1992, Nye 1993, and Roberts 1994.

5. Tilly and Scott 1978, 71.

6. A. Audiganne, *Les Populations ouvrières et les industries de la France dans le mouvement social du XIXe siècle* (Paris, 1854), 311. For other examples, see Accampo 1989, 81.

7. Tonim [Albert Monot], *La Question sociale et le congrès ouvrier de Paris: Conditions rationnelles de l'ordre économique, social et politique: État de la capacité morale et politique du prolétariat* (Paris, 1877), 105. For other descriptions of and complaints about factory conditions, see Accampo, 80–83.

8. See, for example, *Séances du Congrès ouvrier socialiste de France: Troisième session tenu à Marseille du 20 au 31 octobre 1879* (Marseilles, 1879), 82–84, 87, 97. Workers testify in these proceedings that a woman could earn thirty centimes per pair of men's trousers. An "able" worker could make four in one day, "without quitting work for one instant." A woman who interrupted her work for household chores could only make two in one day.

9. For one prominent politician's concerns, see Sharif Gemie, "Politics, Morality, and the Bourgeoisie: The Work of Paul Leroy-Beaulieu (1843–1961)," *Journal of Contemporary History* 27 (1992): 345–62.

10. For a discussion of women during the Paris Commune, see Gullickson 1991, 246–66.

11. Henri Cetty, *La Famile ouvrière en Alsace* (Rixheim, France, 1883), 74; Tilly and Scott, 102, 172.

12. Accampo, 124–30. Infant mortality rose from 122 deaths per 1,000 births in the first half of the century to 200 in the second half. The rate of children dying before their fifth year of life rose from 95 per 1,000 to 130. Stillbirths rose from 27 per 1,000 live births to 74. (Rates calculated for stillbirths, however, are not entirely accurate because stillbirths were not always properly recorded as such in the birth registers. Many of the "stillbirths" were actually infant deaths that occurred within minutes or hours of birth.) Maternal mortality more than doubled, from 7.4 maternal deaths per 1,000 births to 16.2.

13. Tilly and Scott, 172; Accampo, 63–65, 125–26. For wet-nursing, see also Fuchs 1984, chap. 6, and Sussman 1982. For the difficulty of combining work in the home with child care, see descriptions quoted in Coffin 1991, 230–70; see esp. 254.

14. Cetty, 122. See also Fuchs 1992, 219–26, and Fuchs 1984.

15. These figures come from Ronsin 1980, 14–17. See also Henri Napias, "Les Revendications ouvrières au point vue de l'hygiène," *Revue d'hygiène* 12, no. 8 (1890): 9; Fuchs 1992, 61, 251 n. 21.

16. Nye 1984. Nye provides a very detailed discussion of the scientific origins of degeneration theory and the process by which it became translated into a social theory; see esp. 119–70. See also Pick 1989. For the crucial transition from degeneration theory to eugenics, see Kevles 1985 and Schneider 1990.

17. Valentin Magnan and Paul-Maurice Le Grain, *Les Dégénérés* (Paris, 1895), 79, quoted in Nye 1984, 124.

18. Nye 1984, 143.

19. Jordanova 1989. Émile Durkheim's work exemplifies the application of the organic metaphor to social theory. Jordanova points out that the notion of societies as organisms with functionally interdependent parts was not a new concept in the

late nineteenth century but had "achieved a novel prominence and fresh inspiration from the biomedical sciences" (39). Throughout, her book stresses how the meta-phor of society as an organism and the biomedical model in general were highly gendered.

20. Joshua Cole, "Motherhood and Social Responsibility: The Infant Mortality Crisis in France, 1858–1874," paper presented at the Thirty-seventh Annual Con-ference of the Society for French Historical Studies, Vancouver, 23 March 1991. See also Rollet-Echalier 1990, 21.

21. Napias, 9–11.

22. Stewart 1989. Contrary to what modernization theorists have suggested, this legislation did not simply represent a response to the "increasing complexity of a mature industrial society," one that began with child labor laws and eventu-ally regulated men's work as well. Stewart has demonstrated that this legislation directed toward women had a logic of its own and cannot simply be treated as part of a continuum that resulted in the welfare state. Gender-specific legislation, she argues, reinforced and further created a dual labor market that privileged men and restricted women to lower-paying jobs. She and other scholars have pointed out that such legislation tended to regulate women's reproductive as well as their pro-ductive lives. It applied to women regardless of whether they ever became mothers and thus defined all women as potential mothers. Furthermore, such legislation, by reducing economic opportunities open to women, intensified their economic dependency and thus reinforced and perpetuated patriarchy.

23. See Linda Gordon, "The New Feminist Scholarship in the Welfare State," in Gordon 1990, 18, and Marshall 1965.

24. Jacques Donzelot, "The Promotion of the Social," *Economy and Society* 17 (August 1988): 404. This article is also a chapter in Donzelot 1984.

25. Ewald 1986, 25.

26. Riley 1988, 50. See also Gordon, "New Feminist Scholarship."

27. On individual rights as a male construction, dependent on female subordi-nation, see Pateman 1988. It is interesting to note that outside France, and especially in the United States, reproduction remained more of a private than public concern. Linda Gordon notes how the private nature of reproduction has disadvantaged women in the United States: "With respect to welfare, the ideology of the private-ness of reproduction is itself an influence, and one disadvantageous to those who do reproductive work, for it undermines their formation of a sense of entitlement to public help" ("New Feminist Scholarship," 20).

28. Discussions about virtue permeate Rousseau's writings, but the most direct commentary about its gendered nature is in Jean-Jacques Rosseau, *Émile*, trans. Barbara Foxley (London: J. M. Dent & Sons, 1989). For further elaboration, see Mary Wollstonecraft's response to Rousseau in *A Vindication of the Rights of Woman* (New York: W. W. Norton & Co., 1988); Elshtain, chap. 4; Schwartz 1984; Blum; and Landes. Landes elaborates that women and children in Rousseau's

discourse are "yoked to a conservative and ultimately passive function—that of the state. Woman's duty consists of subordinating her independent aims and interests to a higher goal, the ethical life of the community" (69).

29. Landes, 69.

30. Quoted in Blum, 213. This crucial juncture in the French Revolution when Jacobins excluded women from political activity has received considerable attention in recent scholarship. See, for example, Sewell, Landes, Melzer and Rabine, and Hunt.

31. Linda Kerber in *Women of the Republic* first used this term with reference to women in the United States who, in the early stages of the American republic, felt an acute need to fashion a meaningful role for themselves. The notion, according to Kerber, developed as the result of a search "for a political context in which private female virtues might comfortably co-exist with the civic virtue that was widely regarded as the cement of the Republic. . . . The mother, and not the masses, came to be seen as the custodian of civic morality" (11). Kerber, while pointing out that historians cannot determine with precision whether women claimed this role for themselves or whether it was assigned to them, suggests that women did create it, and they "integrated these expectations into their own understanding of what a mother ought to do" (11). Although she does not label it as such, Mary Wollstonecraft advocates "republican motherhood" when she stresses in her response to Rousseau the civic responsibilities motherhood entailed and therefore the political rights women should have; see her *Vindication of the Rights of Woman*. Some women in the French Revolution proclaimed their adherence to the ideals of republican motherhood. See Desan 1992, 11–35.

32. Landes, 271.

33. Pope 1977, 296–324. For further discussion of separate spheres and the influence of Rousseau through the nineteenth century, see, for example, Jordanova.

34. Smith 1981.

35. Clark 1984, 68.

36. On solidarism, see Stone 1985; Elwitt 1986; Zeldin, *France, 1848–1945: Politics of Anger*, 276–318; and Donzelot 1984.

37. Elwitt 1986, 74.

38. Elwitt 1986, 73.

39. Ellis 1990, 180. For the influence of physicians and their gendered perspective, see also Harris 1989.

40. Ellis, 236.   41. Elwitt 1986, 147.

42. See Stone, below.   43. See McBride, below.

44. See Stewart, below.

45. See Joan Scott, " 'L'Ouvrière! Mot impie, sordide . . .': Women Workers in the Discourse of French Political Economy, 1840–1860," in Scott 1988, 139–63. See also Fuchs 1992.

46. Jensen 1989, 251, 257. See also Lehrer 1987. For more recent work on the

development of the welfare state, see Skocpol 1992 and Koven and Michel 1993. For a comparative perspective, see Chapter 7 in this volume.

47. See Clark, below.

48. Koven and Michel 1990, 1099.

49. Offen 1984, 648–76. For another example of women's successful efforts to circumvent attempts to regulate their lives and impose a state-conceived form of gender behavior, see Sharif Gemie, "Docility, Zeal, and Rebellion: Culture and Sub-Cultures in French Women's Teacher Training Colleges, c.1860–c.1910," *European History Quarterly* 24 (1994): 213–44.

50. Perrot 1976, 105–22. See also Seccombe 1986, 53–75, and Magraw 1992, 61–71.

51. *Séances du Congrès ouvrier de France: Session de 1876 tenue à Paris du 2 au 10 octobre* (Paris, 1877), 104.

52. *Séances du Congrès ouvrier socialiste de France: Troisième session,* 31.

53. Ibid., 35.

54. Ibid., 23–25.

55. Tonim, 7–10, 30; *Séances du Congrès ouvrier de France: Session de 1876,* 99.

56. Guesdists and other socialists (although not all) supported women's rights in the 1880s, but the Section française de l'internationale ouvrière (SFIO) remained largely indifferent, if not hostile, to women's rights until the years prior to World War I when the Confédération générale du travail (CGT) tried actively to recruit women. See Hilden 1986 and Sowerwine 1982.

57. The most comprehensive treatment of the French neo-Malthusian movement is Ronsin. See also Roger-H. Guerrand, *La Libre maternité* (Paris: Casterman, n.d.). These works, however, do not explore the gender implications of the movement. Most interesting for their ability to break gender stereotypes were the women involved in neo-Malthusianism, such as Nelly Roussel and Madeleine Pelletier, each of whom published numerous books, pamphlets, and newspaper articles on feminism, birth control, and related subjects. See, for example, Nelly Roussel, *L'Éternelle Sacrifiée,* preface, notes, and commentary by Daniel Armogathe and Maité Albistur (Paris: Syros, 1979); Cova 1992, 663–72; Felicia Gordon 1990; and Sowerwine and Maignien 1992.

58. Pateman (1988) explains that the very moves to extend full individuality to women carried within them the paradox that individuality itself had been constructed to mean men: "Women are not incorporated as 'individuals' [into civil society] but as women, which, in the story of the original contract, means as natural subordinates (slaves are property). The original contract can be upheld, and men can receive acknowledgment of their patriarchal right, only if women's subjection is secured in civil society" (181).

Two   The Republican Brotherhood

Research for this essay was made possible by support from the Faculty Research Support Fund of Western Michigan University and from the Burnham-Macmillan Research Fund of the History Department of Western Michigan University.

1. Hanley 1989, 4–27, Fox-Genovese 1983 and Hunt 1992.

2. Louis de Bonald, *Du Divorce considéré au XIXe siècle* (Paris, 1818), 182.

3. Eugène Pelletan, *La Femme au dix-neuvième siècle* (Paris, 1869), 29.

4. These two quotes support Carole Pateman's incisive analysis demonstrating the shift from traditional patriarchal theories of the state and family to those of the contract theorists. Locke and Rousseau dissociated paternal and political rule, making political rule the exclusive creation of the fraternal contract. See especially "The Fraternal Social Contract," in Pateman 1989, 36. Since Pateman's main concern in these excellent essays is to demonstrate the patriarchal character of liberalism, she devotes less attention to the increasing dissatisfaction with liberal theory after 1850. Eugène Pelletan's metaphor indicates that many nineteenth-century social commentators were no longer content with the sharp distinction between domestic and public realms. See also " 'The Disorder of Women': Women, Love, and the Sense of Justice" and "Feminist Critiques of the Public/Private Dichotomy," in Pateman 1989.

5. Sewell 1988, and Pateman 1989, 35.

6. See especially Daumier's 1848 painting of the seated female Republic breast-feeding two muscular infants, frontispiece.

7. Archives de la Préfecture de police, Ba 1216.

8. Blum 1986, 122–23.

9. Pateman 1989, 19–21.

10. Georges Clemenceau, Camille Pelletan, and Alfred Naquet were three examples of sons of actively republican fathers.

11. Camille Pelletan, "Mémoires inédites," in Paul Baquiast, "Camille Pelletan (1846–1915): Esquisse de biographie," Mémoire de maîtrise d'histoire, Université de Paris IV, 1986, 219, 249; Bell and Offen 1983, 1:335.

12. Auguste Vacquerie, lead article, *Le Rappel*, 12 February 1874. Michelet's obituary, *Le Rappel*, 11 February 1874.

13. Jules Michelet, *Le Peuple* (Paris, 1846; reprint, Paris: Flammarion, 1974); see especially chapter on love and marriage. Jules Michelet, *Le Prêtre, la femme et la famille: Les Jésuites* (Paris, 1845).

14. Jules Michelet, *La Femme*, 3d ed. (Paris, 1860), 23. This parallels literary portraits of the period, especially those of Flaubert.

15. Ibid., 53 and title of chap. 4. Given Michelet's descriptions of women's situations, an equally logical conclusion might have been that women could not live *with* men.

16. For Michelet's adoration of the child, see ibid., 67, and for the cult of maternity, see 96, 104, 121.

17. Ibid., 68.

18. Ibid., 120.

19. Blum, 45–47.

20. Michelet, *La Femme*, 118, 268. One might ask why must people be trained to do what is natural.

21. The painting, *The Intoxication of Charity* by Andreo del Sarto, was in the Louvre. Ibid., 186–89.

22. Ibid., 359–63.

23. Michelet, *Le Peuple*, 208.

24. Michelet, *La Femme*, preface; this might be a specific reference to Flaubert's *Madame Bovary*, which had been brought to court a few years earlier on charges of encouraging adultery.

25. Ibid., 68–69.

26. Michelet, *Le Peuple*, 209.

27. Michelet, *La Femme*, 356–57.

28. Offen 1987, 144–58, and Bell and Offen, 1:335, 342–49; see also Zeldin, *France, 1848–1945: Ambition and Love* (1979), 293.

29. Quoted in Bell and Offen, 1:343.

30. In the mid-twentieth century standard French literature manuals identified Hugo as "la plus grande figure littéraire du dix-neuvième siècle." Castex and Surer 1950, 65. See also the major biography, Maurois 1954. Hugo's power can also be measured by the intensity of his critics in the early twentieth century; see Ionesco 1982.

31. Camille Pelletan, in a study of Hugo's political life, identified his republicanism with his *"l'age d'homme."* His earlier royalism was attributed to his mother's influence on a youthful Hugo. *Victor Hugo: L'Homme politique* (Paris: Librairie Paul Ollendorff, 1907), 62; see also Maurois, 339–81.

32. In 1881 the Republic officially celebrated Hugo's eightieth birthday, and at his death in 1885 Hugo received an official state funeral. This funeral inaugurated the reopened and newly secularized Pantheon, dedicated, as it had been during the Revolution, to the "Great Men of the Nation."

33. Hugo had been working on the manuscript since the 1840s, and the essential narrative had been completed before his exile, but important and lengthy passages were added during the 1850s. Pelletan, *Victor Hugo*, 270.

34. Pelletan, "Mémoires inédites," 266, and *Victor Hugo*, 284.

35. The passage seems an attempt to present the novelist's credentials as a recorder of political violence, to legitimate Hugo as a veteran of republican political struggles, and to explain the fundamental dilemmas of the short-lived Second Republic. Victor Hugo, *Les Misérables* (Paris, 1862; reprint, Paris: Livre de Poche, 1972), 3:223–24.

36. Ibid., 3:170.

37. Ibid., 2:407–8.

38. Throughout the novel the Thénardiers represented this counterfamily that

progressed from being in difficult circumstances, to a family of child abusers, crimi-
nals, and degenerates, to one in which parents sell and ultimately kill their own
children. By the end of the novel the surviving Thénardier *père* has fled to the United
States to become a slave dealer. Ibid., 3:524 and passim.

39. Ibid., 3:257.   40. Ibid., 3:260.

41. Ibid., 3:528.   42. Ibid., 3:468–70, 525–26.

43. Victor Hugo's 1853 collection of poems, *Les Chatiments*, had taught "a new
generation . . . to identify the idea of the imperial regime with shame, crime and
blood. A deep gap had opened between the youth and the government." Pelletan,
Victor Hugo, 258.

44. *Le Rappel*, 2 May 1869.

45. *Le Rappel*, 17 May 1869. The article from which these specific examples are
drawn covered Eugène Pelletan's electoral campaign.

46. Quoted in Moses 1984, 149. One wonders if Hugo recalled this funeral oration, when in 1869 he told the editors of *Le Rappel* that the nineteenth century was
the century of "L'HOMME."

47. Auguste Vacquerie, "Les Droits de la femme," *Le Rappel*, 11 May 1871.

48. Edouard Petit, *Eugène Pelletan, 1813–1884: L'Homme et l'oeuvre d'après
des documents inédits* (Paris: Aristide Quillet, 1913). Pelletan, "Mémoires inédites,"
294–95.

49. Petit, 173.

50. Archives de la Préfecture de police, Ba 1216.

51. Ernest Alfred Vizetelly, *Paris and Her People under the Third Republic*
(1919: reprint, New York: Kraus, 1971), 205.

52. Archives de la Préfecture de police, Ba 1216.

53. Eugène Pelletan, *La Nouvelle Babylone* (Paris, 1862), 364.

54. Auspitz 1982, 31.   55. Pelletan, *La Nouvelle Babylone*, 330.

56. Ibid., 23.   57. Ibid., 105–11.

58. Ibid., 299; emphasis added.

59. Eugène Pelletan, *La Charte au foyer* (Paris, 1864), 20–22.

60. Eugène Pelletan, *La Famille: La Mère* (Paris, 1865), 303.

61. Ibid., 312, 315, 327, 335.

62. Pelletan, *La Femme au dix-neuvième siècle*, 21.

63. Ibid., 31.

64. Camille Pelletan, *Questions d'histoire: Le Comité central et la Commune*
(Paris, 1879), 184–86.

65. Ibid., 166.

66. Camille Pelletan, *La Semaine de Mai* (Paris, 1880), 405.

67. Bonnie G. Smith's rich and intriguing *Ladies of the Leisure Class* (1981)
demonstrates this without question for the Nord and suggests the same for all
of France. Further, Robert Nye establishes the centrality of a powerful masculine
identity for the Parisian elite of the Third Republic in his important study *Mascu-*

linity and Male Codes of Honor in Modern France (1993), 48–49, 58–59. Edward Berenson also explores the crisis of this gender system in *The Trial of Madame Caillaux* (1992), 106–9, 115–17.

68. The group was originally organized in 1895 by Clovis Hugues, independent socialist from Marseilles. Originally it had thirty-six members. After becoming inactive, it was reorganized in 1906 with ninety-six members; by 1910 it had two hundred. Hause with Kenney 1984, 90.

69. There is some evidence that Pelletan may not have been as "liberated" as his free union suggested. In a 1985 interview Pelletan's niece by marriage claimed, "My uncle did not marry her because he felt she would not carry the name of Pelletan in as dignified a manner as he would like. She really was quite a character [très originale]." Baquiast, 372.

70. Pelletan, "Mémoires inédites," 328–33; Fantin-Latour's painting *Coin de table* (Musée d'Orsay, Paris) portrays Pelletan's poets' circle of 1871, which included Verlaine and Rimbaud.

71. Nye 1993, 128–31, 155, 191, 187. See also McMillan 1981, 85.

72. Pelletan, "Mémoires inédites," 332. Valade was a minor poet who had a small reputation as a "translator" of Heine and who earned his living as an administrator in the Paris municipal government.

73. Nye 1993, 217, 225–26.

74. Offen 1984, 648–76. This important article demonstrates the increasing significance of this issue for feminists and antifeminists during the Third Republic.

75. Paul Deschanel, "Les Conditions du travail et le collectivisme," *Revue politique et parlementaire* 10 (1896): 7.

76. Stewart 1983 and her important *Women, Work, and the French State* (1989).

77. Paul Pic, *Traité élémentaire de législation industrielle: Les Lois ouvrières*, 2d ed. (Paris: Arthur Rousseau, 1903), 503.

78. Stewart (1989) has ably identified these underlying causes, 98, 196–97.

79. Pateman, "Fraternal Social Contract," 36, 43.

80. Léon Bourgeois, "Réunion sur l'éducation sociale," May 1897, in *La Politique de la Prévoyance sociale: La Doctrine et la méthode* (Paris: Charpentier, 1914), 1:68.

81. Bourgeois speech in the Chamber of Deputies, 1912, in *La Politique de la Prévoyance sociale*, 1:244. See also his "Discours de l'Alliance d'hygiène," October 1910, in ibid., 96–97.

82. Bourgeois speech in Senate, 1912, ibid., 240–41, 378.

83. Bourgeois, *Solidarité*, 2d ed. (Paris, 1897), 109.

84. Report of the Chamber's Committee on Labor on ten-hour legislation, Assemblée nationale, Chambre des députés, Documents, se, 11 December 1899, 341.

85. Chambre des députés, Débats, 15 June 1896, 254.

86. Stone 1985, 123–34; Stewart 1989, 119, chap. 5.

87. Moses, 197–200.   88. Clark 1984.

89. Hause with Kenney, 18.   90. Moch 1988.

91. Smith, 94, 113.

92. Drumont's antirepublican and anti-Semitic *Libre parole* endorsed suffrage from 1906 to 1914. In 1919 a significant portion of conservative and right-wing deputies voted for women's suffrage. Hause with Kenney, 226.

93. Smith, 116–17, 120.

94. Archives nationale, F7 12541, report on political activities, April–May 1902.

95. Ibid. For a description of the founding of this clerical women's group, see Odile Sarti, *The Ligue Patriotique des Françaises, 1902–1933: A Feminine Response to the Secularization of France* (New York: Garland Press, 1984).

96. Compte rendu du septième congrès annuel du Parti républicain radical et radical-socialiste, Nancy, 1907, Programme du parti.

97. This was the third bill addressing women's suffrage which had been sent to the committee and the only one reported on in committee. While the Radicals had promised the suffrage organizations support, they had explained that no general debate could occur until after the difficult issue of proportional representation was decided. Hause 1987, 172–76, 190.

98. Not surprisingly, Buisson contributed the preface to Edouard Petit's 1913 biography of Eugène Pelletan.

99. Ferdinand Buisson, *Le Vote des femmes* (Paris: H. Dunod et E. Pinat, 1911), 19. Buisson was here specifically referring to Condorcet.

100. Ibid., 36.

101. Ibid., 306–8.

102. Ibid., 15.

103. Jenny P. d'Héricourt, *A Woman's Philosophy of Woman* (1860), quoted in Offen and Bell, 1:345–47.

104. Stewart 1989, 156–57, 201–2, and passim.

105. Offen (1984, 1986) discusses the impact of domesticity on feminism itself and argues persuasively for the existence of a familial feminism in France.

Three   Divorce and the Republican Family

1. Naquet to Elisée Reclus, 26 January 1899, Bibliothèque nationale, Nouvelles acquisitions françaises (hereafter cited as BN NAF) 22.914.

2. Alfred Naquet, *Autobiographie*, ed. Emile Pilias (Paris: Librairie du Recueil Sirey, 1939), 3.

3. Alfred Naquet, *La Loi du divorce* (Paris: Charpentier, 1903), 77–78.

4. Alfred Naquet, *Religion, propriété, famille*, 2d ed. (Paris, 1869), 310.

5. Ibid., 281.

6. On the early feminists and Fourier's critique of marriage, see Bidelman 1982, 52.

7. Lorulot 1934, 10.

8. The Civil Code restricted divorce to four specified grounds and allowed divorce by mutual consent only in limited circumstances; divorce was not permitted in the marriage's first two years and not if the wife was over 45 years old, and it was granted only if the parents deposited half of their property in trust for the children of the dissolved marriage.

9. Quoted in Manfred Simon, "Divorce in French Law," *Juridical Review* 57 (April 1945): 18–33.

10. Alfred Naquet, *Le Divorce*, 2d ed. (Paris, 1881), 6; Desforges 1954, 107.

11. Léon Richer promoted divorce as part of his campaign for women's civil liberties; see Richer, *Le Divorce: Projet de loi* (Paris, 1874). Émile Acollas had organized the Ligue de la paix et de la liberté with Naquet in 1867 and later wrote a book on the reform of marriage, *Le Mariage, son passé, son présent, son avenir* (Paris, 1880).

12. Naquet, *La Loi du divorce*, 8.   13. Naquet, *Autobiographie*, 10.

14. Ibid., 8.   15. Elwitt 1975, 298–99.

16. Naquet, *La Loi du divorce*, xvi.

17. See Paul Strauss on Naquet, *Les Fondateurs de la République: Souvenirs* (Paris: La Renaissance du Livre, 1934), 115, 123.

18. *Annales du Sénat* (hereafter cited as *AS*), 19 June 1884, 191.

19. See William Reddy's suggestive treatment of legal separations in the period of the Restoration, "Marriage, Honor, and the Public Sphere in France: Séparations de corps, 1815–1848," *Journal of Modern History* 65 (September 1993): 437–72.

20. Boulanger to Naquet, BN NAF 23.783; Seager 1969, 180.

21. Naquet remained close to his friends from the Boulangist period such as Georges Laguerre and Alfred Laisant, who were the witnesses for his second marriage in 1903. Naquet, *Autobiographie*, 29.

22. Retired from politics at 64, Naquet continued to write, including a pamphlet-length "autobiography" up to 1887 which leaves open many questions about his political motivations and personal life.

23. Naquet, *Le Divorce*, 1.

24. *AS*, 19 June 1884, 196.

25. Chambre des députés (hereafter cited as CDD), 26 November 1881, documents appendix 141, report of Louis Marcère, 236.

26. McBride 1992, 747–68.

27. Naquet, *Le Divorce*, 14.

28. Wright 1987, 230; one critic of the Naquet law commented that it was passed not to help women but "to give the Church a slap in the face." "Divorce in France," *Spectator* 57 (7 June 1884): 738.

29. This charge was made by Charles Freppel, who was archbishop of Angers and a deputy from Finistère, *AS*, 13 June 1884, 487; Edouard Drumont, *La France juive devant l'opinion* (Paris, 1886), 45; Wilson 1982, 293.

30. *AS*, 31 May 1884, 82.

31. Paul and Victor Margueritte, "Mariage et divorce," extract from *La Revue et revue des revues* (Paris: n.p., 1900), 457.

32. Netter 1930, 169.

33. Louis Legrand, *Le Mariage et les moeurs* (Paris, 1879), 293.

34. *AS*, 31 May 1884, 76.

35. *AS*, 21 June 1884, 231–33.

36. *AS*, 31 May 1884, 76.

37. Dr. Edouard Toulouse, *Les Conflits intersexuels et sociaux* (Paris: Fasquelle, 1904), 18.

38. Michel Dussac, *Etude médico-légale sur la séparation de corps* (Paris, 1878).

39. Gustave Téry, *Les Divorcés peints par eux-mêmes* (Paris: A. Fayard, n.d.).

40. Ibid., 135–36.

41. Ibid., 145–46.

42. Louis Albanel, *Le Crime dans la famille* (Paris: J. Rueff, 1900), 27.

43. M. Yvernès, "La Justice en France de 1826 à 1880," *Annales de démographie internationale* 4 (1882): 229.

44. Louis Proal, *Le Crime et le suicide passionels* (Paris: F. Alcan, 1900), 261.

45. Ibid., 266; Louis Proal, *La Criminalité féminine* (Paris, 1890).

46. Proal, *Le Crime*, 21–22.

47. Paul Bernard, a prosecutor at Château-Thierry during the Second Empire, argued for extensive changes in separation laws as early as 1860–62. "La séparation de corps réformée," *Revue critique de législation et du jurisprudence* 17 (1860): 250–311; 20 (1862): 42–56.

48. *AS*, 23 June 1884, 263.

49. Louis de Bonald, *Du Divorce considéré au XIXe siècle* (Paris, 1818), 182.

50. CDD, 5 February 1881, 160.   51. Legrand, 231.

52. *AS*, 23 June 1884, 264–65.   53. *AS*, 29 May 1884, 53.

54. *AS*, 18 January 1887, 17.   55. CDD, 7 February 1881, 193.

56. A. de Malarce, *Les Résultats de la loi sur le divorce* (Paris, 1898), 3.

57. *AS*, 21 June 1884, 224.

58. Impotence was also not allowable as grounds for separation before 1884.

59. *AS*, 7 February 1884, documents appendix 31, report of Émile Labiche; Naquet, *La Loi du divorce*, 88–89.

60. Alfred Naquet in *L'Humanité et la patrie*, quoted in McLaren 1983, 116.

61. Naquet supported Paul Robin's Neo-Malthusian League but remained unconvinced by the arguments of the small birth control movement that family limitation would alone produce a better society. Alfred Naquet, *Le Néo-malthusisme, est-il moral?* (Paris: Edition de Génération Consciente, 1909).

62. Naquet, *Religion, propriété, famille*, 257.

63. Ibid., 268.

64. Alfred Naquet, *Vers l'union libre* (Paris: Société d'Edition et de Publications, 1908), 48.

65. Naquet, *Religion, propriété, famille*, 309.

66. Ibid., 301. 67. *AS*, 21 June 1884, 236.

68. *AS*, 23 June 1884, 251. 69. *AS*, 21 June 1884, 230.

70. CDD, 5 February 1881, 160. 71. *AS*, 27 May 1884, 42.

72. Alfred Naquet, "Divorce: From a French Point of View," *North American Review* 155 (December 1892): 727.

73. *AS*, 23 June 1884, 260.

74. Naquet, "Divorce," 728–29.

75. Émile Zola, "L'Adultère dans la bourgeoisie," in *La Femme au XIXe siècle*, ed. Nicole Prioullard (Paris: Levi and Messinger, 1983), 151.

76. Naquet, *La Loi du divorce*, 155.

77. Naquet, *Religion, propriété, famille*, 264–65.

78. Alfred Naquet, "Referendum sur l'avortement—réponses," *Chronique médicale* 16, no. 4 (15 February 1901): 117–18.

79. Dominique Vallaud, "Le Crime d'infanticide et l'indulgence des cours d'assises en France au XIXe siècle," *Information sur les sciences sociales* 21, no. 3 (1982): 475–99; Donovan 1991, 157–76.

80. Naquet, *Religion, propriété, famille*, 278; Naquet reiterated this position in *Vers l'union libre*.

81. "The Clemenceau Case," *New York World*, 14 March 1892, 1.

82. Bidelman, 240 n. 63.

83. Roderick Phillips (1988) found a precedent in prerevolutionary customary law, 160–61.

84. *AS*, 15 June 1882, 517–18; *AS*, 7 February 1884, documents appendix 31, 67; *AS*, 20 June 1884, 208; *AS*, 23 June 1884, 250.

85. *The French Civil Code*, trans. Henry Cachard (London, 1895), bk. 1, title 5, art. 230.

86. *AS*, Débats, 19 July 1884, 766.

87. *The French Civil Code*, bk. 1, title 5, art. 298; CDD, 8 May 1882, 57; CDD, 19 July 1884, 765.

88. Clark 1937, 45. 89. CDD, 7 February 1881, 201.

90. *AS*, 23 June 1884, 259. 91. Naquet, *Le Divorce*, 69–71.

92. Hause 1987, 23, 101; Moses 1984, 209.

93. Naquet, *La Loi du divorce*, 31.

94. Naquet recalled a meeting in which he was shouted down by a large group of women and concluded that priests had persuaded the women that divorce would destroy the family. Naquet, *Autobiographie*, 20.

95. Naquet, *Religion, propriété, famille*, 196–97.

96. Ibid., 206.

97. Naquet, *Le Divorce*, 69.

98. Congrès international de la condition et des droits des femmes, "Compte-rendu du séance du 8 septembre 1900," *La Fronde*, 11 September 1900; Hause with Kenney 1984, 276.

99. Bidelman, 93.

100. BN NAF 22.914.

101. Alfred Naquet, *Collectivism and the Socialism of the Liberal School*, trans. William Heaford (London, 1891), 158.

102. *AS*, 26 May 1884, 24.

103. *AS*, 6 July 1886, documents appendix 319, 213.

104. Naquet: "It was not that my ideas had changed . . . , instead I recognized the impossibility of obtaining from parliament a more radical law than that of 1803 [the Napoleonic Code]" (*Le Divorce*, 204).

105. "Divorce in France," *American Law Review* 47 (September–October 1913): 768; *Royal Commission on Divorce and Matrimonial Causes* (London: Eyre and Spottiswoode, 1912), 479–80, report of Henri Mesnil on the French law.

106. Charles Desmaze, *Le Crime et la débauche à Paris* (Paris, 1881), 266.

107. Jacques Bertillon, *Etude démographique du divorce et de la séparation de corps dans les différents pays de l'Europe* (Paris, 1883), 97; *AS*, 30 May 1884, 61; Legrand, 31.

108. *AS*, 21 June 1884, 234.   109. *AS*, 13 December 1904, 234–35.

110. *AS*, 31 May 1884, 79.   111. *AS*, Débats, 24 June 1884, 284.

112. H. Taudière, "Les Lois récentes sur le mariage et la famille," *Réforme sociale* 55 (April 1908): 400.

113. *AS*, Débats, 26 May 1884, 14.

114. Bernard, 67, 70.

115. Albert Bataille, "Une Agence tricoche," in *Les Causes criminelle et mondaines*, vol. 4 (Paris, 1883), 353–74.

116. The support of Martin-Feuillée representing the Ferry government was crucial to the passage of the Naquet bill; see *AS*, Débats, 29 May 1884, 46.

117. Quoted in Mayeur 1985, 85.

118. *AS*, Débats, 24 June 1884, 283.

119. BN NAF 22.914.

Four   The Right to Life

In finalizing this essay, I greatly appreciate the help of all the other contributors to this volume. The generosity of an Arizona State University Women's Studies Research Grant facilitated research for this chapter, and I appreciate the support.

1. Abortion was already illegal and a criminal offense. Antiabortion literature became more prevalent after 1890.

2. Ewald 1986; Hatzfeld 1971; Martin 1983; Elwitt 1986; and Stone 1985.

3. Bibliothèque nationale, Nouvelle acquisitions française (NAF) 18463 ff. 369–71, 374–77; 25003 ff. 124–26; 24639 ff. 428–29; Baguley 1973, 118–20.

4. Hervé Le Bras (1991) argues that Strauss and his political colleagues were

primarily familialists; their brand of nationalism was a "natalist nationalism" (175–88).

5. Jules Simon, *De l'initiative privée et de l'état, en matière de réformes sociales.* Conférence faite au Grand-Théatre de Bordeaux, 7 novembre 1891 (Bordeaux, 1892), 19–20. Simon and Strauss served together in the Senate and also on the Conseil supérieur de l'assistance publique in the 1890s. See Conseil supérieur de l'assistance publique (hereafter cited as CSAP), *Rapports* and *Procès verbaux* of the meetings, 1896–99. They were not noticeably in opposition on any key issues.

6. Dr. A. Balestre and A. Giletta de Saint-Joseph, *Etude sur la mortalité de première enfance dans la population urbaine de la France* (Paris: Doin, 1901). The pamphlet by Camille Rabaud, *Le Péril national ou la dépopulation croissante de la France: Le Péril, les causes, les moyens* (Paris, 1891), 13, uses striking language referring to the national peril of France and fears that a war could break out at any instant; it also notes that the low birthrate will hurt France.

7. For example, Doctors Théophile Roussel, Henri Napias, Gustave Drouineau, Paul Brouardel, and Henri Thulié were prominent either as deputies, senators, or active members of the Conseil supérieur de l'assistance publique—a national parliamentary committee. Doctor Pierre Budin and his pupil Dr. Henri de Rothschild were especially prominent in Paris politics. Ellis 1990. Strauss even titled one of his major books *The Sanitary Crusade.* See Paul Strauss, *La Croisade sanitaire* (Paris: Charpentier, 1902).

8. It is not possible to estimate the number of works on depopulation published between 1871 and 1882, but in the dozen or so published between 1882 and 1890, writers primarily established causes of the low natality and sought ways in which to remedy it. The most widely cited book of that period is Arsène Dumont, *Dépopulation et civilisation: Étude demographique* (Paris, 1890). He attributes low natality to *capilarité sociale,* that is, the theory of social mobility whereby an individual can, and seeks to, better his social position, usually by having only one child, preferably a son. The individualism of a democracy, he said, leads to depopulation. See also Dr. Picon, *Aperçu sur les principales causes de la dépopulation et de l'affaiblissement progressif de la France* (Paris, 1888), and Andre-Théodore Brochard, *Des Causes de la dépopulation en France et des moyens d'y remédier* (Lyons, 1873).

Most works on depopulation appeared after 1891. From 1891 to 1925 an estimated 120 works were published on that subject. See Bibliothèque nationale, Inventaires des matières, 1882–94 and 1894–1925. See, for example, the most widely cited and reprinted book of this period, Jacques Bertillon, *La Dépopulation de la France: Ses Consequences, ses causes, mésures à prendre pour la combattre* (Paris: Félix Alcan, 1911). To underscore the issue of depopulation, Premier René Waldeck-Rousseau established an extraparliamentary commission on depopulation in 1902. On depopulation and the question of women and nationalism, see Offen 1984, 648–76, and Karen M. Offen, "What Price Admission: The Sexual Politics of French

Nationalism from 1905 to the First World War," paper presented at the Conference on Aspects of Nationalism in France: From Boulanger to the Great War, St. John's College, Cambridge, 10–12 April 1989. For further discussion of the issue of depopulation, see Fuchs 1992, chap. 3.

9. See, for example, Picon, *Aperçu sur les principales causes de la dépopulation*, 6–7. This concern led to the passage of the 1874 Roussel law, which regulated and inspected the system of wet-nursing. See Sussman 1982, chaps. 5–7, and Fuchs 1984.

10. Becchia 1986, 201–41.

11. Jenson 1989.

12. Jacques Léonard (1981) implies that Paul Bert, Alfred Naquet, Émile Combes, Léon Gambetta, and Henri Thulié were Freemasons (273–74).

13. Henri Monod, *L'Assistance publique en France en 1889 et en 1900* (Paris: Imprimerie Nationale, 1900). Charles Gide, *La France sans enfants*. (Paris: Chez M. Léon Peyric, 1914); Rabaud, *Le Péril national*. For three excellent studies of Protestants, Freemasons, and Radical journalists, see Hause 1989; Nord 1989; and Judith F. Stone, "The Formation of a Radical Identity: Opposition Journalism, 1860s–1885," paper presented at the 103d Annual Meeting of the American Historical Association, Cincinnati, Ohio, 29 December 1989. For further discussion of Protestants and public policy in the early Third Republic, see Clark 1990; Hause 1990; and Fuchs 1990.

14. Paul Strauss, *Les Fondateurs de la République: Souvenirs* (Paris: La Renaissance du Livre, 1934). Throughout his long life Strauss maintained close social contact with other Jewish families in Paris. For a discussion of Strauss's Jewish background, see Birnbaum 1992, 105, 127.

15. Tristan Bernard, *Mémoires d'un jeune homme rangé*, préface de Gilbert Sigaux (1926; Lausanne: Société Coopérative Editions Rencontre, 1960), 8.

16. Renée Paul Strauss, *Au pays basque* (Paris: Hachette, 1906).

17. Martin de Torina, *Mère sans être éspouse: Pour la France et pour soi-même* (Paris: Chez l'Auteur, 1917), 145.

18. Strauss, *Les Fondateurs de la République*.

19. Birnbaum, 265, 394.

20. For a fascinating "decoding" of the male bourgeois nature of the Civil Code and what that meant for the idea of liberty and the treatment of women, see Arnaud 1973, ii, 66.

21. Paul Strauss, *Le Suffrage universal*, avec une préface d'Alfred Naquet (Brussels, 1878), 101, 136–37.

22. Paul Strauss, "Notre programme," *Revue philanthropique* 1 (1897): 1–8. See also his published books: *Paris ignoré* (Paris, 1892); *L'Enfance malheureuse* (Paris, 1896); *Dépopulation et puériculture* (Paris: Charpentier, 1901); *Assistance sociale, pauvres et mendiants* (Paris: Félix Alcan, 1901); *La Croisade sanitaire*; *La Loi sur la protection de la santé publique* (Paris: Jules Rousset, 1905); *Habitations*

à bon marché (Paris: Flammarion, 1907); *Le Foyer populaire* (Paris: Charpentier, 1913); and *Pour la vie et pour la santé* (Paris: Jules Tallandier, 1929).

23. For example, in 1892–93 Strauss worked to have the association of urban ambulances declared a public utility with a subvention from the state. In this activity he communicated directly with Jules Simon and showed his tact and skill in being polite, correct, and persistent. See Archives nationales (AN) 87/AP/7, Papers of Jules Simon.

24. Paul Feillet, *De l'Assistance publique à Paris*, avec une préface par M. Paul Strauss (Paris, 1888), vii.

25. *Revue philanthropique* 2 (1897–98): 112.

26. Strauss, *La Croisade sanitaire*, 41. He was a Radical belonging to the *gauche democratique*.

27. Biographical material on Strauss comes from his own *Les Fondateurs de la République* (which gives his birthdate as 1853, not 1852 as in other sources); Jolly 1960–67, 8: 3036–37; and Archives de l'Assistance publique (hereafter cited as AAP), Cérémonie à l'Institut Pasteur en l'honneur de M. Paul Strauss, 20 December 1924.

28. Paul Strauss as ministre de l'hygiène, de l'assistance et de la prévoyance sociale to the prefect of police, 8 April 1922, Archives de la Préfecture de police, Ba/381 Provisoire. I wish to thank Elinor A. Accampo for providing this source.

29. Strauss, *Dépopulation et puériculture*, 2, 6. See also Strauss, *L'Enfance malheureuse* and *Assistance sociale*.

30. Strauss, *Dépopulation et puériculture*, 245.

31. *Revue philanthropique* 2 (1897): 12.

32. Jenson 1989.

33. *L'Assistance française*, exposé général de la constitution et des résultats des divers services, établissements et oeuvres d'assistance ou de bienfaisance de la France, présenté au Congrès international de Copenhague par un groupe de membres du Comité national français des Congrès d'assistance publique privée sous la présidence du M. Emile Loubet, préface par M. Paul Strauss (Paris: n.p., 1910), preface.

34. Strauss, *L'Enfance malheureuse*, iii.

35. For amplification of these ideals of national solidarity to protect infants' "right to life," see *Revue philanthropique* 1 (1897): 2–3, and Strauss, *L'Enfance malheureuse*, vi, 46, and *La Croisade sanitaire*, 267.

36. Strauss, *Assistance sociale*, 3, 152.

37. Strauss, *La Croisade sanitaire*, 340.

38. Conseil général de la Seine, *Rapport présenté par Georges Clemenceau au nom de la 3ᵉ Commission sur le service des enfants assistés*, session of 24 November 1875.

39. Strauss, *L'Enfance malheureuse*, iii; Conseil général de la Seine, *Rapport présenté par Paul Strauss au nom de la 3ᵉ Commission sur le service des enfants as-*

sistés (1886–97; hereafter cited as Strauss, *Rapport*, and the date). See specifically the *Rapport* of 1887, p. 2.

40. *Revue philanthropique* 22 (1907–8): 400.

41. For a detailed analysis of this welfare program, see Fuchs 1992, chaps. 6 and 7.

42. For greater elaboration of the theme of children belonging to the state, see Sylvia Schafer, "The Best Interests of the Child and Parental Self-Interest: The Problem of Parenthood in the Early Third Republic," paper presented at the Thirty-seventh Annual Conference of the Society for French Historical Studies, Vancouver, 23 March 1991, and Cole 1991. See also Fuchs 1992, chaps. 3 and 7.

43. Archives de la Ville de Paris et Département de la Seine (hereafter cited as ADS), "Rapports d'inspection sur le service des enfants assistés de Paris," manuscript reports of the inspectors from 1876 to 1904.

44. Zola's fictional character Norine Moinaud in *Fécondité* also shared a small apartment with her sister. They worked at making cartons while Norine received welfare. A *dame visiteuse* came regularly. Émile Zola, *Fécondité* (1899; reprint, Paris: Fasquelle, 1957). See Émile Zola, *Fruitfulness*, translated by Ernest Vizetelly (New York: Doubleday, 1900), 380–83. See also Fuchs 1992, chap. 7.

45. ADS, *Procès verbaux*, Commission des enfants assistés, session of 30 December 1885.

46. Strauss, *Rapport* (1886), 3.   47. Ibid. (1894, 1896, 1897).
48. Ibid. (1887), 5.   49. Ibid., 12.
50. Ibid. (1888), 5.   51. Ibid. (1892), 11.
52. Ibid. (1895), 2.   53. Nye 1982, 476, 481.
54. Ibid., 481.

55. The amount of aid the women received, fifteen to twenty francs a month for up to twelve months (but usually for six months), was inadequate to compensate for their loss of time at work and the time they spent nursing their baby. They could not make ends meet without help from their parents or from a lover. Strauss and the Conseil général eventually realized this. See also Feillet, 113.

56. Strauss, *La Croisade sanitaire*, 262, and *Dépopulation and puériculture*, 95–97.

57. For more detail on the change in admissions regulations, see Fuchs 1984 and idem, "Legislation, Poverty, and Child-Abandonment in Nineteenth-Century Paris," *Journal of Interdisciplinary History* 18 (summer 1987): 55–80.

58. Feillet, 113.

59. AAP, *Rapport sur le Réfuge-ouvroir pour les femmes enceintes*, session of 29 November 1891.

60. *Revue philanthropique* 1 (1897): 950.

61. Commission de la dépopulation, Sous-commission de la mortalité. *Rapport général sur les causes de la mortalité*, présenté par Paul Strauss (Melun: Imprimerie Administrative, 1911), 9. For his support of the feminists on this issue, see Biblio-

thèque Marguerite Durand (hereafter cited as BMD), DOS 347 PAT, piece 19, "La Recherche de la paternité," in *Le Droit des femmes* (November 1912).

62. Strauss, "Bulletin," *Revue philanthropique* 26 (1909–10): 263–64; "Les Causes de la mortalité," *Revue philanthropique* 31 (1912): 97–128.

63. For a discussion of Strauss's role in the passage of the 1913 law, see Stewart 1983, 79–105.

64. For a more complete picture of the history of abandoned children in Paris and in France during the nineteenth century, see Fuchs 1984; Potash 1980; and Lynch 1988. For implementation of the Roussel law of 1874, see Sussman.

65. For the best source of the law of 1904, see Dalloz Jurisprudence Générale, *Recueil périodique et critique*, pt. 4 (Paris: Jurisprudence Générale Dalloz, 1905), 16–46.

66. CSAP, sessions of 1–3 March 1890, fasc. 31.

67. Actual facts, however, do not entirely support Strauss's contention. In most systems of counting, the numbers of abandoned children actually increased in the mid-1880s, but these numbers are suspect. It is impossible to ascertain how many of the children in this counting were the abused or neglected older children— the *moralement abandonnés*. See Fuchs 1984 and idem, "Legislation, Poverty, and Child-Abandonment."

68. CSAP, session of 1 March 1890, fasc. 31, p. 96.

69. Préfecture de la Seine and Paul Strauss, *Rapport sur un projet de réglement sanitaire* (Paris: n.p., 1902). Strauss was president of this commission named by the Préfet de la Seine. Shapiro 1985, 101–2.

70. Article 33 of that law stated, "Les femmes enceintes sont reçus pendant la dernière quinzaine de leur grossesse; elles sont admises dans les mêmes conditions que les malades auxquels elles sont assimilées. L'hospitalisation leur est assurée jusqu'á ce que le médecin ait certifié qu'elles peuvent quitter l'hôpital sans danger pour elles et pour leur enfant." Long debates ensued about whether or not fifteen days was enough. Strauss argued for fifteen days as a minimum with women being admitted up to thirty days before expected delivery. He also insisted that two beds be reserved for "*mères clandestines*." See CSAP, *Comptes rendus*, 1898, fasc. 63.

71. For further information, see Rachel G. Fuchs and Paul E. Knepper, "Women in the Paris Maternity Hospital: Public Policy in the Nineteenth Century," *Social Science History* 13, no. 2 (summer 1989): 187–209; Fuchs 1992, chaps. 1, 5, and 6.

72. Louis Marin and Paul Strauss, *La Protection de la maternité ouvrière*, speech and discussion before the Assemblée générale on 26 January 1912 (Paris: F. Alcan, 1912), 58, 75, 85.

73. Marin and Strauss, speech by Strauss, 12 January 1912, 75. For a detailed analysis of the passage of maternity leave legislation, see Stewart 1983.

74. CSAP, first session, 11 March 1897, fasc. 58.

75 CSAP, January 1890, fasc. 31.

76. See, for example, his *Rapports* and CSAP, *Procès verbaux*, 1896 to 1906, particularly the first session of 1897 on the subject of *crèches*.

77. Strauss even strongly advocated inspection of *vacheries* and both governmental supervision and inspection of all aspects of the production and distribution of milk. Commission de la dépopulation, *Rapport général sur les causes de la mortalité*, 17.

78. F. Bar, "Paul Strauss," *Puériculture* (February 1935): 288.

79. Despite his anticlericalism, faced with anti-Semitic comments in the Senate, Strauss did not hesitate to respond on the floor of that body: " 'Messieurs, je ne laisserai pas passer sans protester devant le Sénat une parole qui établit une division entre les Français, qui les distingue suivant leurs origines et leur confession religieuse.' " Quoted in Birnbaum, 109. Above all, Strauss was French.

80. Strauss, *Le Suffrage universal*, 118.

81. Paul Strauss, *Assistance aux vieillards ou infirmes privés de ressources* (Rouen, 1897), 5.

82. Ibid., 282–88.

83. CSAP, sixth session, 1898, fasc. 63.

84. *Congrès national des droits civils et du suffrage des femmes*, tenu en l'Hôtel des Sociétés Savantes à Paris les 26, 27, et 28 juin 1908. Compte rendu in extenso, recueilli, mis en ordre et publié par les soins de Mme Oddo Deflou, secrétaire générale. (Paris: Chez Mme Vincent, 1910), 2.

85. BMD, DOS 347 PAT, piece 19, *Le Droit des femmes* (November 1912): 1–8.

86. Strauss, *La Croisade sanitaire*, 41, 234, and *Assistance sociale*, 1; Stone, 87.

87. Strauss, *Dépopulation and puériculture*, 167, 251–63.

88. *Assistance sociale*, 264, 271. He did not directly say that laissez faire equals laissez mourir, but he implied it.

Five   Setting the Standards

I wish to thank all the contributors to this volume for reading and suggesting revisions to earlier versions of this essay. I am also grateful to Wendie Nelson of Langara College for her survey of Dron's and Waddington's legislative speeches on other subjects and to the Social Science and Research Council of Canada for financial support for the research in Tourcoing, Rouen, and Chartres.

1. *Journal officiel de la République française* (hereafter cited as *JO*), Lois et décrets, 3–4 November 1892 and 30–31 March 1900.

2. For example, Cross 1989.

3. The votes are recorded in *JO*, Débats, 29 March 1881, 5 February 1889, 19 December 1891, and 20 and 21 December 1899; biographical information is drawn from Robert 1891 and Jolly 1960–67.

4. Membership lists were compiled from Archives nationales (hereafter cited as AN), Procès-verbaux de Commission du Travail, C3291 for 1880, C5429 for 1885–

88, C5515 for 1889–93, and C5673 for 1898–1902; from *JO*, Débats, 19 July 1879 (Diancourt Report); and from *Annales de la Chambre des députés* (hereafter cited as *ACD*), Documents, 1895, no. 1724 (Dron Report).

5. See, for instance, *JO*, Débats, 22 and 29 March 1881, speeches by Barthe, Hugot, and Laroche-Joubert.

6. Ibid., 10 and 19 June 1888.

7. For instance, Millerand and Prudent-Dervilliers speeches in ibid., 15 June 1888 and 12 June 1896.

8. See Judith F. Stone, "The Republican Brotherhood: Gender and Ideology," in this volume.

9. Electoral appeals in Archives départementales de Seine-Maritime (hereafter cited as ADSM), 3M301, and *L'Avenir de Roubaix-Tourcoing*, 25 July and 20 September 1889; see also *Le Petit Rouennais*, 26 January, 4 February and 22 March 1891.

10. Waddington speech in *Annales du Sénat* (hereafter cited as *AS*), Débats, 28 March 1892, and Dron speech in *JO*, Débats, 8 July 1890 and 26 June 1896.

11. *Discours . . . relative à l'établissement du tarif général des douanes* (Paris, 1880), *Discours . . . loi portant modification du tarif général des douanes* (Paris, 1885), and *Discours . . . nouveau tarif de chemins de fer* (Paris, 1886).

12. ADSM, 3M306. See especially the poster for 1881 and *Le Petit Rouennais*, 1, 5, and 19 January 1891.

13. Archives départementales du Nord (hereafter cited as ADN), M37–26, M37–33, M37–47, and M37–59, legislative elections of 1889, 1893, 1898, and 1902. See also C. Kuhn, "1880: Le Docteur Dron arrivait à Tourcoing," *Nord Eclair*, 17–18 August 1980.

14. Baker 1967 and Ameye 1963, 28–37.

15. Woshinsky 1973.

16. *JO*, Débats, 19 June 1888 and 5 February 1889, and AN, C5515, 19 March 1893. See also Linda L. Clark, "Bringing Feminine Qualities into the Public Sphere: The Third Republic's Appointment of Women Inspectors," in this volume.

17. Conseil supérieur du travail, *Rapports sur l'application . . . des lois réglementant le travail* (Paris: Imprimerie Nationale, 1895–1913).

18. See, for example, AN, C7414, 4 September 1906.

19. The departments of all deputies voting for standards in roll call votes from 1881 through 1891 were checked for the proportion of the active population in industry in Bouvier et al. 1979.

20. *AS*, Débats, 23 February 1882.

21. See, for instance, *AS*, Documents, 1889, no. 182 (Ferry Report), and *AS*, Débats, 4–5 July and 26–28 November 1889.

22. D. Lenoir, *Notice nécrologique sur M. R. Waddington* (Rouen: Société Libre d'Émulation du Commerce et de l'Industrie de la Seine-Inférieure, 1913), 4, 25; Musée sociale, Institutions patronales, Waddington fils et Cie., 1889; and

Archives départementales de l'Eure et Loir (hereafter cited as ADEL), J603, Exposition de Roubaix 1911 and Exposition de 1900.

23. Chaline 1982, 153–54.

24. Smith 1981. Ewald (1986) makes the distinction between social economy and social insurance schemes.

25. Musée sociale, Institutions patronales, Waddington fils et Cie., 1889, and ADEL, J603, Exposition de Roubaix 1911, and J600, Etablissements Waddington fils et Cie.

26. AN, F22 445, Enquête du Service d'inspection, 1905.

27. Waddington offered the explanation about specialization and protection from competition in *AS*, Débats, 28 March 1892, 355.

28. P. T. Moon, *The Labor Problem and the Social Catholic Movement in France* (New York: Macmillan, 1921), 113–19.

29. Berch 1976.

30. M. Waddington, *My First Years as a Frenchwoman* (New York: Scribners, 1914).

31. Chaline, 325–27, and Delescluze 1985, 179–80, 184, 188, 374.

32. ADSM, 6 A1P 12, Sessions du Conseil général, 16 April 1885 and 21 August 1890.

33. See Rachel G. Fuchs, "The Right to Life: Paul Strauss and the Politics of Motherhood," in this volume.

34. *Le Petit Rouennais*, 17 and 20 April and 6 June 1891; 2 and 9 July and 10 August 1892.

35. AN, C3291, 19 March 1880, and C5429, 9, 23, and 25 March, 25 May and 8 June 1887.

36. *ACD*, Documents, 1887, no. 2204, 731–42, and *JO*, Débats, 3, 10, and 12 June 1888 (Passy and Andrieux speeches).

37. Cross, 61–63, 105–11.

38. *JO*, Débats, 23 and 30 March 1881.

39. See Hause 1990 and Fuchs 1990.

40. G. Lange, *In Memorium: Richard Waddington: Discours prononcé au temple St. Aloi* (Rouen: n.p., 1913), and *Richard Waddington, 1838–1918* (Rouen: n.p., 1914) in ADEL, J607.

41. Chaline, 303–5, 325.

42. ADSM, 14J54–55, Société des amis des pauvres, and 2XP 284, Bureau de bienfaisance de Saint-Léger-de-Darnétal.

43. Ibid., 14J39–42, Société des dames protestantes, and 3XP 212–13, Société des dames de la maternité de Darnétal.

44. Richard's magnum opus was *La Guerre de sept ans: Histoire diplomatique et militaire*, 5 vols. (Paris: Firmin-Didot, 1899–1914).

45. *JO*, Débats, June 1880, (first) Waddington Report; *ACD*, Documents, 1884, (second) Waddington Report; and ibid., 1887, no. 2204, (third) Waddington Report.

46. *JO*, Débats, 3, 10, and 12 June 1888 (De Mun, Guyot, and Lyonnais speeches).

47. Waddington, Keller, and Villain did cite some statistics on infant mortality in industrial departments and linked them, arbitrarily, to women's industrial labor. See ibid., 22 March 1881, and *ACD*, Documents, 1887, no. 2204.

48. M. Spuller, "Rapport présenté par la Commission d'enquête parlementaire sur la situation des ouvriers . . . , in *ACD*, Documents, 1884, no. 2695.

49. AN, C5429, 9 and 25 February 1887, 14 May 1890, and 18 November 1891; *JO*, Débats, 29 January 1891; and *AS*, Débats, 3, 6, and 9 July 1891.

50. Coons 1985, 63–64.

51. AN, C5429, 22 June 1887, and *ACD*, Documents, 1887, no. 2204.

52. AN, C3291, 13 March 1880, C5515, 23 January 1891, and correspondence and pamphlets throughout the Commission du travail files.

53. *Le Temps*, 30 November 1888 and 1 February 1889.

54. P. Bousquet, "L'Opinion publique en face de la journée de dix heures: Histoire de la loi de dix heures," D.E.S., Université de Paris, n.d., 3.

55. *AS*, Documents, 1903, no. 364; 1904, no. 65; and 1911, no. 11; and ADEL, J607, commemorative brochure on Waddington.

56. Conseil supérieur de l'assistance Publique, *Compte-rendu général de la session . . . 1901*, session of 4 June, 19–20.

57. Archives municipales de Tourcoing (hereafter cited as AMT), 2Fi4, funeral speeches of the vice president of the Bureau de bienfaisance and the president of the Dames charitables.

58. AMT, 2Fi4, Gustave Dron; "Obsèques du Docteur Dron," *Revue philanthropique* 51 (1930): 799–806; and Ellis 1990.

59. ADN, X3-2, list of Etablissements privés d'assistance, 1891, and X3-3, Etablissements . . . reconnus d'utilité publique, 1900.

60. AMT, Procès-verbaux du Conseil municipal, 8 December 1890, 2 September 1891, 30 September and 18 November 1892.

61. Ibid., 2Fi4, funeral oration of Jules Passy; *Les Maires de Tourcoing* (n.p., 1985); and "Obsèques du Docteur Dron."

62. ADN, X 15/94, Commission administrative des Hospices de Tourcoing, 1888, and AMT, 1 AS 15, Bureau de bienfaisance, Laïcisation, and 2S12 (D), Bureau de bienfaisance, Subventions, and Délibérations du Conseil municipal, 20 December 1907, 29 September, 31 October and 6 December 1908.

63. AMT, Délibérations du Conseil Municipal, 27 February 1886 and 21 February 1888.

64. ADN, IN137, Session du Conseil général, 10 April 1893 and 13 April 1899.

65. Ibid., IN137, Sessions du Conseil général, 22 and 31 August 1888, 31 August 1889, 18 April 1890, 21 August 1891, 22, 23, and 30 August 1892, 10 April 1893, 6 April 1894, 18 April 1896, 29 April and 26 August 1897, and 13 and 14 April and 24 August 1899.

66. "Obsèques du Docteur Dron."

67. AMT, 2Fi4, extract from will.

68. Ibid., Procès-verbaux du Conseil municipal, 6 December 1903, 10 and 29 March 1904, 10 August 1906, and 20 December 1910.

69. *Oeuvres d'hygiène sociale de Tourcoing* (Tourcoing: n.p., 1928); J. Lahousse, *Histoire des Hospices de Tourcoing* (Tourcoing: Duvivier, 1926), 388–411; and AMT, 2 Fi4, H. E. Labbé, *Hommage à la mémoire de Gustave Dron* (Tourcoing: n.p., 1933).

70. G. Dron, *L'Organisation de l'apprentissage* (Nancy: Association Française pour le Développement de l'Enseignement, 1909), and AMT, Procès-verbaux du Conseil municipal, 27 November 1896, 21 October 1899, 12 October 1906, and 23 August 1907.

71. AMT, 2J1, Associations des Dames charitables, and J. Ameye, "Les Dames charitables," *Brotteux* 187 (16 March 1986) and 188 (31 March 1986).

72. *Le Courrier du Nord*, 12 June 1912, and AMT, 36Z1, Dames charitables.

73. *JO*, Débats, 1888, p. 1788, and 1889, p. 309.

74. Ibid., 1890, pp. 1347, 1349.

75. AN, C5515, 5 February 1890, and C5517, correspondence of 5 February and 22 April 1890.

76. "Rapport sur le travail de nuit des femmes dans les manufactures, usines et ateliers," *Bulletin de l'Académie de médicine*, 3d ser., 23–24 (1890).

77. Dr. Adrien Proust, "Le Travail de nuit des femmes dans l'industrie, au point de vue d'hygiène," *Revue d'hygiène et de police sanitaire* 12 (1890).

78. *JO*, Débats, 18 June 1888 and 8 July 1890, and *ACD*, Documents, 1891, no. 1187.

79. AN, C5515, Commission . . . des femmes en couches, 16 July 1891; *ACD*, Documents, 1892, no. 2027; and *JO*, Débats, 29 October and 3–4 November 1892.

80. Commission de la dépopulation, Sous-commission de la mortalité, *Rapports* (1902), and Stewart 1983.

81. Guilbert 1966, 49–197.

82. Mitchell, 1987, 13–17.

83. AN, C5429, 27 and 29 November 1888.

84. Ibid., C5515, 3 and 14 February and 15 March 1890; also ADN, M605, correspondence re inquiry, 20 and 21 March and 25 November 1890.

85. AN, C5515, 21 February, 18 and 19 March, and 7 May 1890; C5517, letters and petitions from seamstresses and wool carders; and *ACD*, Documents, 1891, Jamais report.

86. *ACD*, Documents, 1893, no. 2874, esp. 309 ff.

87. Ibid., 1895, no. 1724, 5–16, 29–43, 89.

88. *JO*, Débats, 17 and 26 June 1896 and 28 June 1898.

89. Ibid., 21–23 December 1899, and AN, C5673, 22 November and 6 December 1899.

90. *ACD*, Documents, 1902, no. 296. See also AN, C7338, 27 May 1903 and 29 May 1905.

91. Ibid., C7414, 14 October 1906, and *ACD*, Documents, 1910, no. 272.

Six   Bringing Feminine Qualities into the Public Sphere

Part of the research for this article was made possible by a fellowship from the National Endowment for the Humanities and by grants from the Faculty Development Committee of Millersville University of Pennsylvania.

1. Ferdinand Buisson, *Nouveau dictionnaire de pédagogie*, 2 vols. (Paris: Hachette, 1911), s.v. "Légion d'honneur (Maisons d'éducation de la)" and "Filles (Instruction primaire, secondaire et supérieure des), Première partie, De 1789 à 1870," by Hippolyte Durand.

2. Ibid., "Filles . . . , Deuxième partie, De 1870 à nos jours," by Maurice Pellisson; Ministère de l'instruction publique, *Règlements organiques de l'enseignement primaire* (Paris, 1887), 344; Clark 1984.

3. Landes 1988.

4. Darrow 1979, 41–65; Pope 1976, 368–77.

5. Tilly and Scott 1978, 123–36, 194–205; Frader 1987, 312–13.

6. Charles Lucas, "De l'éducation pénitentiare des femmes et de ses rapports avec leur éducation sociale," *Revue pénitentiare* 3 (1846): 342–43.

7. Joan W. Scott, "The Woman Worker," in *A History of Women*, ed. Georges Duby and Michelle Perrot, vol. 4, *Emerging Feminism from Revolution to World War*, ed. Geneviève Fraisse and Michelle Perrot (Cambridge: Harvard University Press, 1993), 399–426.

8. Bairoch et al., 1968, 167.

9. Stewart 1989, 41–58.

10. McMillan 1981, 10–16.

11. Luc 1982, 38–39; "Rapport de Salvandy et ordonnance royale sur l'organisation des salles d'asile," in ibid., 66–74.

12. "Rapport de Salvandy," 68; Pope; Lejeune-Resnick 1991; Kerber 1980.

13. Allen 1991, 17–94.

14. Koven and Michel 1993; Klaus 1993; Skocpol 1992.

15. Buisson, s.v. "Mallet, Mme Jules (née Emilie Oberkampf)," by Charles Defodon.

16. "Lettre de la Commission supérieure des salles d'asile aux dames inspectrices" (July 1841), in Luc, 83; Mme Chevreau-Lemercier, *Essai sur l'inspection générale des salles d'asile* (Paris, 1848), 5.

17. Émile Gossot, *Mlle Sauvan, première inspectrice des écoles de Paris, sa vie et son oeuvre* (Paris, 1877).

18. Chevreau-Lemercier, 5–8, 13–17.

19. Langlois 1984, 129.

20. Archives nationales (hereafter cited as AN), F1bI 272-4 L (Lechevalier).

21. Ibid.; "Société de patronage des jeunes filles libérées et abandonnées de la Seine," *Bulletin de la Société générale des prisons* 2 (June 1879): 727.

22. Caplat et al. 1986, 78, 83–85.

23. Ibid., 83–85, 535–37; Huguet 1988, 24–28, 37.

24. AN, F1bI 272-4 L, 273-5 M (Muller), F1bI* 534, 535.

25. Caplat et al., 78; "Rapport et décret relatifs aux déléguées générales pour l'inspection des salles d'asile" (22 March 1879) and "Circulaire aux préfets relative à l'inspection départementale des salles d'asile" (5 November 1879), in Luc, 141–46; *Annuaire de l'instruction publique*, 1884–1912.

26. AN, F17 10864, 10865; Pauline Kergomard, *Rapport sur les salles d'asile des académies de Toulouse et de Grenoble* (Paris, 1881), and *Rapport sur les écoles maternelles des académies de Toulouse, de Clermont et de Bordeaux* (Paris, 1882); Kergomard, "Encore l'inspection des écoles maternelles: Les Inspectrices départementales," *L'Ami de l'enfance* 4 (15 February 1885): 82–84.

27. Prost 1968, 218.

28. Luc, 40.

29. AN, F17 21634 (Rocher-Ripert).

30. Clark 1984, 29–59; Kerber.

31. Pauline Kergomard, "Les Femmes dans l'enseignement primaire," *Revue pédagogique* 14 (May 1889): 417–27. On Kergomard, see Clark 1990, 364–72.

32. *Journal officiel de la République française* (hereafter cited as *JO*), Sénat, Débats, 17 June 1889, 738. Bardoux had been education minister from December 1877 to February 1879.

33. The law stated, "Des inspectrices primaires pourront être nommées aux mêmes conditions et dans les mêmes formes que les inspecteurs." "Les Inspectrices des écoles primaires," *Revue pédagogique* 18 (February 1891): 184.

34. Fuchs 1984; Fuchs 1992; Rollet-Echalier 1990.

35. Conseil supérieur de l'assistance publique (hereafter cited as CSAP), *Comptes rendus*, fasc. 97 (1905), 85. On Monod, see Fuchs 1990, 373–82.

36. Mme Caubet, "De l'admission des femmes dans les commissions et services centrales," *Revue philanthropique* (hereafter cited as *RP*) 9 (July 1901): 329–32.

37. *Décret* of 8 March 1887, *Revue des établissements et oeuvres de bienfaisance* (hereafter cited as *REOB*) 3 (1887): 79–81. For obstacles to secularizing nursing, see Ellis 1990, 165–69.

38. *Arrêté* of 18 November 1887, *REOB* 3 (1887): 370; *Arrêté* of 4 May 1888, *REOB* 4 (1888): 192; *JO*, Chambre des députés, Documents parlementaires, annexe no. 2130, 24 November 1887, 354–55.

39. International Labour Office 1923, 37–39; Reid 1986, 68–72.

40. Mme Villate-Lacheret, *Les Inspectrices du travail en France* (Paris: A. Pedone, 1919), 32; Stewart, 89.

41. Villate-Lacheret, 40–41; *Bulletin des lois* (1892), no. 1511, p. 801; ibid., no. 1522, p. 1303; ibid., no. 1524, p. 1255.

42. Koven and Michel.

43. Hayward 1961, 19–48; Stone 1985.

44. Anna Lampérière, *Le Rôle social de la femme, devoirs, droits, éducation* (Paris: Alcan, 1909).

45. Musée pédagogique, *Congrès international de l'enseignement primaire, compte rendu des séances, Mémoires et documents scolaires,* fasc. 95 (Paris, 1889), 20–24, 68–76; Clark 1989, 96–125.

46. Louis Bouquet, "Organisation de l'inspection des fabriques en France et résultats obtenus," in *Congrès international des accidents du travail et des assurances sociales* (Milan, 1894), 175.

47. AN, F22 547, letter of 4 October 1900.

48. CSAP, *Comptes rendus,* fasc. 97 (1905), 73.

49. Ibid., 73, 78; *JO,* Sénat, Débats, 18 June 1889, 752–53; A. Bourderon, *L'Inspection du travail, rapport présenté par M. Bourderon au nom de la commission permanente* (Paris: Imprimerie Nationale, 1906), 14; Conseil supérieur du travail (hereafter cited as CST), *Compte rendu,* 16th session, November 1906 (Paris: Imprimerie Nationale, 1907), 197.

50. Kergomard, "Les Femmes," 424–26; AN, F22 547; CSAP, *Comptes rendus,* fasc. 97 (1905), 73.

51. Clark 1989, 106; Stewart, 81; *Décret* of 8 March 1887, *REOB* 3 (1887): 79; *Décret* of 28 July 1906, *Bulletin des lois* (1906), no. 2769, p. 2334.

52. *JO,* Sénat, Débats, 18 June 1889, 752; "Les Inspectrices," *Revue pédagogique,* 184.

53. Inspectress Marie Rauber, unpublished "Journal," in the possession of Professor Michelle Perrot.

54. Clark 1989, 106; Rauber, concerning Chaumié; Un jeune "ancien inspecteur primaire," "L'Inspection féminine et les inspecteurs primaires," *Correspondance générale de l'instruction primaire* 2 (15 February 1894): 129–30.

55. *Annuaire de l'instruction publique,* 1885–1914; Luc, 150; "Circulaire aux inspecteurs d'académie relative aux attributions respectives des inspectrices départementales des école maternelles et des inspecteurs primaires" (7 March 1906) and "Circulaire aux préfets relative aux inspectrices départementales des écoles maternelles" (5 March 1910), in Luc, 226–28, 233–35.

56. Louis Bouquet, *Le Travail des enfants, des filles mineures et des femmes dans l'industrie, commentaire de la loi du 2 novembre 1892* (Paris, 1893), 202, 306, 343–44.

57. Villate-Lacheret, 56; Stewart, 89–93.

58. *Décret* of 10 May 1902, *Bulletin des lois* (1902), no. 2373, pp. 556–59; *La Fronde* (Paris), 25, 26 October 1899.

59. Guillaume 1976, 87.

60. *Décret* of 3 April 1909, *Bulletin des lois*, new ser. (1909), no. 7, pp. 630–33. Conseil national des femmes françaises (hereafter cited as CNFF), *Troisième assemblée générale* (1906), 64; Antoine Bonnefoy, *Place aux femmes: Les Carrières féminines administratives et libérales* (Paris: A. Fayard, 1914), 102.

61. CST, *Compte rendu* (1906), 197; AN, F22 571, letters of 26 February, 25 March 1911.

62. CSAP, *Comptes rendus*, fasc. 97 (1905), 74–77.

63. Ibid., 85.

64. *JO*, Sénat, Documents, annexe no. 293, 29 March 1923, 247 (letter of retired *sous-inspectrice* Arnaud).

65. CSAP, *Comptes rendus*, fasc. 97 (1905), 69–70, 86, 117–19; *JO*, Sénat, Documents, 9 February 1904; *JO*, Sénat, Débats, 26 February 1904, 235–37.

66. *JO*, Sénat, Débats, 12 April 1906, 531–32; *La Femme* 28 (May 1906): 54; CNFF, *Troisième assemblée générale*, 22–25.

67. *JO*, Sénat, Documents, annexe no. 4, 10 January 1923, 1; *JO*, Sénat, Débats, 18 May 1923, 790–91.

68. Guillaume Jost and Emilien Cazes, *L'Inspection de l'enseignement primaire* (Paris: Imprimerie Nationale, 1900), 32–34; *Le Concours pour l'emploi d'inspecteur ou d'inspectrice du travail dans l'industrie*, 5th ed. (Paris: Berger Levrault, 1915); AN Fontainebleau, 810638-001, Inspection du travail, Concours.

69. Luc, 108, 150–51, 194.

70. Ibid., 144, 150; Clark 1989, 106.

71. "Inspection générale des prisons," *Bulletin de la société générale des prisons* 3 (1879): 960; AN, F1bI 272-4 L. The *décret* of 5 December 1879 set a pay scale of 4,000 to 5,000 francs for an *inspectrice générale* and 7,000 to 10,000 francs for *inspecteurs généraux*.

72. "L'Inspection générale des services administratifs au ministère de l'intérieur," *RP* 8 (April 1901): 624.

73. O'Brien 1982, 59–60, 111.

74. CSAP, *Comptes rendus*, fasc. 97 (1905), 69; CNFF, "Rapport" of 15 May 1903, *La Femme* 25 (1903): 127–28; "Commission d'enquête sur l'assistance publique," *Bulletin officiel de la Ligue des droits de l'homme* 3 (1903): 624; CNFF, Deuxième assemblée générale (29 January 1905), 62–65.

75. H. Moniez, "Le Contrôle général de l'inspection des enfants assistés et protégés et le décret du 24 février 1901," *Revue politique et parlementaire* 34 (February 1902): 349–61; Moniez, "Le Projet de règlement d'administration publique à rendre en exécution de la loi du 27 juin 1904," *RP* 16 (February 1905): 397–417; Paul Strauss, "Bulletin," *RP* 19 (May 1906): 130; Strauss, "Hélène Moniez," *RP* 31 (October 1912): 465–67.

76. "Réorganisation de l'inspection générale des services administratifs," *RP* 22 (January 1908): 364–72; Hause with Kenney 1984, 98–99, 122; "Conseil supérieur de l'assistance publique," *RP* 19 (August 1906): 508–11.

77. "Réorganisation," *RP* 22 (1908); D., "Mme H. Moniez," *Tribune de l'assistance publique*, no. 161 (October 1912): 10.

78. Bairoch et al., 169.

79. Huguet, 23–24.

80. Calculations are based on 53 names on Huguet's list of 67 (p. 76), also in Caplat et al., 83–88. Of the 67, 12 were not appointed until after February 1879, 2 names are really for one person, and one was paid only by the Seine. Data on individuals come from *dossiers personnels* in the AN F17 series and Caplat et al.

81. Huguet, 24, 35, 79; Caplat et al., 140, 215, 351, 390, 574.

82. Huguet, 24; Rogers 1992, 77–108.

83. Caplat et al., 193, 283, 303, 305–6, 359, 396, 425, 492–93, 625. Of the 12 appointees for 1879–1914 listed by Huguet (p. 76), 3 were not *inspectrices générales*: 2 had only departmental appointments, and one had a temporary assignment.

84. 1879–80 appointees: Davy (AN, F17 22816), Dodu (F17 22833), Kergomard (F17 23609), Thomas (F17 21940), Friedberg (*Dictionnaire de biographie française*, s.v. Friedberg, Mme de); 1894: Brès (AN, F17 22313); 1904: Garonne (F17 21940).

85. Clark 1989, 110, 113–15.

86. AN, F4 3301 (Mlle Oppezzi di Chério), F1bI 262-2 B (Barrault), 272-4 L, 273-5 M, 273-1 M (Malrieu), 279-3 S (De Staël-Holstein).

87. AN, F1bI 262-2 B, 273-1 M, 279-3 S, F4 3301; "Nécrologie," *Revue pénitentiaire* 30 (July–October 1906): 1082 (Dupuy).

88. AN, F4 3302 (Gevin-Cassal), F1bI 413 (Fournier), F4 3307 (Thiry); Strauss, "Hélène Moniez."

89. *Le Petit Parisien*, 13 March 1914; Ministère de l'intérieur, *Annuaire des membres de l'administration préfectorale au 31 mars 1935*, 128.

90. *Annuaire du Ministère de l'intérieur* (1893), 300–302.

91. Conseil général de la Seine, *Procès-verbaux* (1889), 234; (1890) 233; (1891) 259–61; AN, F12 4773-B (Loubens); AN Fontainebleau, 830053, *dossiers personnels*.

92. AN Fontainebleau, 830053; AN, F17 23197-A (Bécam); *Fémina*, no. 119 (1 January 1906): 22.

93. AN Fontainebleau, 810638-001.

94. AN Fontainebleau, 830053, DAG 1754, 1777.

95. Bairoch et al., 169. The count includes 39 labor inspectresses, education's 9 inspectresses general and 8 primary inspectresses, and interior's 12 inspectresses general or adjunct inspectresses general (including one appointed in 1876 and one in 1878, but serving, respectively, until 1906 and 1908) and 3 departmental assistant inspectresses of public assistance.

96. The age is an average for sixty inspectresses.

97. Mme Al. Paul Juillerat, "L'Activité féminine en France au vingtième siècle," *Revue économique internationale* 8 (August 1911): 248–51; Bibliothèque nationale,

Nouvelles acquisitions françaises (hereafter cited as BN NAF) 24997, Papiers Félix Nadar, fols. 16–20, letter of Gevin Cassal, 28 May 1897; *La Fronde*, 3 January 1899, supplement, 5; Marguerite Ginier, "L'Inspection féminine des écoles maternelles et des écoles de filles, *Revue pédagogique* 58 (March 1911): 217–29.

98. *JO*, Sénat, Documents, March 1923, 247; Musée pédagogique, *Congrès, compte rendu*, 1889, 68–69.

99. Al. Paul Juillerat, "L'Inspection du travail," *Revue économique internationale* 4 (October–December 1907): 319; Hélène Moniez, "L'Education des femmes prépare-t-elles à exercer une action sociale?" *Revue internationale de l'enseignement* 54 (1907): 7; Société internationale pour l'étude des questions de l'assistance, "Assemblée générale du 25 mai 1907," *RP* 21 (June 1907): 233; Moniez, "Le Contrôle des établissements de bienfaisance privés," *RP* 22 (February 1908): 441.

100. Ginier, 221; *Le Matin* (Paris), 26 August 1911; AN, F7 13266 (Union française pour le suffrage des femmes); Oulhiou 1981, 161; Rauber.

101. BN NAF 24997, fols. 517–18, Gevin-Cassal letter; Jeanne Deflou, "Les Ouvrages de Mme Gevin-Cassal," *L'Entente* (Paris), January 1906; *Le Petit Parisien*, 13 March 1914.

102. Bibliothèque historique de la ville de Paris (hereafter cited as BHVP), Papiers Georges Renard, ms. 2561, fol. 416, Bourat to Mme Renard, 1 July 1911; Bibliothèque Marguerite Durand (hereafter cited as BMD), DOS CON FEM, Union fraternelle des femmes, 1911; *Dixième congrès international des femmes, oeuvres et institutions féminines*, ed. Mme Avril de Sainte-Croix (Paris: Giard et Brière, 1914), 205.

103. Offen 1988, 119–57; Cott 1989, 809–29.

104. Musée pédagogique, *Compte rendu*, 68–70 (Kergomard); Ginier; E. Kieffer, "Ce que la société demande à l'école: pour nos filles," *Manuel général de l'instruction primaire* (27 February 1909): 340–41; Gevin-Cassal, "Autour des berceaux français," *Revue de morale sociale* 1 (1899): 356; Juillerat, "L'Activité"; Moniez, "L'Education des femmes"; *Deuxième congrès national de la natalité, compte rendu* (Rouen: Vicomte, 1920), 163–78 (Charrondière).

105. Kergomard, *Rapport* (1881), *Rapport* (1882); AN, F17 23609.

106. *Deuxième congrès international des oeuvres et institutions féminines, 18–23 juin 1900*, 4 vols., ed. M. Pegard (Paris: Blot, 1902), 3:281; Ginier, 228; Jeanne d'Urville, "Les Institutrices de la ville de Paris," *La Française* (Paris), 4 April 1912.

107. CNFF, "Bulletin" (1906), 36–37.

108. "Congrès féministe universitaire de Bordeaux, les voeux du congrès," *Manuel général de l'instruction primaire* (27 September 1913): 6.

109. CST, *Compte rendu* (1906), 220.

110. AN Fontainebleau, 810638-001.

111. BMD, DOS CON FEM, Congrès du travail féminin, 1907; BHVP, Papiers Georges Renard, ms. 2561, fols. 411–27, Bourat to Mme Renard, 1911; BHVP, Collection Bouglé, fonds Jeanne Bouvier, 17, 18.

112. Villate-Lacheret, 90.

113. Gevin-Cassal, "L'Oeuvre du trousseau," *La Femme* 24 (May 1902): 70–71; *La Fraternité en action* (Geneva: Fischbacher, 1904); *La Fronde*, 12, 13 December 1897; BN NAF 24997, fols. 182–84, 189, 200–201, Gevin-Cassal to Nadar.

114. Moniez, "L'Education des femmes"; Moniez, "Le Contrôle des établissements de bienfaisance," *RP* 21 (July 1907), 22 (November, December 1907; January, February, March, April 1908); *Congrès national d'assistance publique et de bienfaisance privée (quatrième congrès)*, 3 vols. (Reims: Matot-Braine, 1908).

115. Clark 1989, 117–18.

116. Strauss, "Bulletin," *RP* 23 (June 1908): 264; "Société internationale," *RP* 32 (November 1912): 51; Georges Rondel, *L'Assistance et la protection des faibles* (Paris: O. Doin, 1912), 188.

117. AN, C 7422, Chambre des députés, Commission d'assurance et de prévoyance sociale, 31 January 1911.

118. *International Labor Conference, First Annual Meeting* (Washington, D.C.: Government Printing Office, 1920), 85, 105, 210; International Labour Office 1921, 1:xlvi, 2:744; "Une Victoire féministe à la 5e conférence internationale du travail," *La Française*, 22 December 1923.

119. *La Française*, 8 October 1911; Thuillier 1988, 34–37.

120. Donzelot 1979.

121. Clark 1989, 13–15; Briand et al. 1987, 36.

122. Offen 1984, 648–76; Stewart, 169–90; Becchia 1986, 201–46; Clark 1984, 83–84, 94–97.

123. For example, "Concours pour l'emploi d'inspectrice générale des services administratifs," *RP* 22 (April 1908): 794; *Le Concours pour l'emploi d'inspecteur*; Jost and Cazes, 47–62.

124. Annick Davisse, *Les Femmes dans la fonction publique* (Paris: Documentation Française, 1983), 47–72; Pion 1986.

Seven   France in a Comparative Perspective

1. This entire volume has been a truly collaborative enterprise, and I am deeply appreciative of the friendship, support, and help from all the contributors. I especially owe a debt to the other two collaborators, Elinor Accampo and Mary Lynn Stewart, for their constructive assistance and partnership. Brian Gratton and Kate Lynch took the time to read and comment on an earlier draft of this chapter, and I am grateful for their suggestions.

For some recent works on this topic, see Ambler 1991; Bock and Thane 1991; Koven and Michel 1993; Pedersen 1993; Skocpol 1992.

2. Although the idea of degeneration was part of the intellectual current in western European nations and the United States, French intellectuals focused on women's role in degeneration. Right-wing writers such as Gustave LeBon and

Gabriel Tarde regarded women as the embodiment of disorder and degeneration. Pick 1989, 40–42, 92.

3. I am indebted to Mary Lynn Stewart for much of the work in this paragraph. Douglas E. Ashford, "Advantages of Complexity: Social Insurance in France," in Ambler, 32–37; Rosanvallon 1984.

4. Laroque 1983, 61.

5. Ewald 1986. For a cultural analysis of the origins of the French welfare state also based on compensation to male workers, see Hatzfeld 1971. On social scientists' recognition of the origins of the welfare state, see also Ashford 1986.

6. John S. Ambler, "Ideas, Interests, and the French Welfare State," in Ambler, 5–8. Much of this paragraph, and the research for it, is due to the work of Mary Lynn Stewart.

7. Hatzfeld.

8. Political scientists and historians writing in the 1970s and analyzing the development of welfare in the United States have been quick to point out the relationship of social welfare to social control. See, for example, Piven and Cloward 1971 and Cohen and Scull 1985.

9. In France it was the Radical party. Derfler 1977; Donzelot 1984; Elwitt 1986; Stone 1985.

10. Habermas 1989, 151–52, 175, 232.

11. Ibid., 142, 148, 224, 232.

12. Fraser 1992, 110–11.

13. Fraser 1989, 126, 129, 144ff; Pascall 1986. I am grateful to Mary Lynn Stewart for her reading and analysis of Pascall. Susan Pedersen has persuasively discussed the British focus on the male breadwinner and dependent wife and mother as the essential component of social welfare ideology (chap. 1).

14. Remi Lenoir, "Family Policy in France since 1938," in Ambler, 146–52.

15. Skocpol, 2.

16. Koven and Michel, introduction to idem 1993, 2, 4; emphasis in original.

17. Cova 1994; Fuchs 1992, chaps. 3 and 4.

18. For details on the situation in England, see Rose 1992; Thane 1992; and Lewis 1980. For details on the situation in Germany, see Allen 1991.

19. Allen 1991, 17, 223; Thane, 42; Schafer 1992.

20. Thane, 73–80.

21. Lewis, chaps. 2 and 3; Sonya Michel, "The Limits of Maternalism: Policies toward American Wage-Earning Mothers during the Progressive Era," in Koven and Michel 1993, 280–92; Klaus 1993, 44–45, 57–58.

22. Lindenmeyr, fall 1993, 114–25. (For information on the Drop of Milk, see 121.) See also Lindenmeyr, spring 1993, 562–91.

23. Allen 1993–94, 27–50.   24. Thane, 80.

25. Lewis, 167–68.   26. Bock and Thane, 4.

27. Lindenmeyr, fall 1993, 121.   28. Bock and Thane, 104–6; Lewis, 167.

29. Lewis, 13. For details of the French situation, see Fuchs 1992, chaps. 3, 6, and 7; Rollet-Echalier 1990; Thébaud 1986.

30. Skocpol, ix, 10, 425; Abramovitz 1988.

31. Skocpol, 10, 495–511. For a detailed discussion of the Sheppard-Towner Act, see Molly Ladd-Taylor, *Mother-Work: Women, Child Welfare, and the State, 1890–1930* (Urbana: University of Illinois Press, 1994), chap. 6.

32. Russia, which did not have a problem of fertility decline and depopulation, was the exception. Lindenmeyr, fall 1993, 116, 122.

33. Cova 1994, 96–97.

34. The analysis of gender-specific labor legislation in this and the next few related paragraphs depends heavily upon the research and expertise of Mary Lynn Stewart. E. Brooke, *A Tabulation of the Factory Laws of European Countries . . . Special Legislation for Women, Young Persons, and Children* (London, 1898).

35. Skocpol, 383, 386, 421; Abramovitz.

36. Lehrer 1987, esp. 61ff, 144ff, and 241–42. Information from Lehrer supplied by Mary Lynn Stewart. See also Kathryn Kish Sklar, "The Historical Foundations of Women's Power in the Creation of the American Welfare State, 1830–1930," in Koven and Michel 1993, 73–74.

37. Rose, 46, 64, 76, 188; Lewis, 78; Pedersen, chap. 1.

38. Thane, 43, 46.

39. Lindenmeyr, fall 1993, 116, 120, 122.

40. Phillips 1991, 170. This discussion of divorce is based on the pathbreaking work of Roderick Phillips.

41. Ibid., 133, 134.

42. Lewis, 169; Thane, 43; Christoph Sachße, "Social Mothers: The Bourgeois Women's Movement and German Welfare-State Formation, 1890–1929," in Koven and Michel 1993, 136–58; Sklar, 44–49; Stewart 1989, 55–57.

43. Clark 1994.

44. Koven and Michel 1989, 114.

45. Allen 1991, 176–81; Lewis, 34; Klaus, 71; Lindenmeyr, fall 1993, 121.

46. Allen 1991, 177.

47. Lewis, 15–16.

48. Allen 1993–94.

49. Soloway 1990, 41–47; Teitelbaum and Winter 1985, 21, 30–32.

50. Bock and Thane, 10–11.

51. Thane, 58–60.

52. Allen 1991, 177.

53. Quotation from Lewis, 30–31, 50–51. See also Mazumdar 1992, 40–46; Pick, 179; Soloway 1990, 38–132; Kevles 1985; and Teitelbaum and Winter, 33–47.

54. Allen 1991, 157–60.   55. Nye 1984, 140–41.

56. Schneider 1990, 4, 8, 33, 92.   57. Ibid., 29, 85.

58. Abramovitz; Habermas; Fraser 1992, 129.

59. Thane, 7, 10, 66.

60. Cohen and Scull, "Introduction," 2.

61. Piven and Cloward, xv, 7, 30, 38–41. Michel Foucault, however, in "seeking to illuminate the 'genealogy of power,' explicitly rejects any explanatory schema in which notions of central state power and the economic determination of action play any major role," in Cohen and Scull, 3.

62. Cohen and Scull, "Introduction," 4, and Scull, "Humanitarianism or Control?" in Cohen and Scull, 121, 122.

63. Robert Castel, "Moral Treatment: Mental Therapy and Social Control in the Nineteenth Century," in Cohen and Scull, 259.

64. Nye 1984 and Donzelot 1979.

65. Lewis.

66. Allen 1991, 2; Lindenmeyr, fall 1993, 120–22.

67. Ellis 1990 and Léonard 1981.   68. Ellis, 93–97, 136–40, 248–49.

69. Ibid., 5.   70. Goldstein 1987.

71. Thane, 10. Reference to the Fabians is in Mazumdar, 45.

72. Skocpol, 21.

73. Edme Piot, senateur de la Côte-d'Or, à Emile Combes, president du conseil, "Une Décoration pour les mères de famille," Informations, *Revue philanthropique* 13 (1903): 273–74.

74. For an elaboration of this theme, see Donzelot 1979; see also Fuchs 1992, chaps. 3–6.

75. Bock and Thane, 6, 8; Walkowitz 1991, 156; Seth Koven, "Borderlands: Women, Voluntary Action, and Child Welfare in Britain, 1840 to 1914," in Koven and Michel 1993, 123–27; Sachße, 136–37.

76. Sklar, 43–53, 60–78; Skocpol, 10, 35, 37, 57, 317–18, 427, 445, 495–511, 530.

77. Skocpol, 317–18, 331, 335, 368.

78. Gratton and Haber 1993; Molly Ladd-Taylor, " 'My Work Came out of Agony and Grief' ": Mothers and the Making of the Sheppard-Towner Act," in Koven and Michel 1993, 321–42; Michel, 277–320.

79. Habermas. Habermas does not specify that women were part of civil society. For women in the civil society, see Fraser 1992.

80. The only reform many feminists rejected was female labor legislation. Cova 1994; Fuchs 1992, chaps. 4–6; Offen 1984, 648–76; Allen 1991; Lindenmeyr 1980.

81. Lewis, chaps. 2 and 3, esp. 13, 14, 35–44, 89, 165.

82. Allen 1991, 1, 17, 102–3.

83. Skocpol, 16.

84. See, for example, the essays in Mandler 1990; Gordon 1988; and Ellen Ross, *Motherhood in Outcast London, 1870–1918* (New York: Oxford University Press, 1993).

85. Quoted in Scull, "Humanitarianism or Control?" 133.

Select Secondary References

Abramovitz, Mimi. *Regulating the Lives of Women: Social Welfare Policy from Colonial Times to the Present*. Boston: South End Press, 1988.

Accampo, Elinor A. *Industrialization, Family Life, and Class Relations: Saint Chamond, 1815–1914*. Berkeley: University of California Press, 1989.

Agulhon, Maurice. *Marianne au combat: L'Imagerie et la symbolique républicaines de 1789 à 1880*. Paris: Flammarion, 1979.

Allen, Ann Taylor. "Feminism, Venereal Diseases, and the State of Germany, 1890–1920." *Journal of the History of Sexuality* 4, no. 1 (1993–94): 27–50.

———. *Feminism and Motherhood in Germany, 1800–1914*. New Brunswick, N.J.: Rutgers University Press, 1991.

Ambler, John S., ed. *The French Welfare State*. New York: New York University Press, 1991.

Ameye, J. *La Vie politique à Tourcoing sous la Troisième République*. Lille: Silis, 1963.

Arnaud, André-Jean. *Essai d'analyse structurale du Code Civil français: La Règle du jeu dans la paix bourgeoise*. Paris: Librairie Générale de Droit et de Jurisprudence, 1973.

Ashford, Douglas E. *The Emergence of the Welfare States*. Oxford: Blackwell, 1986.

Auspitz, Katherine. *The Radical Bourgeoisie: The Ligue de l'Enseignement and the Origins of the Third Republic, 1866–1885*. New York: Cambridge University Press, 1982.

Baguley, David. *"Fécondité" d'Émile Zola*. Toronto: University of Toronto Press, 1973.

Bairoch, P.; T. Deldycke; H. Gelders; and J.-M. Limbor. *La Population active et sa structure*. Brussels: Institut de l'Université Libre, 1968.

Baker, R. "A Regional Study of Working-Class Organization in France: Socialism in the Nord, 1870–1924." Ph.D. diss., Stanford University, 1967.

Becchia, Alain. "Les Milieux parlementaires et la dépopulation de 1900 à 1914." *Communications* 44 (1986): 201–46.

Bell, Susan Groag, and Karen Offen, eds. *Women, the Family, and Freedom: The Debate in Documents*. 2 vols. Stanford: Stanford University Press, 1983.

Berch, B. "Industrialization and Working Women in the Nineteenth Century:

England, France, and the United States." Ph.D. diss., University of Wisconsin, 1976.

Berenson, Edward. *The Trial of Madame Caillaux*. Berkeley: University of California Press, 1992.

Bidelman, Patrick. *Pariahs Stand Up! The Founding of the Liberal Feminist Movement in France, 1858–1889*. Westport, Conn.: Greenwood Press, 1982.

Birnbaum, Pierre. *Les Fous de la République: Histoire politique des Juifs d'Etat de Gambetta à Vichy*. Paris: Fayard, 1992.

Blum, Carol. *Rousseau and the Republic of Virtue: The Language of Politics in the French Revolution*. Ithaca, N.Y.: Cornell University Press, 1986.

Bock, Gisela. "Pauvreté féminine, droits des mères et états-providence." In *Histoire des femmes en occident*, vol. 5. Paris: Plon, 1991.

Bock, Gisela, and Pat Thane, eds. *Maternity and Gender Policies: Women and the Rise of the European Welfare States, 1880s–1950s*. London: Routledge, 1991.

Braudel, Fernand, and Ernest Labrousse, eds. *Histoire économique et sociale de la France*. Vol. 4, *L'Ère industrielle et la société d'aujourd'hui (1880–1980)*, by J. Bouvier et al. Paris: Presses Universitaires de France, 1979.

Briand, J.-P.; J.-M. Chapoulie; F. Huguet; J.-N. Luc; and A. Prost. *L'Enseignement primaire et ses extensions: Annuaire statistique, 19e–20e siècles*. Paris: Economica, 1987.

Caplat, Guy; Isabelle Havelange; Françoise Huguet; and Bernadette Lebedeff. *Les Inspecteurs généraux de l'instruction primaire: Dictionnaire biographique, 1802–1914*. Paris: Institut National de Recherche Pédagogique, 1986.

Castex, P., and P. Surer, eds. *Manuel des études littéraires françaises*. Paris: Hachette, 1950.

Chaline, J.-P. *Les Bourgeois de Rouen: Une Elite urbaine au XIXe siècle*. Paris: Presses de la Fondation Nationale des Sciences Politiques, 1982.

Clark, Frances Ida. *The Position of Women in Contemporary France*. London: P. S. King and Son, 1937.

Clark, Linda L. "A Battle of the Sexes in a Professional Setting: The Introduction of *Inspectrices Primaires*, 1889–1914." *French Historical Studies* 16 (spring 1989): 96–125.

———. "Pauline Kergomard: Promoter of the Secularization of Schools and Advocate of Women's Rights." *Proceedings of the Western Society for French History* 17 (1990): 364–72.

———. *Schooling the Daughters of Marianne: Textbooks and the Socialization of Girls in Modern French Primary Schools*. Albany: State University of New York Press, 1984.

———. "Women Combining the Private and the Public Spheres: The Beginnings of Nursery School Inspection, 1837–1879." *Proceedings of the Annual Meeting of the Western Society for French History* 21 (1994): 141–50.

Cobban, Alfred. *A History of Modern France*. Vol. 2, *1799–1945*. Baltimore: Penguin Books, 1981.

Coffin, Judith. "Social Science Meets Sweated Labor: Reinterpreting Women's Work in Late Nineteenth-Century France." *Journal of Modern History* 63 (June 1991): 230–70.

Cohen, Stanley, and Andrew Scull, eds. *Social Control and the State*. London: Blackwell, 1985.

Cole, Joshua H. "The Power of Large Numbers: Population and Politics in Nineteenth-Century France." Ph.D. diss., University of California, Berkeley, 1991.

Coons, L. A. "Orphans of the Sweated Trades: Women Homeworkers in the Parisian Garment Industry (1860–1915)." Ph.D. diss., New York University, 1985.

Cott, Nancy F. "What's in a Name? The Limits of 'Social Feminism'; or, Expanding the Vocabulary of Women's History." *Journal of American History* 76 (December 1989): 809–29.

Cova, Anne. "Droits des femmes et protection de la maternité en France, 1892–1939." Doctorat d'Etat Nouveau Régime. École des Hautes Etudes en Sciences Sociales, Paris, France, and l'Institut Européen de Florence, Italy, 1994.

———. "Féminisme et natalité: Nelly Roussel (1878–1922)." *History of European Ideas* 15 (1992): 663–72.

Cross, Gary. *A Quest for Time: The Reduction of Work in Britain and France, 1840–1940*. Berkeley: University of California Press, 1989.

Darrow, Margaret. "French Noblewomen and the New Domesticity, 1750–1850." *Feminist Studies* 5 (spring 1979): 41–65.

Delescluze, J. *Les Consuls de Rouen: Histoire de la Chambre de Commerce*. Rouen: P'tit Normand, 1985.

Derfler, Leslie. *Alexandre Millerand: The Socialist Years*. The Hague: Mouton, 1977.

Desan, Suzanne. "Constitutional Amazons: Jacobin Women's Clubs in the French Revolution." In *Recreating Authority in Revolutionary France*, edited by Bryant T. Ragan Jr. and Elizabeth Williams. New Brunswick, N.J.: Rutgers University Press, 1992.

Desforges, Jacques. *"La Loi Naquet": Renouveau des idées sur la famille*. Edited by Robert Prigent. Paris: Presses Universitaires de France, 1954.

Donovan, James. "Infanticide and the Juries in France, 1825–1913." *Journal of Family History* 16, no. 2 (spring 1991): 157–76.

Donzelot, Jacques. *L'Invention du social*. Paris: Fayard, 1984.

———. *The Policing of Families*. Translated by Robert Hurley. New York: Pantheon, 1979.

Ellis, Jack D. *The Physician-Legislators of France: Medicine and Politics in the Early Third Republic, 1870–1914*. Cambridge: Cambridge University Press, 1990.

Elshtain, Jean Bethke. *Public Man, Private Woman: Women in Social and Political Thought*. Princeton: Princeton University Press, 1981.

Elwitt, Sanford. *The Making of the Third Republic: Class and Politics in France, 1868–1884*. Baton Rouge: Louisiana State University Press, 1975.

———. *The Third Republic Defended: Bourgeois Reform in France, 1880–1914*. Baton Rouge: Louisiana State University Press, 1986.

Ewald, François. *L'Etat providence*. Paris: Bernard Grasset, 1986.

Fauré, Christine. *Democracy without Women: Feminism and the Rise of Liberal Individualism in France*. Translated by Claudia Gorbman and John Berks. Bloomington: Indiana University Press, 1991.

Fox-Genovese, Elizabeth. "The Ideological Basis of Domestic Economy." In *The Fruits of Merchant Capital: Slavery and Bourgeois Property in the Rise and Expansion of Capitalism*, by Elizabeth Fox-Genovese and Eugene D. Genovese. New York: Oxford University Press, 1983.

Frader, Laura Levine. "Women in the Industrial Capitalist Economy." In *Becoming Visible: Women in European History*. 2d ed. Edited by Renate Bridenthal, Claudia Koonz, and Susan Stuard. Boston: Houghton Mifflin, 1987.

Fraser, Nancy. "Rethinking the Public Sphere: A Contribution to the Critique of Actually Existing Democracy." In *Habermas and the Public Sphere*. Edited by Craig Calhoun. Cambridge: MIT Press, 1992.

———. *Unruly Practices: Power, Discourse, and Gender in Contemporary Social Theory*. Minneapolis: University of Minnesota Press, 1989.

Fuchs, Rachel G. *Abandoned Children: Foundlings and Child Welfare in Nineteenth-Century France*. Albany: State University of New York Press, 1984.

———. "From the Private to the Public *Devoir*: Henri Monod and Public Assistance." *Proceedings of the Western Society for French History* 17 (1990): 373–82.

———. *Poor and Pregnant in Paris: Strategies for Survival in the Nineteenth Century*. New Brunswick, N.J.: Rutgers University Press, 1992.

Goldstein, Jan. *Console and Classify: The French Psychiatric Profession in the Nineteenth Century*. New York: Cambridge University Press, 1987.

Gordon, Felicia. *The Integral Feminist: Madeleine Pelletier, 1874–1939: Feminism, Socialism, and Medicine*. London: Polity Press, 1990.

Gordon, Linda. *Heroes of Their Own Lives: The Politics and History of Family Violence, Boston, 1880–1960*. New York: Viking/Penguin, 1988.

———, ed. *Women, the State, and Welfare*. Madison: University of Wisconsin Press, 1990.

Gratton, Brian, and Carole Haber. "Civil War in Sociology: Competing Explanations for the Development of American Social Security." Paper presented at the annual meeting of the Gerontological Society of America, New Orleans, November 1993.

Guilbert, M. *Les Femmes et l'organisation syndicale avant 1914*. Paris: C.N.R.S., 1966.

Guillaume, Michel. "Arthur Fontaine, premier directeur du travail." In *Les Directeurs de ministère en France (XIXe–XXe siècles)*, edited by Francis de Baecque. Geneva: Droz, 1976.

Gullickson, Gay. "*La Petroleuse*: Representing Revolution." *Feminist Studies* 17 (1991): 246–66.

Habermas, Jürgen. *The Structural Transformation of the Public Sphere: An Inquiry into a Category of Bourgeois Society*. Translated by Thomas Burger. Cambridge: MIT Press, 1989.

Hanley, Sarah. "Engendering the State: Family Formation and State Building in Early Modern France." *French Historical Studies* 16, no. 1 (spring 1989): 4–27.

Harris, Ruth. *Murders and Madness: Medicine, Law, and Society in Fin de Siècle*. Oxford: Oxford University Press, 1989.

Hatzfeld, Henri. *Du paupérisme à la sécurité sociale, 1850–1940*. Paris: Armand Colin, 1971.

Hause, Steven C. *Hubertine Auclert: The French Suffragette*. New Haven: Yale University Press, 1987.

———. "A Pastoral Family in French Politics: Edmond, Elise, and Francis de Pressensé." *Proceedings of the Annual Meeting of the Western Society for French History* 17 (1990): 354–63.

———. "Protestant Republicans and the Making of the Third Republic." Paper presented at the 103d annual meeting of the American Historical Association, Cincinnati, Ohio, 29 December 1989.

Hause, Steven C., with Anne R. Kenney. *Women's Suffrage and Social Politics in the French Third Republic*. Princeton: Princeton University Press, 1984.

Hayward, J. E. S. "The Official Social Philosophy of the French Third Republic: Léon Bourgeois and Solidarism." *International Review of Social History* 6 (1961): 19–48.

Hilden, Patricia. *Working Women and Socialist Politics in France, 1880–1914: A Regional Study*. Oxford: Clarendon Press, 1986.

Huguet, F. *Les Inspecteurs généraux de l'instruction publique, 1802–1914: Profil d'un groupe social*. Paris: Institut National de Recherche Pédagogique, 1988.

Hunt, Lynn. *The Family Romance of the French Revolution*. Berkeley: University of California Press, 1992.

International Labour Office. *Factory Inspection: Historical Development and Present Organisation in Certain Countries*. Geneva: International Labour Office, 1923.

———. *International Labour Conference, Third Session*. 2 vols. Geneva: International Labour Office, 1921.

Ionesco, Eugène. *Hugoliade*. Translated by D. Contineau. 1935–37. Reprint, Paris: Gallimard, 1982.

Jenson, Jane. "Paradigms and Political Discourse: Protective Legislation in France and the United States before 1914." *Canadian Journal of Political Sciences* 22 (June 1989).

Jolly, Jean, ed. *Dictionnaire des parlementaires français*. 8 vols. Paris: Presses Universitaires de France, 1960–67.

Jordanova, Ludmilla. *Sexual Visions: Images of Gender in Science and Medicine between the Eighteenth and Twentieth Centuries*. Madison: University of Wisconsin Press, 1989.

Kerber, Linda K. *Women of the Republic: Intellect and Ideology in Revolutionary America*. Chapel Hill: University of North Carolina Press, 1980.

Kevles, Daniel J. *In the Name of Eugenics: Genetics and the Uses of Human Heredity*. New York: Knopf, 1985.

Klaus, Alisa. *Every Child a Lion: The Origins of Maternal and Infant Health Policy in the United States and France, 1890–1920*. Ithaca, N.Y.: Cornell University Press, 1993.

Koven, Seth, and Sonya Michel. "Gender and the Origins of the Welfare State." *Radical History Review* (winter 1989): 114.

———, eds. *Mothers of a New World: Maternalist Politics and the Origins of Welfare States*. New York: Routledge, 1993.

———. "Womanly Duties: Maternalist Politics and the Origins of Welfare States in France, Germany, Great Britain, and the United States, 1880–1920." *American Historical Review* 95 (October 1990): 1076–1108.

Ladd-Taylor, Molly. *Mother-Work: Women, Child Welfare, and the State, 1890–1930*. Urbana: University of Illinois Press, 1994.

Landes, Joan. *Women and the Public Sphere in the Age of the French Revolution*. Ithaca, N.Y.: Cornell University Press, 1988.

Langlois, Claude. "L'Introduction des congrégations féminines dans le système pénitentiare français (1839–1880)." In *La Prison, le bagne et l'histoire*, edited by Jacques G. Petit. Geneva: Librairie des Méridiens, 1984.

Laroque, Pierre. *The Social Institutions of France*. Translated by Roy Evans. New York: Bordon and Breach Science Publishers, 1983.

Le Bras, Hervé. *Marianne et les lapins: L'Obsession démographique*. Paris: Olivier Orban, 1991.

Lehrer, Susan. *Origins of Protective Labor Legislation for Women, 1905–1925*. Albany: State University of New York Press, 1987.

Lejeune-Resnick, Evelyne. *Femmes et associations (1830–1880): Vraie démocrates ou dames patronnesses?* Paris: Tublisud, 1991.

Léonard, Jacques. *La Médecine entre les savoirs et les pouvoirs: Histoire intellectuelle et politique de la médecine française au XIX siècle*. Paris: Aubier, 1981.

Lewis, Jane. *The Politics of Motherhood: Child and Maternal Welfare in England, 1900–1939*. London: Croom Helm, 1980.

Lindenmeyr, Adele. "Maternalism and Child Welfare in Late Imperial Russia." *Journal of Women's History* 5 (fall 1993): 114–25.

———. "Public Life, Private Virtues: Women in Russian Charity, 1762–1914." *Signs* 18, no. 3 (spring 1993): 562–91.

———. "Public Poor Relief and Private Charity in Late Imperial Russia." Ph.D. diss., Princeton University, 1980.

Lorulot, André. *Alfred Naquet, le "père du divorce."* Seine-et-Oise: Aux Editions de l'Idée Libre Herblay, 1934.

Luc, Jean-Noël. *La Petite Enfance à l'école: Textes officiels présentés et annotés.* Paris: Institut National de Recherche Pédagogique and Economica, 1982.

Lynch, Katherine. *Family, Class, and Ideology in Early Industrial France.* Madison: University of Wisconsin Press, 1988.

———. "The Family and the History of Public Life." *Journal of Interdisciplinary History* 14, no. 4 (spring 1994): 665–84.

Magraw, Roger. *A History of the French Working Class.* Vol. 2, *Workers and the Bourgeois Republic, 1871–1939.* Oxford: Blackwell, 1992.

Mandler, Peter, ed. *The Uses of Charity: The Poor on Relief in the Nineteenth-Century Metropolis.* Philadelphia: University of Pennsylvania Press, 1990.

Marshall, T. H. *Class, Status, and Citizenship.* Garden City, N.Y.: Anchor Books, 1965.

Martin, Jean Baptiste. *La Fin des mauvais pauvres.* Paris: Champ Vallon, 1983.

Maurois, André. *Olympio ou la vie de Victor Hugo.* Paris: Hachette, 1954.

Mayeur, Françoise. "La Femme dans la société selon Jules Ferry." In *Jules Ferry, fondateur de la République,* edited by François Furet. Paris: École des Hautes Etudes en Sciences Sociales, 1985.

Mazumdar, Pauline M. H. *Eugenics, Human Genetics, and Human Failings: The Eugenics Society, Its Sources and Its Critics in Britain.* New York: Routledge, 1992.

McBride, Theresa. "Public Authority and Private Lives: Divorce after the Revolution." *French Historical Studies* 17 (spring 1992): 747–68.

McLaren, Angus. *Sexuality and Social Order: The Debate over the Fertility of Women and Workers in France, 1770–1920.* New York: Holmes and Meier, 1983.

McMillan, James F. *Housewife or Harlot: The Place of Women in French Society, 1870–1940.* New York: St. Martin's Press, 1981.

Melzer, Sara E., and Leslie W. Rabine, eds. *Rebel Daughters: Women and the French Revolution.* New York: Oxford University Press, 1992.

Mitchell, Allan. *The Divided Path: The German Influence on Social Reform in France after 1870.* Chapel Hill: University of North Carolina Press, 1991.

Mitchell, B. *The Practical Revolutionaries: A New Interpretation of the French Anarchosyndicalists.* New York: Greenwood Press, 1987.

Moch, Leslie Page. "Government Policy and Women's Experience: The Case of Teachers in France." *Feminist Studies* 14, no. 2 (summer 1988): 301–24.

Moses, Claire Goldberg. *French Feminism in the Nineteenth Century.* Albany: State University of New York Press, 1984.

Netter, Yvonne. "Le Féminisme dans la famille." In *Les Problèmes de la famille et le féminisme: Conférences faites à la Ligue Française d'Education morale*, edited by G. Belot et al. Paris: Fernand Nathan, 1930.

Nord, Philip. "French Freemasonry and the Formation of the Republican Elite, 1861–1877." Paper presented at the 103d annual meeting of the American Historical Association, Cincinnati, Ohio, 29 December 1989.

Nye, Robert A. *Crime, Madness, and Politics in Modern France: The Medical Concept of National Decline.* Princeton: Princeton University Press, 1984.

———. "Degeneration and the Medical Model of Cultural Crisis in the French *Belle Epoque.*" In *Political Symbolism in Modern Europe: Essays in Honor of George L. Mosse,* edited by S. Drescher, D. Sabean, and A. Sharlin. New Brunswick, N.J.: Rutgers University Press, 1982.

———. *Masculinity and Male Codes of Honor in Modern France.* New York: Oxford University Press, 1993.

O'Brien, Patricia. *The Promise of Punishment: Prisons in Nineteenth-Century France.* Princeton: Princeton University Press, 1982.

Offen, Karen. "Defining Feminism: A Comparative Historical Approach." *Signs* 14 (1988): 119–57.

———. "Depopulation, Nationalism, and Feminism in Fin-de-Siècle France." *American Historical Review* 89 (June 1984): 648–76.

———. "Ernest Legouvé and the Doctrine of 'Equality in Difference' for Women: A Case Study of Male Feminism in Nineteenth-Century French Thought." *Journal of Modern History* 58, no. 2 (1986): 479–81.

———. "Exploring the Sexual Politics of French Republican Nationalism." In *Aspects of Nationalism in France: From Boulanger to the Great War,* edited by Robert Tombs. London: Harper Collins, 1991.

———. "A Nineteenth-Century French Feminist Rediscovered: Jenny P. d'Héricourt, 1809–1875." *Signs* 13, no. 1 (autumn 1987): 144–58.

Orloff, Ann. *The Politics of Pensions: A Comparative Analysis of Britain, Canada, and the United States.* Madison: University of Wisconsin Press, 1993.

Oulhiou, Yvonne. *L'École normale supérieure de Fontenay-aux-Roses à travers le temps, 1880–1980.* Fontenay-aux-Roses: Cahiers de Fontenay, 1981.

Pascall, Gillian. *Social Policy: A Feminist Analysis.* London: Tavistock, 1986.

Pateman, Carole. *The Disorder of Women, Democracy, Feminism, and Political Theory.* Stanford: Stanford University Press, 1989.

———. *The Sexual Contract.* Stanford: Stanford University Press, 1988.

Pedersen, Jean Elisabeth. "Legislating the Family: Gender, Population, and Republican Politics in France, 1870–1920." Ph.D. diss., University of Chicago, 1993.

Pedersen, Susan. *Family, Dependence, and the Origins of the Welfare State: Britain and France, 1914–1945.* Cambridge: Cambridge University Press, 1993.

Perrot, Michelle. "L'Éloge de la ménagère dans le discours des ouvrières françaises au XIXe siècle." *Romantisme* 13–14 (1976): 105–22.

Phillips, Roderick. *Family Breakdown in Late Eighteenth-Century France*. Oxford: Clarendon Press, 1980.

———. *Putting Asunder: A History of Divorce in Western Society*. Cambridge: Cambridge University Press, 1988.

———. *Untying the Knot: A Short History of Divorce*. New York: Cambridge University Press, 1991.

Pick, Daniel. *Faces of Degeneration: A European Disorder, c. 1848–c. 1918*. New York: Cambridge University Press, 1989.

Pion, André. "Les Inspectrices générales du ministère de l'intérieur (1843–1939)." *Administration* 133 (October 1986): 63–67.

Piven, Francis Fox, and Richard A. Cloward. *Regulating the Poor: The Functions of Public Welfare*. New York: Pantheon, 1971.

Pope, Barbara Corrado. "Angels in the Devil's Workshop: Leisured and Charitable Women in Nineteenth-Century England and France." In *Becoming Visible: Women in European History*, edited by Renate Bridenthal and Claudia Koonz. Boston: Houghton Mifflin, 1977.

———. "Maternal Education in France, 1815–1848." *Proceedings of the Western Society for French History* 3 (1976): 368–77.

Potash, Janet. "The Foundling Problem in France, 1800–1869: Child Abandonment in Lille and Lyon." Ph.D. diss., Yale University, 1980.

Prost, Antoine. *Histoire de l'enseignement en France, 1800–1967*. Paris: Armand Colin, 1968.

Reid, Donald. "Putting Social Reform into Practice: Labor Inspectors in France, 1892–1914." *Journal of Social History* 20 (fall 1986): 67–87.

Riley, Denise. *"Am I That Name?" Feminism and the Category of "Women" in History*. Minneapolis: University of Minnesota Press, 1988.

Robert A. *Dictionnaire des parlementaires français à 1889*. Paris, 1891.

Roberts, Mary Louise. *Civilization without Sexes: Reconstructing Gender in Postwar France, 1917–1927*. Chicago: University of Chicago Press, 1994.

Rogers, Rebecca. *Les Démoiselles de la Légion d'honneur au 19e siècle*. Paris: Plon, 1992.

Rollet-Echalier, Catherine. *La Politique à l'égard de la petite enfance sous la Troisième République*. Paris: Presses Universitaires de France, 1990.

Ronsin, Francis. *La Grève des ventres: Propagande néo-malthusienne et baisse de la natalité en France, 19e–20e siècles*. Paris: Aubier, 1980.

Rosanvallon, Pierre. *Crise de l'état providence*. Paris: Seuil, 1984.

Rose, Sonya O. *Limited Livelihoods: Gender and Class in Nineteenth-Century England*. Berkeley: University of California Press, 1992.

Schafer, Sylvia. "Children in 'Moral Danger' and the Politics of Parenthood in Third Republic France, 1870–1914." Ph.D. diss., University of California, Berkeley, 1992.

Schneider, William H. *Quality and Quantity: The Quest for Biological Regenera-*

tion in Twentieth-Century France. New York: Cambridge University Press, 1990.

Schwartz, Joel. *The Sexual Politics of Jean-Jacques Rousseau*. Chicago: University of Chicago Press, 1984.

Scott, Joan. *Gender and the Politics of History*. New York: Columbia University Press, 1988.

———. "The Woman Worker." In *A History of Women*, edited by George Duby and Michelle Perrot; vol. 4, *Emerging Feminism from Revolution to World War*, edited by Geneviève Fraisse and Michelle Perrot. Cambridge: Harvard University Press, 1993.

Seager, Frederic H. *The Boulanger Affair*. Ithaca, N.Y.: Cornell University Press, 1969.

Seccombe, Wally. "Patriarchy Stabilized: The Construction of the Male Bread-winner Wage Norm in Nineteenth-Century Britain." *Social History* 2 (January 1986): 53–75.

Sewell, William H., Jr. "Le citoyen/la citoyenne: Activity, Passivity, and the Revolutionary Concept of Citizenship." In *The Political Culture of the French Revolution*, vol. 2, edited by Colin Lucas. New York: Pergamon Press, 1988.

Shapiro, Ann-Louise. *Housing the Poor of Paris, 1850–1902*. Madison: University of Wisconsin Press, 1985.

Skocpol, Theda. *Protecting Soldiers and Mothers: The Political Origins of Social Policy in the United States*. Cambridge: Harvard University Press, 1992.

Smith, Bonnie G. *Ladies of the Leisure Class: The Bourgeoises of Northern France in the Nineteenth Century*. Princeton: Princeton University Press, 1981.

Soloway, Richard. *Birth Control and the Population Question in England, 1877–1930*. Chapel Hill: University of North Carolina Press, 1982.

———. "Counting the Degenerates: The Statistics of Race Deterioration in Edwardian England." *Journal of Contemporary History* 17 (1982): 137–62.

———. *Demography and Degeneration: Eugenics and the Declining Birthrate in Twentieth-Century Britain*. Chapel Hill: University of North Carolina Press, 1990.

Sowerwine, Charles. *Sisters or Citizens? Women and Socialism in France since 1876*. Cambridge: Cambridge University Press, 1982.

Sowerwine, Charles, and Claude Maignien. *Madeleine Pelletier, une féministe dans l'arène politique*. Paris: Les Éditions Ouvrières, 1992.

Stewart, Mary Lynn [McDougall]. "Protecting Infants: The French Campaign for Maternity Leaves, 1890s–1913." *French Historical Studies* 13, no. 1 (spring 1983).

———. *Women, Work, and the French State: Labour Protection and Social Patriarchy, 1879–1919*. Kingston, Ontario: McGill-Queen's University Press, 1989.

Stone, Judith F. *The Search for Social Peace: Reform Legislation in France, 1890–1914*. Albany: State University of New York Press, 1985.

———. *Sons of the Revolution: Radical Democrats in France.* Baton Rouge: Louisiana State University Press, 1996.

Sussman, George D. *Selling Mothers' Milk: The Wetnursing Business in France, 1715–1914.* Urbana: University of Illinois Press, 1982.

Teitelbaum, Michael, and Jay Winter. *The Fear of Population Decline.* New York: Academic, 1985.

Thane, Pat. *Foundations of the Welfare State.* London: Longman, 1992.

Thébaud, Françoise. *Quand nos grand-mères donnaient la vie: La Maternité en France dans l'entre-deux-guerres.* Lyons: Presses Universitaires de Lyons, 1986.

Thuillier, Guy. *Les Femmes dans l'administration depuis 1900.* Paris: Presses Universitaires de France, 1988.

Tilly, Louise A., and Joan W. Scott. *Women, Work, and Family.* New York: Holt, Rinehart, and Winston, 1978.

Traer, James. *Marriage and the Family in Eighteenth-Century France.* Ithaca, N.Y.: Cornell University Press, 1980.

Walkowitz, Judith R. *City of Dreadful Delight: Narratives of Sexual Danger in Late Victorian London.* Chicago: University of Chicago Press, 1991.

Watson, David R. *Georges Clemenceau: A Political Biography.* New York: David McKay, 1976.

Weissbach, Lee Shai. *Child Labor Reform in Nineteenth-Century France: Assuring the Future Harvest.* Baton Rouge: Louisiana State University Press, 1987.

Wilson, Stephen. *Ideology and Experience: Antisemitism in France at the Time of the Dreyfus Affair.* Rutherford, N.J.: Fairleigh Dickinson University Press, 1982.

Woshinsky, O. H. *The French Deputy: Incentives and Behavior in the National Assembly.* Lexington, Mass.: D. C. Heath, 1973.

Wright, Gordon. *France in Modern Times.* 4th ed. New York: W. W. Norton and Co., 1987.

Zeldin, Theodore. *France, 1848–1945: Ambition and Love.* Oxford: Oxford University Press, 1973.

———. *France, 1848–1945: Politics and Anger.* Oxford: Oxford University Press, 1979.

Index

Library of Congress Cataloging-in-Publication Data

Accampo, Elinor Ann.
    Gender and the politics of social reform in France, 1870–1914 /
Elinor A. Accampo, Rachel G. Fuchs, and Mary Lynn Stewart ; with
contributions by Linda L. Clark, Theresa McBride, and Judith F.
Stone.
        p.   cm.
    Includes bibliographical references and index.
    ISBN 0-8018-5060-6. — ISBN 0-8018-5061-4 (pbk.)
    1. Social problems—France—History—19th century.   2. France—
Social policy.   3. France—Politics and government—1870–1940.
I. Fuchs, Rachel Ginnis, 1939–   .   II. Stewart, Mary Lynn, 1945–   .   III. Title.
HN429.A19   1995
303.48'4'0944—DC20   94-47977